SLANTWISE MOVES

&

Games, Literature, and Social Invention in Nineteenth-Century America

Douglas A. Guerra

D0075150

PENN

UNIVERSITY OF PENNSYLVANIA PRESS

PHILADELPHIA

Published by
University of Pennsylvania Press
Philadelphia, Pennsylvania 19104–4112
www.upenn.edu/pennpress

Printed in the United States of America on acid-free paper
1 3 5 7 9 10 8 6 4 2

Library of Congress Cataloging-in-Publication Data
Names: Guerra, Douglas, author.
Title: Slantwise moves : games, literature, and social invention in
    nineteenth-century America / Douglas A. Guerra.
Other titles: Material texts.
Description: 1st edition. | Philadelphia : University of Pennsylvania
    Press, [2018] | Series: Material texts | Includes bibliographical
    references and index.
Identifiers: LCCN 2018007655 | ISBN 978-0-8122-5061-9 (hardcover :
    alk. paper)
Subjects: LCSH: Games—Social aspects—United States—History—
    19th century. | Books and reading—Social aspects—United
    States—History—19th century. | Popular culture—United States—
    History—19th century. | United States—Social life and customs—
    19th century.
Classification: LCC GV1201.38 .G84 2018 | DDC 306.4/870973—dc23
LC record available at https://lccn.loc.gov/2018007655

For Courtney
in token of my admiration for her genius

CONTENTS

On the Uses and Abuses of Games

Ragged at the edges from a century and a half of wear, a black and gold game board waits quietly in the archives of the Missouri History Museum. Wispy lines carve the surface, tracing links between tarnished brass images of "happiness" and "idleness," "truth" and "crime," "bravery" and "suicide." These slanted strokes, etched remnants of aggressive play, suggest a history that goes beyond the imagistic content of an 1865 luxury edition of Milton Bradley's runaway hit, *The Checkered Game of Life*—"handsomely gotten up," as the ad copy of the day would have it, in "muslin and gilt."[1] Like the scarred drag of squid tentacles across the "dead, blind wall" of a sperm whale's head, they invite visualizations of a now bodiless conflict. There is no definite sense of endings or meanings, of *who* won and precisely *when*. Instead, there is only a scratched and worn suggestion of many *doings* that create a weird impression of time, a phantom feeling of intimacy at a distance. Attempting to bracket these feelings, we might set out to learn something by looking at the board itself (Figure 1). We might note, perhaps, the nineteenth-century obsession with reforming "intemperance" imaged in a square illustrating the same. Or we might attend to the evidence of innovation in planar printing technique that is literally reflected in the flat golden impression of its lithographed surface. Yet the scratches continue to itch, reminding us of the play and movement that must accompany a faithful picture of the game's cultural work. To "read" this artifact requires more than a scan of its surfaces: one must wind oneself to the rhythms of a different moment, moving things, arranging bodies, and sliding over the worn paths of now absent hands. Reading takes the form of testing for potentials, and the nature of this testing slides freely between material and conceptual domains of knowledge.

Figure 1. Game board. *The Checkered Game of Life*. Springfield: Milton Bradley
& Co., ca. 1865. Courtesy of Missouri History Museum, St. Louis.

Games are profoundly experimental media. The dimensions of this experimentation, and what can be learned from it, are at the center of the present book. The interpretation of games requires an approach that probes for
meaning at persistently unsettled boundary lines between content and form,
production ethos and reception aesthetics, subjects and objects. We can begin
to frame their complexity by thinking of them as microtheories of association,
codifications of and speculative exercises in how we might find pleasure with
others (dare I say "fun?"). Games fix our attention on a specific subset of
things, people, and actions, allowing us to understand how we operate when
given a reduced but nevertheless urgent(ish) cluster of demands. They are iterative, habitual, and performative—we watch how others play, how we play,
and what we think to do in specifically conditioned situations of stress, challenge, or humorous improvisation. In games we see a world in miniature, and

like all miniatures they cue us to questions of fidelity, prompting us to ask what is emphasized and what is left out.[2]

With a media form like the book, these questions are most often critically framed by the concept of "representation," but games impose strange alternatives. They direct one to think about fidelity in action, in materials, and in construction, fidelity on the level of patterns and figures of interaction enabled by the form.[3] By situating games and books in a shared ecosystem of mass-circulating leisure media in the U.S. nineteenth century, *Slantwise Moves* uses the "itchy" interpenetrations of games like *The Checkered Game of Life* to educe different ways of reading nineteenth-century books—and different ways of thinking about how people may have read or used books in the past. The tricky issue with nineteenth-century textuality is not that literary history's picture is incorrect but that it is often insufficient to a full view of the book as a media object. Media must be understood as an interrelated collection of venues, an ecology of uneven lifecycles and developmental dependencies, upon and within which certain forms of social life are staged and performed, never in isolation and never without some collective consequence. Despite this, the idea of experimentation within literature can often wend rapidly into the insular solidity of canon (the experiment as a representative example waiting to exist, always already literature) or the controlled flux of modernist play (the experiment as the privileged space of—a primarily masculinized—high art).

Games of this period, by contrast, occupy an especially precise, complex, and visible field of media experimentation relatively uncolonized by concepts of canon or intellectual tradition—revealing alternative foundations for thinking about what "books" were doing *in medias res* and how "writing" and "reading" may have created *senses* of sociality and self. The heart of my argument, here and in the chapters that follow, is a rejection of the idea that the "literary" can be cordoned off from the "ludic" in the nineteenth-century marketplace of cheap amusement commodities. As we shall see, intermedial reciprocity was a core feature of nineteenth-century production practice (much like it is in our own time), and I use this historical fact to reorient the literal and figurative modes of "self-making" and "socialization" that were enmeshed in and preserved by media across traditional conceptual divides.

Productively, the question of what a game *is* doesn't creep into the background as easily as it sometimes does with other forms of media. Even in the most literal terms, every game emerges from its defining gestures—from its particular emphases and elisions. Though they undoubtedly might, literary critics don't always (or in some cases ever) ask themselves to define the "book" as a genre or specific historical media figure at the onset of a critical analysis. Yet one is hard-pressed to find a critical work on games that doesn't begin with a definition.[4] While fixations on genre in literary discussions can appear to rotate within a distant orbit of the valorizing term "literature," similar fixations occupy the molten core of gaming discourse.

"The Uses and Abuses of Games" (1886), Milton Bradley's compact history of Anglo-American game playing and invention written for *Good Housekeeping*, provides a case in point. By then a twenty-six-year veteran of the games industry, Bradley opens by raising the question of definition only to trouble it: "The oldest and broadest definition of the word game would cover much more than its present use implies, which is merely that class of amusements . . . in which some one or some side wins. In addition there is a large class of puzzles, charades, tricks, etc., some of which are entirely separated from and others very closely allied to a game in its more limited sense."[5] Savvy to the categorical designations that enabled him to patent his games as technological inventions more frequently than any other designer of his generation, Bradley invokes the technical language of patent "class[es]" even as the alliances of the class petulantly rub against its conceptual collecting power. Indeed, the problem is the same even within the 1872 class specification used by the U.S. Patent and Trademark Office (USPTO). While "Class 46" is first given the subject heading of "Games and Toys," an immediate and perplexing set of expansions begins on the very next line, where it is clarified that this category includes "Games, Gymnastic and Exercising Apparatus, Traps, and Nets." Below this, the list grows to ensnare even more: billiard balls and dumbbells, puzzles and targets, baseballs and police batons.[6] One can imagine the anonymous author or authors of this document yearning for the comparative clarity of "Class 44: Fuel" or "Class 45: Furniture." Similarly, as Bradley's *Good Housekeeping* article progresses, he bounces from board games to word puzzles to card games, grappling with and hedging against sprawling disruptions to what he terms the "limited sense." Totalizing declarations like "All quiet indoor games may generally be divided into two classes" are quickly trailed by "These two classes, however broadly construed, may not cover all in common use."[7] Other objects of discussion are held in suspension by statements like "if this may be called a game."[8] Seemingly by their nature, games are difficult to separate from those other mechanisms of play with which they are, as Bradley puts it, "very closely allied." Both he and the USPTO struggle with an intuition that I am inclined to put more bluntly: the invention of a new game is the invention of a new *genre*.[9] This might explain why "games" as a category—as opposed to specific examples like *The Checkered Game of Life*, tangrams, or billiards—are difficult to capture under a particular genre umbrella or invention class. Games are about invention itself.

Slantwise Moves is about games, but it is resistant to defining them in sweeping ways for this reason. Individual, historically located games are as interesting for the particular limits they set as for the specific associative assemblages they enable. Thus it is important not to rule out what we might learn from the outset by overwriting empirical complexity through a surplus of conceptual rigor. "The conceptual distance we travel from the facts before us," Sacvan Bercovitch reminds us in "Games of Chess," "is directly proportional to our capacity to see the particular in the essential."[10] All too frequently, discussions about games flow in the opposite direction, looking for anthropological continuity where we might find meaningful breaks. To address this meaning in a particular set of moments in U.S. history, this book takes a case-study approach, looking intensively at popular mass-market games of the mid-nineteenth century not to answer what a game is but instead to ask what certain media *do* and how that *doing* might offer perspective on the literary questions we have directed at the period. Like the designers of nineteenth-century games, I find it not unhelpful to allow other amusements that gaming theorist Espen Aarseth dubs "ergodic" into the mix; that is, objects whose expressive form in a given use-iteration is dependent on a process of input and material negotiation involving both user and artifact—algorithmic media.[11] Read *Moby-Dick* and tell me that you never saw anything about whales, and I'll suggest that you must have skipped something. But you can play many hands of poker and never see a red queen (as an idealistic royal-flush seeker knows all too well). The existence of queens undoubtedly constitutes the "scene" of card playing or its particular sphere of potentials, but it's not necessarily a part of the plot of any given game.[12] It is in this redoubled attention to indirectly scriptive and ambiguously performative qualities of popular games in the nineteenth century that I see opportunities for reimagining "literary" developments in figure and form. The "slantwise" of this book's title advocates interpretative "alongsides," while the plurality of "moves" is an invitation—and a particularly game-like one at that—to consider potentials as well as outcomes.

I should note that even as the goal here is to prompt a more dimensional, fragmentary, and dispersed conversation about historical media—and a conversation about nineteenth-century texts that is not overdetermined by the disciplinary traditions of literary study as it emerged in the twentieth century—the methodology I employ is, in fact, derived from one of the most important tools in the literary toolkit: the sensitive use of metaphor as a mode of intellectual invention and experimentation. Though often employed to more aesthetic ends, a suggestive metaphor functions as an instrument through which one domain of knowledge becomes a foundation for testing the suitability of new knowledge in a different domain. Metaphor is less an object than an operation. It is a way to use a "strictly" incommensurate conceptual schema—a set of words or images traditionally associated with one thing (the "vehicle" in I. A. Richards's classic terminology)—to produce unthought but potentially valid ways of speaking and thinking about another thing (the "tenor").[13] When Romeo says "Juliet is the sun," he invites us to use knowledge about the sun to illuminate potential ways of speaking about his tenor, Juliet, that may not have previously occurred to us: her spatial orientation above him, yes, and undoubtedly certain thoughts about enlightenment and growth, but maybe also the specific distance at which a certain kind of warmth must be kept. Let's remember that to get as close to the sun as Romeo does to Juliet would be to vaporize in a terrible storm of heat and plasma. And while it's true that I'm indulging in a little scientific anachronism here, it's not wrong to say that in four words Romeo conveys potential reflections about vitality and danger that *resonate* in relation to Shakespeare's script, no matter how circuitous the path. Even if we knew nothing else of the play, our model of Juliet's potential significance changes with these words—and with that, our sense of how to "read" her characterization (and Romeo's). The metaphorical operation, by prompting nontraditional but specific schematic ways of knowing a tenor, fills in a territory that may have seemed nonexistent in an otherwise "full" literal depiction of characteristics. Metaphor reminds us that any concept—even one as deeply ingrained as "literature"—is always only a working model.

In "Deep Play," Clifford Geertz sees games as occupying a similar space of operative social modeling. Expanding on a discussion of rural cockfights in 1970s Bali, he explains that "an expressive form works (when it works) by disarranging semantic contexts in such a way that properties conventionally ascribed to certain things are unconventionally ascribed to others, which are then seen actually to possess them."[14] Since nineteenth-century books and games *did* exist in a tightly shared context of production, transmission, and reception—something I discuss below—it makes even more than usual sense to ask the near-metaphorical question: What if a book were seen a game? What ideas about gaming might be usefully applied to notions of reading and writing? But this risks discussions of "play" that won't take us much further than the semiotic deployments of this term that characterized the important, though often abstract, enlistments of late twentieth-century poststructuralist theory. Instead, I'm inclined to ask these questions in a way that lingers with material and historical details of distinctive gameplay media—not a loose or common-denominator sense of definition but concrete models of actual games that offer ways to test for the social potentials we might otherwise be overlooking in specific historical moments. "The heart is a city" can prompt certain thoughts about emotion, but no one would deny that "The heart is Chicago," "The heart is New York," and "The heart is Phoenix" are statements that carry *different* opportunities for thinking: about lakefronts and emotion; about compression, circulation, and cultural displacement; or about love, dust, rattlesnakes, and strip malls. Nineteenth-century games can provide information about repetitive cultural behavior that is as important to thinking about reading practice as it is to thinking about historically oriented sociological questions more broadly—and *Slantwise Moves* addresses this in appropriately messy and speculative, but interlocking, ways that require tracings of the unruly media scenes that books and games shared.

Conversational Slants

In this book, I argue that beyond anything else a game reveals, it also *signals a social scene*: a dicey collection of concepts, materials, and people in a distinctively mobile arrangement. An example can help to clarify this. Variations on a simple game called "conversation cards" existed throughout the long nineteenth century in the United States, advertised in newspapers at least as far back as 1775.[15] A commonplace in many stationery and job printing establishments, conversation cards (and playing cards) conspicuously lodged themselves among other more functional paper and ink implements. A representative listing of printed goods for sale might include:

> A great variety of message and visiting cards, plain, bordered, and
>   gilt,
> Large printer's blanks, common size ditto,
> Playing cards English and American,
> Conversation cards for reading the hearts of ladies,
> Ditto for reading the thoughts of men,
> Dutch quills.[16]

Typically a tiny pack with the dimensions of a matchbox and wrapped in paper or leather, conversation cards could be tossed into a pocket or reticule and be used to break the ice in friendly company—to "read" each other, as noted above. It's not uncommon to find playing cards and conversation cards printed on the backsides of unused formal cards of introduction, aligning pervasive social rituals that involved the exchange of cards.[17] The gameplay itself evokes an advanced level of such practices, moving beyond family names and business recognitions into the ambiguous terrain of "hearts" and "thoughts." Composed of question cards and answer cards, the roughly sixty-card deck would be dealt entirely to the players, which the pronouns and supporting materials presuppose will be a mixed-gender gathering. An 1866 edition from Adams & Co. outlines the basic procedures of gameplay:

> The player having the [question] cards takes one from his pack, and
> after reading it, aloud or not, as may be agreed upon, passes it to
> the other player, who in the same manner returns [an answer]
> card. . . . A laugh is allowable if it be not audible. The player who
> laughs aloud on the passing of a card, or during the game, shall take
> one of his live cards and put it with the dead ones. The player who
> first loses his cards, loses the game, and the other player wins. The
> preceding Rule and Forfeit may be dispensed with if desired, and a
> right-down merry time be had without limitation. The former man-
> ner of playing may be called a Tight, and the latter a Loose Game.[18]

With these procedures in place, players are given license to work through a series of irony-laden call and response situations that, notably to my mind, only require at least one player who can read.[19] On the one hand, strict attention to the content of the card—distanced from the probable scene of gameplay—reveals this as a game invested in specific forms of heterosexual courtship. Benjamin Lindsey's 1811 pack, widely copied and likely a reprinted copy itself, asks, "Do you long to be married?" and "Do you think yourself handsome?" with answers like "Yes, sir, with all my heart" or "Indeed you make me blush" (Figure 2). On the other hand, these composed and appropriate responses must have faced persistent interruption from otherwise unspeakable flirtations and gender inversions: "Are you fond of making conquests?" "Yes, sir, only in the dark."[20] If this weren't the case, *laughing* certainly couldn't be one of the functional methods of competitive assessment. Depending on the players, laughter could be its own form of behavioral policing: we laugh at things we recognize to be "wrong"; we laugh to show we're in on "what's right." But just as often we laugh at things that gesture at the ambiguity of rightness—things that transcend or neutralize a traditional polarization of wrong and right. We laugh at the thing that may be right even though no one ever says it that way (or says it at all).[21] Because the operation of play is controlled by the rules, "conversation cards" do a lot of the talking for you—literally in the case of the silent variation suggested above—and there are myriad reasons why we can imagine this to be desirable. When one person asks, "Are you my friend?" and the other answers, "As circumstances will admit," the words themselves can tell only a partial story. The rest lies in what is registered by the laughter, nonlaughter, or almost laughter that accompanies the physical exchange of a card: the losers of a "tight" game might actually be the winners of a broader communicative scene.

Tone is key. But we wouldn't know *that* simply by reading the conservative gender content of the cards themselves. Ironically, this would strip the cards of their conversational quality.[22] Alongside the text, we sketch a

Figure 2. *Conversation Cards*. New Bedford: Benjamin Lindsey, ca. 1811.
Courtesy of American Antiquarian Society.

plausible social territory by narrating the potential contours of the game in its playing, in the scene of associations that unfold when we envision the game in movement—again, as a particular set of rules, things, spaces, and people. "Close reading," the vexed but tenaciously useful core method of literary studies, demands sticking "close" to the specific language of a text in an effort to produce a "reading" or interpretation responsive to the questions of form and figure raised by a given cluster of words in a given order. Extending this responsivity to extratextual and nonnarrative figures, what we could call "close playing" is about the interplay, exchange, and potential transformations facilitated by traveling across different layers of form in a piece of media. Through this attention to the materials and mechanisms of transformation, close playing allows one to identify "operational figures" in nineteenth-century media and society—sets of actions held together in loose but structured sequences that become the basis of social legibility.[23] Not limited to what objects or images sit next to each other, close playing examines the *actions* that sit next to each other and how certain active sequences gesture at emergent cultural "logics" of association, invention, and connection.[24] In a sympathetic mode, Robin Bernstein has recently argued, using a provocative admixture of performance and "thing" theories, that playthings can be a way to understand "normative aggregate behavior," or iterative social scenes, by keeping a close eye on how a given thing prompts and resists certain sets of actions.[25] A scriptive thing, she insists, "is a tool for analyzing incomplete evidence—and all evidence is incomplete—to make responsible, limited inferences about the past."[26]

Drawing together design, performance, and explicitly algorithmic elements, games like conversation cards are scriptive things par excellence, challenging the analyst to produce an account that interweaves media, behavior, and meaning. They oblige us to imagine "loose[ness]" in even the most "tight" game. While the rules, materials, and history of a game dictate the breaking point of our inferential looseness, stretching the fabric, so to speak, is the only way to make room for the bodies we aim to remember. Games redirect and expand our view of the potential work of books and other allied media in part because a responsible approach to these artifacts makes it impossible to imagine *reading* at an intellectual distance from its material and social sites of enactment: the game of conversation cards is not the same without the tiny cards (requiring some degree of interpersonal touch to pass them on) and without the faces and voices of its players. We can't fully know what they were or what they sounded like, but we know that they were there and how they were most likely arranged. Each of these elements gives us a slant on the game, an incomplete but provocative take on the kind of social world that was coming into being through the playing. For both players and critics, these games exist *in* their slantwise moves—in the indirect opportunities they create for habitual orientation and reorientation through the oblique playful use and reconfiguration of the objects, relationships, and content at hand.

The figure of the "slantwise" is important here because it puts the work of critical orientation at issue. If I stressed earlier that every new game is the invention of a new genre, the thrust of this claim was in the way that a new game begins with a procedural orientation—an outline of how to go about using it, of how to arrange yourself, your friends, and various associated objects in order to produce a specifically contoured performance space. As a result of the liminal privilege afforded to gameplay, these performance spaces can, at times, radically readjust a group's perspective on itself.[27] Prior to the opening of a game of conversation cards, certain skills may have been overemphasized in a given group dynamic: someone with a good memory for current events may dominate conversations; old friendships may effectively place the actors in a hierarchy of leads and supporting players. But the procedures of the game, in their singular reduction of "conversation" to ready-made phrases printed on cards and enforcement of turns, place the emphasis instead on charming gestures, evocative tones, and weird juxtapositions. This is not to say that gameplay escapes the ideological magnetisms of its moment—these gestures, tones, and feelings of weirdness could just as easily reinforce the most awful elements of a culture. Questions remain regarding whose action is emphasized and who gets to be in the room.

Yet there was surprising latitude in the way that room was imagined by the makers of these games: in 1858, William Dick and Lawrence Fitzgerald pitch their best-selling anthology of home amusements as being "for family circles, for schools, for pic-nic parties, for social clubs, and, in short, for all occasions where diversion is appropriate";[28] six years later, Dick, writing under the pseudonym "Trumps" in *American Hoyle*, gleefully reports that "regardless of sex, age, or social position, [billiards] is participated in by all classes of society."[29] In the same year, Milton Bradley advertises his innovative multigame travel pack under the conspicuously combined name of "Games for the Soldiers or Family Circle" and insists that it is "just the thing to send to the boys in CAMP or HOSPITAL for a CHRISTMAS PRESENT, or to keep at home for the winter evenings";[30] just after the war, he contends that Caroline Smith's 1866 *Popular Pastimes for Field and Fireside; or, Amusements for Young and Old*, is "not a *Boy's* book or a *Girl's* book, but a home book for boys and girls of *all ages*."[31] Despite the slow yoking of gameplay to childhood in the late nineteenth and early twentieth centuries, the games addressed in *Slantwise Moves*—board games, card games, fill-in-the-blanks books, configuration puzzles, and targeting games—were promiscuously marketed and often played across generation, gender, and class.[32] As a result, these games prompt us to ask different questions about the spaces where new forms of association and intimacy were being built; they prompt us to notice slantwise moments of productive irony where we might otherwise see only a loud, ponderous normativity machine.

As contrapuntal analytics, attention to historical games can supplement the critical orientation Michel Foucault famously afforded homosexuality in "Friendship as a Way of Life," as the "occasion to reopen affective and relational virtualities, not so much through the intrinsic qualities of the homosexual but because of the 'slantwise' position of the latter, as it were, the diagonal lines he can lay out in the social fabric [that] allow these virtualities to come to light."[33] Of course, "slantwise" is not Foucault's word, but the French *en biais* evokes the practice of cutting woven textiles "on the bias," or at a forty-five-degree angle, in order to allow maximal stretch in the fabric (Foucault's "lignes diagonals qu'il peut tracer dans le tissu").[34] Because gameplay of the kind addressed in this book can never rest easy on the suggestion of a final picture or outcome—because the iterative archive of possibilities that define a game make any single analysis move like a marble on an uneven table—it must persistently hold many discrete though divergent possibilities in suspension, doubling back to stretch the comfortable fabric of texts whose interpretative range may appear to be settled.[35] Folding social *action* of the kind we can infer from games into our readings makes them thicker; orienting the diagonal relationships of books and games within a shared "fabric" of nineteenth-century media production allows for a better accommodation of this thickness, of the bodies that have been corseted out of the picture.[36]

A striking example of the loss that can accompany an overtight perspective on the relationships of text, genre, and medium in the mid-nineteenth century, Emily Dickinson has been a site of important reimaginings in recent criticism. Martha Nell Smith, Marta Werner, and Virginia Jackson have all, in different but related ways, challenged the early editorial and critical work on Dickinson that forced her creative output into shapes that ruled out its nearly game-like medial and genre experimentation. In light of their interventions, Dickinson's writing now appears to anticipate the very problems that accompanied her emergence as a figure of literary interest:

Tell all the truth
but tell it slant—
Success in Circuit
lies
Too bright/bold for our
infirm Delight
The Truth's superb
surprise.[37]

In a reading compatible with my invocation of "operational figures" above, the "Success" to be attained in the task of learning historical truths lies in understanding the "Circuit" or regular routes that direct their flow—hence algorithmic readings that narrate a sphere of potentials in an effort to trace the underlying biases or schemas that give shape to action. At the same time, Dickinson's "Circuit lies" are iterative attempts to get at the truth with an imperfect instrument. The "lies" of customary metaphor and idiomatic rhetoric—the sorts of things one must tap into in order to be understood— require one to hang a lantern on the "slant" one is taking in the effort. Dickinson suggests that these efforts be multiplied, layered over and again upon each other, since no single slant can capture the "superb surprise" of an inexhaustible wonder in the world. This intuition of inexhaustibility reflects the fact that the "truth" of a thing has more to do with our perspective on how it should be used—what it fits with—than on what it *is*. Any "thing" can always be used a different way, as Dickinson demonstrates through her redeployment of scraps from receipts, old envelopes, and lists as platforms for new pieces of linguistic art. As I've gestured at in my transcription, the manuscript in which this "poem" appears makes such a layered redeployment even more obvious: "bright" and "bold" sit right on top of each other, neither struck out (I've clumsily rendered this in type with a slash). One is invited to read one, then the other, in a kind of assay of meaning that is materially prohibited from pushing either word out of the picture. The truth is bright, bold, and— strangely but meaningfully—a kind of flashbulb palimpsest or harmonic concatenation: "bright-bold." Much of Dickinson's writing demands a similar concatenation on the level of its material experimentation: a letter is a poem is a collage is a letter-poem-collage. The artifact insists that you read a poem as if it weren't a poem in a manner comparable to the invocation in conversation cards of a dialogue that both is and is not a conversation in the traditional sense. Would it be useful to imagine Dickinson's work as "conversation cards" of a sort? As objects of exchange and gestural irony instead of lyric? Given the friendship Dickinson enjoyed with Samuel Bowles—the editor of the *Springfield Republican* who collaborated with Milton Bradley on some of his first projects in the same period—it might be more productive to imagine her work within the sphere of game making rather than on the firm ground of the "literary" that has traditionally defined it.[38]

Since books and games occupied overlapping worlds, an attentive approach to games becomes an opportunity to rethink our expectations about what literature was *doing* in this moment as well. Such a shifted perspective allows us to ask what some of the texts and authors at the center of our literary-critical traditions—texts I have selected for their solid familiarity in contrast to the historical amnesia that surrounds their ludic counterparts—could have been figuring in the more motion-driven operational domain highlighted and placed at issue by gameplay. To put it another way, by including canonical literature alongside *native* models of potential social interaction (that is, specific historical games), I hope to show that a common conversation was happening within and across media that did not, in their moment, occupy dramatically different registers. Given that some nineteenth-century designers thought games could "be made to inspire an early taste for a profitable class of reading," one might reasonably ask what specific sets of social behaviors and arrangement practices gave special contour to this idea.[39] Such declarations prompt us to the insight that reading and game playing might have been seen in a continuum that has since been lost, naturalized, or simply ruled out by the slow historical reifications of genre and the late nineteenth-century invention of "childhood"—a major event in the sense of a division between (adult/serious) reading and (childish) gameplay.[40] The more games and books are drawn together, the more possible it becomes to unsettle the assumed reception of both and to see them, in Thomas Augst's phrase, as "artifacts from the messy business of living."[41]

Materials in Play

If the curious contrivances analyzed in this book were always an experiment in pleasurable social modeling, they were also, like Dickinson's work, nearly always the result of an expanded view of material usage, a wide and slippery territory of transmedia objects constructed out of the raw materials most readily at hand. A different approach to considering the vast genre experimentation in nineteenth-century games would be to think of them instead as experiments in the affordances of media. While games of the mid-nineteenth century were undoubtedly in conversation with innovations in reform pedagogy, they were just as often answers to the question of what could or might be done with the light industrial materials that were circulating the U.S. mediascape in high quantities: paper and ink, leather and wood, india rubber and pasteboard.[42] The material world of paper amusements, documentary object production, and communicative labor was incredibly porous in the nineteenth century.[43] Meredith McGill has compellingly argued that reprinting—from pirated European works to modular recirculations of newspaper content—was part of the "horizon of the ordinary . . . a principle of organization" in the antebellum period.[44] Building on this, we might say that "reprinting" was a principle predicated on a general ethos of "repurposing" and "reinvention" that spanned the antebellum and postbellum periods. Like the Silicon Valley programmers of our own time—many of whom draw upon vast libraries of existing software like APIs, development frameworks, and middleware to build new end products without reinventing the wheel— successful agents of this system were as likely to be defined by their capacity to reconfigure, reappropriate, and reimagine what already existed as much as make something entirely new. Calling cards, as I mentioned above, could become playing cards. Maps could become board games with a few lines added.[45] And cardstock for traditional playing cards could be used to print less morally problematic pictorial matching games, which Bradley wryly points out "are nearly all copied after some of the old games or are combinations and modifications of them."[46] Some of this circulation was undoubtedly the result of technological and geographic proximities, an alliance indebted to quasi-centralized locales of production and distribution.

Walk down the bustling printers' row on Washington Street in Boston on a day in early 1858 and you would encounter a vital entanglement of printers, ink sellers, stationers, binders, and dealers of paper goods that ranged from blank books and fill-in-the-blanks puzzles to visiting cards, playing cards, maps, and board games, alongside the "literary" books that have formed criticism's primary objects of study.[47] Boundaries between different forms of media were persistently crossed and interleaved. Gould & Lincoln, which worked with the American Tract Society and primarily published religious pieces and year-end scientific anthologies, also published a stand-alone version of one of the first commercial *Mad Libs*–type games in the country. Anne Abbot's breakout game of family grouping, *Dr. Busby* (1843), was ported into some of

the earliest attempts at literary crossover publishing, as both Harriet Beecher
Stowe's *Uncle Tom's Cabin* (1852) and Maria Susanna Cummins's *The Lamplighter* (1854) were converted into similar card games that were sold around the
corner from the shop of John Punchard Jewett, the original publisher of both
best-selling novels.[48] Jewett got his own start in Salem selling "new games" like
Abbot's alongside pictorial bibles, almanacs, and gift annuals before moving
his business to Boston.[49] And when he moved out of his location at 117 Washington Street in 1858, it was William Crosby and H. P. Nichols, publishers of
the tangram-like "Geometrical Puzzle for the Young," that moved from three
doors down to take over his supplies.[50]

Anne Wales Abbot, arguably the United States' first homegrown commercial game designer, would parlay her career in games into a position as a
well-respected educator and editor. (In a critique of *The Scarlet Letter* for the
North American Review, she gives a hilariously backhanded compliment about
the novel's preface, reporting that "this naughty chapter is more piquant than
any thing in the book.")[51] And though influential reviewers, editors, and authors like Abbot may have prompted Hawthorne's bitter laments about "scrib-
bling women," it was some of these same Salem women who would ensure
that future generations remembered Hawthorne's place in the canon, by
adapting *Dr. Busby* into a new game of literary memorization and matching
called *Authors* (1861).[52] Perhaps all of this interplay explains at least one reason
Milton Bradley took pains to mimic ornate gilding patterns and morocco-
leather binding on the earliest versions of *The Checkered Game of Life* (1860),
presumably so that it would not look out of place propped atop a parlor piano
or in a bookcase (Figure 3). Books and games lived together, if not as blood
family, then at least as raucous adolescent roommates.

Though scholars have begun to think about the role that extraliterary
documents and documentary practices played in the literary establishment,
games and books are not usually discussed together in any material way. The
distance between game studies and literary studies exists in part because of a
critical gap between important tropological studies of nineteenth-century
games and more recent approaches to video games and new media. In the first
category, historical studies of the interaction between literature and games in
the nineteenth-century United States have focused on *rhetorics* of game and
sport, parsing the significance of gameplay tropes, often in contrast to a discourse of "seriousness." Ann Fabian's *Card Sharps and Bucket Shops: Gambling
in Nineteenth-Century America* makes important claims about the significance
of gaming rhetoric in creating models of "economic rationality" in the early

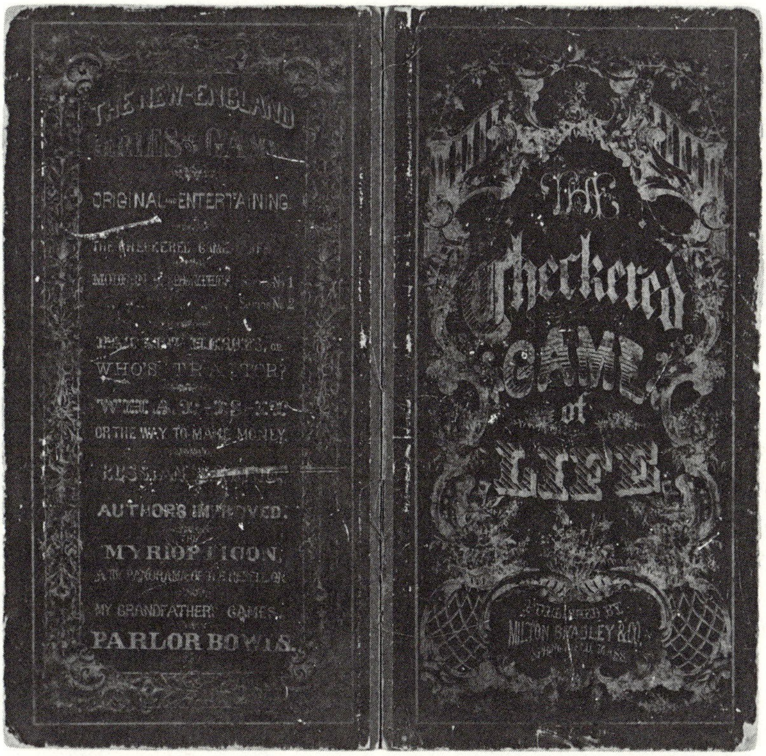

Figure 3. Game back. *The Checkered Game of Life.* Springfield: Milton Bradley & Co., ca. 1865. Courtesy of Missouri History Museum, St. Louis.

age of stock market speculation;[53] while Michael Oriard's expansive study, *Sporting with the Gods: The Rhetoric of Play and Game in American Culture*, traces the use of the word "game" in the nineteenth and twentieth centuries, arguing that the language of gaming metaphors in U.S. literature "reveals human thought processes and cultural values . . . [and] creates the perceived reality."[54] Moving beyond these suggestive rhetorical ambivalences, I focus instead on the function and cross-pollination of specific structures within the available game commodities of the time, enlisting canonical literary luminaries to show that their central position (with regard to acclaim and pedagogy) might be better employed through the different modes of critical attention that are invited by coincident period games. For example, a reading of William Simonds's *Peter Coddle's Trip to New York* (the Gould & Lincoln precursor to *Mad Libs* mentioned previously) adds nuance to Herman Melville's notoriously fragmentary dialogue in *The Confidence-Man: His Masquerade* (1857). Like Melville's characters, Peter Coddle falls victim to a savvy operator, drawn in by his desire for objects written on a set of cards that are selected by players as the game progresses: "a stick of candy," "a mint of gold," or perhaps even "a stack of fat lobsters." Nested within a larger youth novel entitled *Jessie; or, Trying to Be Somebody* (1858), Simonds's textual game makes an operative argument about the increasingly instrumental perspective on becoming "somebody" demonstrated in nineteenth-century reform literature; Coddle's identity is literally structured as a set of social input events bounded by a regulated but undefined grammar. Understanding this facilitates a reassessment of the similarly fragmentary speech of undefined passengers aboard the steamboat *Fidèle* in Melville's *The Confidence-Man*, who construct their own identities as if they were a kind of fill-in-the-blanks game, valuing a comfortably mechanical consistency over impromptu character making. A surrogate for the lost agency of these passengers, the Confidence-Man himself begins to seem more hero than villain in Melville's narrative because he represents an aesthetic of limited invention and tactical play that is materialized and humorously reinforced in Simonds's game.

My precedents in this approach are interdisciplinary scholars working with digital games—some coming from a framework of textual studies and book history, such as Matthew Kirschenbaum, Johanna Drucker, and Steven E. Jones, and some from within new media studies, such as Ian Bogost, Jesper Juul, and Espen Aarseth. The insights of this recent work have not been fully applied to game forms that predate the twentieth century, although there is much to be gained from such an encounter. Engaging with what Kirschenbaum highlights as formal and forensic materialities, nineteenth-century games like bagatelle, croquet, and even *The Checkered Game of Life* developed strategic habits of mind in players that were explicitly coincident with bodily habits of seeing, moving, and touching.[55] Hence, the USPTO's inclusion of dumbbells and exercising devices amid playing cards, dice, and puzzles. Here the materiality of gameplay *mattered* in a way that is only recently being reclaimed by critics of both games and books. And because these forms existed within a shared media ecology, they both reflected and refracted the same cultural imaginary in different though comparatively interesting ways: if games carried the expectation of physical or dispositional exercise, then we are inclined to ask how books may have facilitated or enacted formally continuous modes of engagement. As New Media theorist Lisa Gitelman observes of media technologies in the late nineteenth century, "different media and varied forms, genres, and styles of representation act as brokers among accultured practices of seeing, hearing, speaking, and writing."[56] To understand literary history within the scope of the procedural and ludic practices materially modeled by games is to better comprehend the practices being "broker[ed]" by authors working in this historical moment.

Beginning by thinking through the manner in which object displacements of "interior" character rearticulated the grounds of social legibility in the mid-nineteenth century, my first chapter, "Both In and Out of the Game: Reform Games and Avatar Selves," tracks the interface of decision and thing in Milton Bradley's *The Checkered Game of Life* (1860) and Walt Whitman's "Song of Myself" (1855). A fusion of somatic and cognitive training created to aid in the "exercise of judgment," Bradley's career-making board game combined the tactile socialization of previous board games with a mechanic of timing and decision that was substantially novel for its time. This shift in emphasis rendered the player's marker what we would today call an "avatar," an interactive social representation of users defined by their actions in a shared virtual and often strategically liminal world. By disrupting the genre expectations of lyric that typically frame discussion of Whitman's poetry, I allow Bradley's game to inflect a renewed reading of "Song of Myself"—a poem both formally and thematically concerned with judgment, decision, and touch. In this mode, Whitman's voracious "I" becomes an avatar-like position within a medially sensitive algorithmic piece of writing, with flurries of inclusive "or"s foregrounding a self that chooses among complex, but limited, collections of subject positions that are inscribed upon and indebted to the tactile dislocations of the book's various "leaves."

Chapter 2, "A Fresh and Liberal Construction: State Machines, Transformation Games, and Algorithms of the Interior," continues to examine the constitutive relationship between agency, objecthood, and association. Popular but largely outside of critical view, William Simonds's sixth youth-oriented novel, *Jessie; or, Trying to Be Somebody*, takes a puzzling turn midway through the tale when one of its protagonists introduces a "Game of Transformations" called *Peter Coddle's Trip to New York*. A forerunner of twentieth-century word substitution games, Simonds's story makes Coddle the victim of a New York operator who seduces the rural mark with promises of fabulous luxuries that are filled in by the game players via preprinted cards. As a result, Coddle's active identity is a function both of formal consistencies (the text surrounding the interactive gaps) and of contingent textual variables input by readers—without material social interaction, Coddle remains structured but undefined. Published a year earlier, Herman Melville's *The Confidence-Man: His Masquerade* portrays the passengers of the steamboat *Fidèle* as similarly undefined, giving them notoriously fragmentary dialogue that has often confounded critics: "Believe me, I—yes, yes—I may say—that—that—," "Upon my word, I—I," and "I conjecture him to be what, among the ancient Egyptians, was called a —."[57] Through these stylistic gaps, Melville imagines public identity, within the demands of reformist institutionalism, as an instrumentalization of one's social self, a singular reading and affirmation of identity in a proscriptively static interpretative mode. In this mode, which Melville lambasts through his much commented on metanarrative asides, bodily feelings of anxiety linked to chaotic and competitive interiorities were regulated by performing the self as a consistent decision algorithm, a state machine like Simonds's fill-in-the-blank story. Melville's marks cede their capacity for agency to the Confidence-Man, who reaffirms their desired identity—defining their structured incompleteness for a price they are all too willing to pay. In his triumph, the Confidence-Man represents the importance of "playerliness," a term I ascribe to the ability to read broadly across layers of medial address (operational, affective, and more traditionally textual). The playerliness of the novel's fourth-wall-breaking narrator, as well as its "Mississippi operator," stages a critical supplement to the enactments of state and consistency that dominated U.S. reform discourse and documentation in the mid-nineteenth century. As institutionalism sought to flatten time in a manner that would ensure a consistent future, both *The Confidence-Man* and *Peter Coddle* reconfigure focus onto the differential and associative moments when character could be invented anew. Yet though Simonds was somewhat freer to invite the interplay of tone, scene, and textual object as a consequence of generic fluidity in games, the failure of Melville's novel may reflect a reading public less willing to accept the alternative notions of literary protocol required by his inventive experiments in the novel as mechanism.

This important historical connection between a personal and a mechanical aesthetic of invention is made explicit in my third chapter, "The Power to Promote: Configuration Culture in the Age of Barnum," which situates the success of P. T. Barnum within a framework of advancements in U.S. patent law that reinforced a growing configurative focus in society at large. By keeping the cost of patenting significantly lower than in Europe and by creating managed public archives of existing inventions like the USPTO, the Patent Act of 1836 contributed to a wider culture of exhibition in the United States and encouraged middle-class inventors to make their names by reconfiguring preexisting materials. Aligning this development with the emergence and persistence of a seven-piece configuration puzzle popularly known as "The Chinese Puzzle" or tangram, I explore Barnum's use of physical, oral, and documentary paratextual arrangement—supporting materials he dubs "outside show"—as a variety of inventive associational puzzle play. The obsessive configurational intimacies of "The Chinese Puzzle," which prompted international outcry over "puzzle madness" in the early nineteenth century, offer a way to read Barnum that is sensitive to the thresholds of agency limned by the association of bodies and things. Seeing this through, I pause on the troubling case of Joice Heth, the elderly African American woman who arguably made Barnum's career as a promoter. If outside cues were a crucial element of invention and playful communication, Heth's exhibition—first as George Washington's improbably ancient nurse, then as an impossibly sophisticated automaton—demonstrates the sinister range in which these practices could be used to naturalize dehumanizing attitudes toward nonwhite, nonnormative bodies. At the same time, I explore evidence of audience mediations that may have gone beyond the intended *studium* of Barnum's carefully designed stage pictures to produce a puzzling performative *punctum*, transformatively challenging viewers to play a different game. Haunting the "tact" of Barnum's career, Heth's airy and tonal control of atmosphere seeps into his success at the American Museum, where he places focus on murky contexts of enactment and on the reciprocal and embedded interface of spectator and exhibit, rather than simply on the subject-object relationship between viewer and artifact.

Expanding on the thematics of scope and focal control introduced via "outside show" in Barnum's career, Chapter 4, "Social Cues and Outside Pockets: Billiards, Blithedale, and Targeted Potential," investigates an unlikely pairing: the high literary genre of Romance and the low hustle of the billiards hall. An Irish immigrant with a knack for the pool cue and an ambitious take on the value of his beloved game, Michael Phelan made his name patenting modifications to billiards tables and codifying American slants on both strategy and rules in his immensely popular *Billiards without a Master* (1850). Throughout this otherwise functional and geometrically inclined manual, Phelan fixates on the ways in which proper targeting—particularly in the iterative and improvisational mode of "nursing" the table—can be used to "cue" behavioral change outside of the game through shifts in "disposition," imagination, and mood. Though developed around the table, a set of visual habits and their reversals bleed into associated spaces: the city, the tavern, and the home. I use Phelan's explorations of the interface between eyes, cues, and social bodies to take a different approach to the work of "Romance" in Nathaniel Hawthorne's Brook Farm reverie, *The Blithedale Romance* (1852). In a narrative framed by scenes of nursing, Miles Coverdale's ostentatious visual targeting and iterative rearrangements of view enact a logic of scopic manipulation that is central to Hawthorne's genre intervention. Stories within stories, fixations on point of view, and figures of "reticules" (small netted purses, but also gun targets) permeate a novel that is fronted by a character with a deep attachment to his evenings "at the billiard-hall." By investigating the shared territory of utopic operation in both Hawthorne and Phelan, I consider "Romance" not merely as a genre defined by tropes of atmospheric marvelousness, but also as a way of thinking about relationality and reframing as ways of affecting social change in directedly indirect ways, a kind of motivated vicariousness native to both billiard playing and reading.

In my closing chapter, "The Net Work of Not Work," such "reframing" itself becomes the major topic of focus, as I double back to Milton Bradley to analyze his post–Civil War fascination with thinking across thresholds and training habits of scalar or scopic thinking. In a bizarre follow-up to the kinetic judgments of *The Checkered Game of Life*, Bradley's *Game of Bamboozle, Or the Enchanted Isle* (1872) produces a Gordian knot of visually arresting entanglements that force its players into a series of waiting games and paratactic associations. Advertised as having "no instructional value whatsoever," *Bamboozle* demonstrates Bradley looking in two directions at once: at a future of games sold by virtue of their graphic effusiveness and a past of games as places of "simple" bodily proximity and storytelling. In the first case, the full-color depth of *Bamboozle's* board speaks to developments in lithographic technology that were allowing competitors like the artistically savvy McLoughlin Brothers to encroach on Bradley's business by producing beautiful but operationally unoriginal board games. With a board that represented the most colorful effort in chromolithography by Bradley to date and rules as difficult to pin down as the sperm whales and sea creatures gracing the edges of the playfield, his long-selling amusement was a tangle of race-style games folded in on themselves that may have been intended as a procedural satire of the industry. At the same time, I unpack its deep indebtedness to the alternative sensibilities of undirected gameplay, social narrative, and transmedial reframing that characterized the massively popular card games and novels created by Anne Abbot some thirty years earlier. Pushing back against the aspirational culture that he had emphasized in *The Checkered Game of Life*, Bradley's later output highlights the value of proximity and indirected association, making waiting itself a mode of social agency and group formation.

Over the course of these chapters, the problems of creating, performing, and reinventing public character mirror a certain strain of critical discourse within American Studies. How does one attain genuine social agency—the power to change one's world—despite the normative mechanisms of control that structure that world and make it available for such an agency? As Walter Benn Michaels put it three decades ago, critical transcendence cannot be taken at face value, "not so much because you can't really transcend your culture but because, if you could, you wouldn't have any terms of evaluation left."[58] The issue of scholarly agency here is synecdochic for the wider issue of agency as a whole; six years after Michaels, Sacvan Bercovitch frames the problem as a decision "to make use of the categories of culture or to be used by them."[59] In *Slantwise Moves*, I read nineteenth-century U.S. writers, readers, game players, and designers in the midst of an evolutionary engagement over the issue of repurposing and embedded *use*. Rather than being the passive deployment of supposedly neutral instruments, such "use" was instead a variety of insistent experimentation within an interleaved topography of body and medium. Whether it be Whitman's redefinition of character as choice making on and across the page (use as the rehearsal of personal judgment), Melville's iterative staging of social confidence games (use as manipulation), Barnum and tangram players' exploitation of the thresholds between text and paratext (use as limited reinvention), Phelan and Hawthorne's representations of dispositional change through targeting practices (use as site of perspectival potential), or Anne Abbot and the later Milton Bradley's emphasis on social entanglement and waiting (use as generative waste), the perpetual use of at-hand cultural materials became a central mode of self-making in an era when traditional ways of adjudicating character were being left by the wayside.

This was not a self *made* but a gerund-y and insistent *making*; it was a historical moment when, as Scott A. Sandage writes, "A rising 'business man' embodied true selfhood and citizenship: the man in motion, the driving-wheel, never idle, never content." The requirement of constant change was accompanied by the persistent risk of failure—of inventing a business, a technology, or a self that failed to live up to its promise, by failing to resonate with the social body as a whole.[60] The rise and importance of the games addressed in *Slantwise Moves* speaks to a desire to plot such failures on a continuum, to enable inventive change despite the (often profound) human risk associated with each move this change necessitated. The works discussed here prefigure a need that advances into our own time, when critics call for reconceiving "associations as sites of *inventive* alternatives . . . and not simply as reflections of preexisting or predetermined values."[61] While the rhetoric of "invention" has attained the valence of a dead metaphor (a replacement for "creative" or "imaginative"), tactically critical and locally embedded use was staged by way of both formal and material *mechanisms* in nineteenth-century games, and often, as I argue, in literature as well. This project continues the work called for in the conclusion of Bercovitch's *Rites of Assent*, where he contends, "We will never properly understand [American writers'] force of enterprise, speculation, and invention until we set this firmly within a history of American enterprise, speculation, and invention in the nineteenth century."[62] Supplementing the local comparative work done by individual chapters, *Slantwise Moves* situates major authors of the mid-nineteenth century within a history of invention by looking at procedural amusements as an interface between the representational and the mechanical, refusing to see writing and reading as immaterial practices. If Bercovitch's imperative carries at least the faint suggestion of an impossible or purely metaphorical span between the abstract figural inventions of "writing" and the physical inventions of "history"—history as a forensic "context" emanating explanations for the literary—then one aim of my book is to trouble that distance and do the work of tracing the intermediaries native to writing, bodies, and things. The goal is not homology (or not only homology) but a flattened look at the conditions through which certain social practices, social habits, and social bodies are produced around and with media.

Examining the figures and forms of mid-nineteenth-century games in the United States allows us to understand literature in conversation with a complex and evolving commercial marketplace of things, a conversation that facilitates one of literature's core functions as historical repository. To find meaning in literary objects, critical scholarship must reconstruct the social environments that allow(ed) them to signify; yet it has often proven difficult to track a set of associations that are based on *motion* and *spatiality* and *operational possibility* using what are assumed to be nonprocedural forms (that is, novels, poems, autobiographies). As a result, critical methodologies fixate on the immobile, the institutional, and a historiography of increasingly obliterated time. These perspectives are crucial, and yet they risk leaving out the temporal local activities of daily life that are enacted and reiterated by gameplay and reading. Here timing, movement, and sociality were always, and often explicitly, at issue. For those seeking a deeper understanding of the interactive medial shift that was occurring across the nineteenth century—corresponding to a shift in the possibilities of the literary—games offer models of emerging procedural grammars, drawing attention to the increasingly algorithmic structures enabling the civic agencies that have been represented by American literary studies. The consequence of pairing games and literature allows us (to repurpose a phrase used by Gerry Canavan and Priscilla Wald) "to track both a shift in the formative terms of an ideology and the means by which that shift occurs."[63] In short, it allows us to create new ways of reading and to imagine old ways of playing that have important bearing on literary history, as well as literary critical practice and pedagogy.

CHAPTER I

Both In and Out of the Game

Reform Games and Avatar Selves

Apart from the pulling and hauling stands what I am,
Stands amused, complacent, compassionating, idle, unitary,
Looks down, is erect, bends an arm on an impalpable certain rest,
Looks with its sidecurved head curious what will come next,
Both in and out of the game, and watching and wondering at it.
                    —Walt Whitman, "Song of Myself" (1855)

In the summer of 1860, as the owner of the only lithographic press in western Massachusetts, Milton Bradley undertook creating a standard reproducible image of Abraham Lincoln. Bradley was a capable draftsman who previously had made a living by sketching detailed patent drawings for the early inventors of the American industrial boom. Now he saw an opportunity to turn his political passion for Lincoln into a profit: working from a photograph, he sketched a painstaking likeness of the candidate's distinctive, clean-shaven face and pressed enough copies to populate every home in New England. For a time they sold incredibly well—but Lincoln's beard changed all that. Biographer James Shea writes, "Bradley could not believe it. But . . . no one wanted a lithograph of a beardless Lincoln. Some even wanted their money back."[1] Frustrated but not defeated, Bradley turned his disappointment with the scheme into a renewed energy to produce and sell a game he had invented just a few months earlier, *The Checkered Game of Life* (Figure 4).[2]

On the colorful game board, Bradley created a likeness of nineteenth-century American life—conspicuously, adult male life, though the players

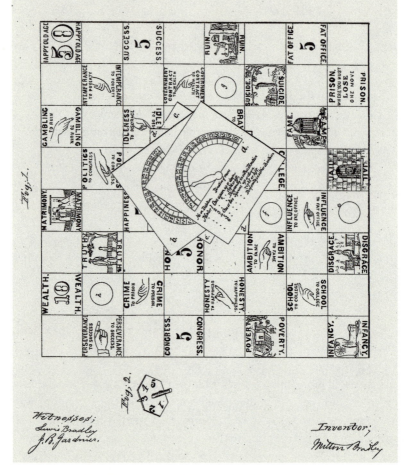

Figure 4. Milton Bradley. Social Game. U.S. Patent 53,561. 3 April 1866.
Source: United States Patent and Trademark Office.

were assumed to span a wider demographic—that placed new emphasis on timing and decision rather than the traditional ideals of place and avocation. Play consisted in accumulating points by moving around a freeform sixty-four-square checkerboard, encouraging "a frequent choice of moves involving the exercise of judgment."[3] More than a roll of the dice, character in *Life* was framed as a position from which to make public and materially registered decisions; it was something you acted out as well as watched. In an urban society composed of interactions among relative strangers, publicly visible decisions—from fashion and conduct to the pointing out of sites, objects, and newspaper articles—were quickly becoming the foundation of social selfhood.[4] And indeed *Life*'s capacity to stage a complex "exercise of judgment" on the cognitive space of a single "page" of pasteboard may account for the game's immense popularity. When Bradley first traveled to New York City to determine interest in the game, his supply of merchandise lasted only two days; within a few months he had sold forty thousand copies.[5] Clearly, this kinetic mixture of bright red ink, brass dials, and layered decision making presented a model of life that the public was eager to practice.

To understand the dimensions of Bradley's precipitous success, and what this success can tell us about American media history (not to mention literary history), it is essential to pause for a moment and reflect on what we can learn from the punctuated emergence of new commercial games like *The Checkered Game of Life*—in contrast to more traditional staples of amusement. Though he may have inaugurated a new era in integrated game design, theory, and branding, Bradley certainly did not invent American play. Sketching the anthropological edges of traditional play practices, anthologies such as *The Boy's Treasury of Sports, Pastimes, and Recreations* (1847) and *The Boy's Book of Sports and Games* (1851) pillaged liberally from London native William Clarke's nostalgic reflections and codifications in *The Boy's Own Book* (1828/1829).[6] In isolation, Clarke's compendium of childhood entertainments—republished by the Boston firm of Munroe and Francis nearly every year for twenty-five years and selling in this period, by one account, eighty thousand copies in the United States[7]—offers a broad introduction to texture of everyday play in the nineteenth century, which included checkers, marbles, wordplay games, puzzles, and playground standards like Blind Man's Buff. Clarke's books and their many echoes documented ubiquitous games and modes of amusement that most would have known or might be expected to know. Advertised and (if inscriptions in extant copies suggests common practice) largely bestowed during the domestic leisure of the Christmas season, *Boy's Own* books were touchstones in social calibration: equal parts reference book and usage guide for a set of discrete playful protocols that could aid in the attainment of a shared sociophysical language. And just as a dictionary does not invent words, and an encyclopedia does not invent topics, these books did not *invent* new games; instead they *cataloged* a cultural topography of leisure time associations and pleasures with a tone of romantic universality and completeness. Indeed, there is only a glancing sense that the games in these books came from anywhere other than a distant, spuriously researched past.

A fact-driven history of particular games in these collections, of the sort that might support meaningful social analysis, is persistently frustrated by a competitive tendency among the makers of these books toward compendious completeness. Authority without authorship reigned. And this authority was anchored by the anonymizing and appropriative tendencies of reprinting. As William Dick, the editor of *American Hoyle* (1864), clarifies in the book's preface: "It has been the intention of the publishers of this work to make it the standard authority for all American Games. With this view, they have neglected no available research to render it as perfect and complete as possible, and think they may safely commend it to the American people as a reliable and trustworthy arbiter of all questions arising within its scope."[8] The sources for this "research" were directly acknowledged in Dick and Fitzgerald's concurrently published *American Boy's Book* (1864): "We are indebted to the compilers of the 'BOY'S OWN BOOK,' 'EVERY BOY'S BOOK, and the 'BOY'S HANDY BOOK OF GAMES,' for sundry extracts, descriptions, and hints, of which we have made use in the preparation of this volume."[9] Similarly, a posthumously expanded 1854 edition of Clarke's *Boy's Own Book* reflects upon the fact that in the absence of many substantive additions, the core differences between these yearly offerings were, in fact, style and format: "As new editions have been called for, the value of the book has been increased by successive improvements, and it has thus been rendered as distinguished for the style of its production as it was formerly attractive for its novelty."[10]

Even so, when collated across publishers, editions, and time, documentary trends begin to surface. New pages are added to reflect newly popular games. New names and name localizations emerge ("Touch" becomes the more familiar "Tag," for example). Emerging technologies like the daguerreotype are folded in, and national distinction emerges as a selling point as the guides begin to highlight differences between American rules, American games, and their European counterparts.[11] If play was a laboratory for the production and manipulation of cultural associations, then a chronological intertextual study of *Boy's Own* books discloses a shifting landscape of instruments, methodologies, and points of focus.[12] And these attempts to break with tradition (or to register important but previously undocumented traditions) were even more apparent in the bureaucratically rationalized world of patents and commercial competition—a world of technical innovation, to wind us back to where we started, that deeply affected Milton Bradley's career.

By studying freshly patented and produced games like *The Checkered Game of Life*, we can more directly locate certain operative mechanics and material affordances as being meaningfully of their time. Where guidebooks reflect an aggregate that can be broken down and collated into a history of trends, the commercial sphere of advertising and patenting represents a series of punctuated moments: instances in which a given inventor was willing to invest both time and capital for the purpose of seizing or creating a new feeling or set of operative associations. We might bear in mind that there was minimal risk in adding new pages to *Boy's Own* books, minimal need for concern over whether anyone would take pleasure in one entry out of hundreds. By contrast, every advertisement and patent signals a leap predicated on the anticipation of a return on investment. In the end, both archives are useful, but in differing ways: one speaks to us about the *being* of diversion and the other, about the *becoming*—residual and emergent forms, to invoke Raymond Williams's terms. "Our list," Bradley's advertisements insist to both consumers and historians, "is not made up of . . . duplications of old methods under new names."[13] Though enjoyment of old forms of play—"old methods"— may not have faded, the emergence of new forms gestured at the subtleties and distinctions that were gaining traction in the everyday lives of Americans— specifically, those with the time and means to play at new models of social pleasure.

Bradley's flagship game may have seen such special success because it materialized a figure of growing importance to its nineteenth-century audience, a figure we now understand through the term "avatar." Analyzing the experience of playing in online virtual spaces, Mark Meadows describes an avatar as an "interactive social representation of a user."[14] Indeed, our own media-heavy society is flooded with such representations in digital form, but we need not limit the figure to the twentieth century's development of computerized games. As I will argue below, Bradley's *Life* innovatively sketches one of the first fully realized avatars in U.S. game history. With this avatar, players are figured, via a unitary piece on the board, as a kind of possibility machine, defined by the way they physically and publically navigate the series of "or"s that constitute any position in the field of play. And while the "interaction" of Meadows's productively intuitive definition reflects the navigation of a scripted *algorithm* (a term I'll return to shortly), the "social" here cannot simply be collapsed into a set of readymade interpersonal or cultural protocols—if so, "social" would only mirror and magnify the sense conveyed by "interactive." Instead, the specific sociality of an avatar, as I employ it, is more closely parsed by what Bruno Latour has dubbed a "sociology of associations"; it reflects a dynamic and performed collective that incorporates things, people, pictures, rules, and concepts, creating a set of coordinated psychophysical habits by which one might begin to account for life in the new world of commercial things and urban exchange.[15]

Avatars of the sort invited by Bradley's game enacted a purposefully tactile dislocation and relocation of the idea of self into a shared space of marking that went beyond a purely mentalist notion of interiority. It was, by contrast, an exteriorized and performed *celebration* of self in a relevant but less familiar sense of "celebration"—not as a simple synonymic substitute for "positive glorification," but instead as a public ritual of materialization, like a wedding or the traditional Christian sense of "celebrating" the Eucharist. The Hindi concept of *avatara* from which videogame designers drew "avatar" in the twentieth century parallels this notion, as it denotes the incarnation of spirit into a bodily form. So while the "exercise of judgment" that Bradley aims for in his game was on the one hand *executive*, it was also and always explicitly somatic and material. It is important to remember, even as I wander into the operative abstractions of gameplay and rules below, that the persistence of decision making was something unfailingly accompanied by public movements of the hand, not simply of the mind.

In what follows, I contend that Bradley wasn't alone in his engagement with an emerging figure of agency constituted through touchy media operations. If the mid-nineteenth-century board game was a site of experimentation in this frame, so too was the book—in ways that can be lost if our approach is primarily oriented toward textual dimensions of meaning. This chapter invests in the idea that both reading and gameplay were variations on coincident habits of self-production that were constituted and expanded by both the formal and the forensic materialities of their respective media.[16] Subjecting *Life* to deeper scrutiny enables contrapuntal opportunities to think about the variety of social practices that were or could be imagined to ally with the term "reading." Appropriately enough, a compelling and recognizable counterpoint to Bradley's reemployment of the checkerboard is a "song" reinvented by the affordances of the book.

The same year that Milton Bradley was making his fateful trip to the city, Walt Whitman trekked in the opposite direction, leaving Brooklyn to oversee the third edition of *Leaves of Grass* in Massachusetts.[17] In this collection, one can see elements of the same avatar-like perspective on self that was so integral to Bradley's game. Opening with "Song of Myself"—a poem he identified simply by its first line, "I celebrate myself," in early manuscripts—Whitman frames agency as a kind of avatar positionality with regard to social choices.[18] And like *Life*, Whitman's poem was deeply invested in the interface of things, ideas, and personal potential: "Put in my poems," he directs himself in early notebooks, "*American things, idioms, materials, persons, groups, minerals, vegetables, animals, etc.*"[19] Though Whitman desired the poem to be a "channel of thoughts and things," this channel was not only a text but also a weight and volume that strategically gestured at the unsettling tactilities of the body itself.[20] There is some cause to believe, especially when considering *The Checkered Game of Life* and "Song of Myself" in a shared mediascape, that Whitman's *Leaves of Grass* is less a masterpiece of abstract and lyric yearning, and more a material instrument of occasion—a work indebted to and embedded in its medium that persistently asks its reader to register their position qua reading body: "Both in and out of the game," as the speaker frames himself.

With Virginia Jackson's piercing critique of lyric genre in the reception of Emily Dickinson in mind, I should note that in the effusive pages of the 1855 *Leaves of Grass* Whitman never once refers to his writing as "lyric." He instead writes of "poems," "poets," "orations," "rhyme," "meter," and of course "song." Each of these terms reflects the conscious impact of form, both within the domain of verbal-textual governance ("meter") and within the domain of medium and performance ("oration"). Through this terminology Whitman documents a materialist schema of poetry as an explicit technology of social arrangement, taking an expansive view of what a "poem" might be above and beyond a companion to private intellectual meditation. In his best-case scenario, as articulated thirty years later to Horace Traubel, a poem was an inducement for "people to take me along with them and read me in the open air"—bringing sensation and cognition into a radically overlapping alignment.[21] This entanglement of paper and text, reading and the body of the reader, coincides with a rhetorical fusion of the first- and second-person perspective in Whitman's poem to imagine a promiscuously creative interplay between texts and bodies, ideas and things, exercise as deciding-upon and exercise as physical preparation.[22] As I mentioned earlier, Bradley's game pivots on a similar equivocation in the act of exercising "judgment," and this coincidence is a prompt to further inquiry.

My purpose, then, in putting Whitman's work into conversation with Bradley's materialization of avatar-selfhood in *The Checkered Game of Life*, is to supplement and expand traditionally textual approaches to *Leaves of Grass* while broadening our view of reading practices in the nineteenth century. It's not as though we need to take a poet's word as gospel, but it is intriguing to recall that even Whitman himself protests, "No one will get at my verses who insists upon viewing them as a literary performance, or attempt at such a performance, or as aiming mainly toward art or aestheticism."[23] Yet in the field of literary criticism we haven't always done much to address this (admittedly paradoxical-seeming) challenge to the general methods of our practice. Consider this the experiment of the present chapter.

When read alongside *Life*, Whitman's voracious "I" can be seen as an avatar-like position within an algorithmic piece of writing: not a lyric ego but a more uncanny physical marker of a place where we might linger, a *leaving* (like the stain from sitting in the grass) that enables a reader to both leave (as in exit) and leave (as in grow and flourish in one place). The cascade of inclusive "or"s that characterize Whitman's writing implicate the reader in something more than catalog-like reportage scanned along linear and sequential vectors. Instead, they become an opportunity to define a self that chooses, that decides among complex, but limited, collections of marked subject positions within the American social milieu, even as one *feels* the stasis and limitation that situate this freedom. Later, Whitman would generalize this view to the whole of *Leaves of Grass*, writing, "You do not read [it], it is someone that you see in action, in war, or on a ship, or climbing the mountains, or racing along and shouting aloud in pure exultation."[24] Here he places distinct emphasis on the inclusive possibilities of this "someone," noting a game-like series of disjunctions that one might choose to seize upon in defining the poem's character. Through this determined emphasis on inclusive disjunction, he can be seen as making an intervention into nineteenth-century debates on characterization—moving the conversation beyond Lockean notions of the self as a passive intellectual vessel (a soft malleable brain upon which the world is impressed) and toward the same avatar-like self that Bradley imagines in *Life*.

The sections that follow enlist the models of avatar action and social legibility that are constructed and highlighted by Bradley's board game to arrive at a different way of reading Whitman's "leaves." In parallel, I also consider the broad sociohistorical significance of Bradley's game. Because avatar is defined by action (the "interactive" aspect of Meadows's definition), it makes sense to trace its operational dynamics first in *Life*, contrasting it with the other board games of the period as a way of understanding the competing small media materializations of selfhood that existed in Bradley's moment. Using Bradley's innovations to codify these differences, I reexamine Whitman's deployment of form and materiality in "Song of Myself." What I hope to gain in this move is a more substantial way of thinking about the literary materialities that supplement Whitman's linguistic deployment of exchangeable poetic grammars. Bradley's game foregrounds the mechanics of avatar agency in ways that are obliged to accept media materiality as a given—the game takes place on a lithographed sheet that will inevitably bear the torn and scratched traces of its interactions. Whitman, America's "printer-poet," plays a coincident game by emphasizing the embodiment of writing in ways that echo these deep engagements with form, both on and as the page. By placing categorical subjectivity alongside disruptive visual patterning and persistent extratextual indication, Whitman's poem resists the breathless ideality of language and rehearses the interleaving of materials and agency in the act of reading.

Milton Bradley and the Game of Self-Representation

Born on 8 November 1836 and raised in Lowell, Massachusetts, by working-class parents, Bradley had a persistent interest in the practical uses of art.[25] The pragmatic tenor of his aesthetic pursuits appears to have been conditioned by a singular coupling of tendencies: a taste for the world of technical engineering paired with a knack for interweaving social threads. By 1853, Bradley had proven himself an ambitious teenager, navigating the bustling Lowell industrial scene with grace, "peddling paper, envelopes, pens, ink, wafers, etc., through the boarding houses in the corporations."[26] He recalls, "All the mill girls at that time were intelligent Americans, and in some of the larger houses there were fifty girls in a tenement. Usually I would find from ten to twenty-five assembled around the dining table sewing or reading or writing letters. I, in fact, had an *established* trade which competitors who learned my methods tried in vain to take from me, as the girls would wait for me."[27] Images like those Bradley describes here—of people in medium-sized groupings around tables, waiting, working, chatting, pointing—stuck with him and emerged as a trope in much of his later artwork involving human figures. Some of the first box art that accompanied *The Checkered Game of Life*—itself localized in ways that connected it to regional traditions of social assemblage as part of the "The New England Series of Games"—featured a majority of women: one standing and looking thoughtfully at the board, while an ambiguously styled person at the front (likely male because of the attire) makes a move as two girls and a boy watch (Figure 5). "There is a sociability in a game," Bradley would write, "which unites all the family, old and young, around the library table of a winter evening, which is found in few places besides."[28] As one of those "few places besides," the mill tenements (and later Civil War encampments) represented a functional and productive society via a diverse circling, usually but not always around a table. Success for Bradley was deeply linked to his ability to produce and maintain such geometric groupings.

At the onset of his twenties, he ventured into urban Springfield, securing a job as a draftsman with Wason Car-Manufacturing Company, a local factory specializing in the manufacture of railroad cars and locomotives.[29] It was here that he honed his technically oriented artistic craft, eventually going into business for himself as a "Mechanical Draftsman & Patent Solicitor."[30] At his Main Street office, he survived the financial downturns of the late 1850s by drawing patent schematics for hopeful inventors and designing a luxurious railcar for an eccentric Egyptian pasha.[31] In the process, he became interested in lithography, and in 1860, in a move that would radically shift the course of his life, he bought himself and his company a lithographic press.[32] Though he lamented that his "first real troubles would came with the lithograph business"—from drunken pressmen to the fickle facial fashions of the president-elect—it would also predicate his first massively public success, enabling him to produce prototypes of *The Checkered Game of Life* later that same year.[33]

Shortly after the stunning initial sales of his new game—some forty thousand copies, or nearly three times the population of his native Springfield[34]—the outbreak of the Civil War saw Bradley briefly abandoning amusement to focus on assisting the mechanical end of the war effort, drafting plans for the Union Army's new percussion-lock rifles.[35] While on the job, he took notice of the intense boredom that accompanied leisure time off the battlefield and began work on *Games for the Soldiers*, a portable kit that included chess, checkers, backgammon, dominoes, and, of course, *The Checkered Game of Life*. Materials and form were always as much a part of his designs as the rules

Figure 5. Game box with record dials. *The Checkered Game of Life*. Springfield: Milton Bradley & Co., ca. 1865. Courtesy of Missouri History Museum, St. Louis.

themselves, and "he took great pains to make it small and light enough to fit in a pocket and not add weight to a soldier's equipment."[36] The thoughtful approach paid off. The first compilation of its kind, *Games for the Soldiers* was immensely popular, as kits were bought up by civilian charities and donated to Union troops throughout the duration of the war.[37]

Beyond *Life*, Bradley's catalog in the period between 1861 and 1865 reflected some degree of focus, emphasizing both the themes and the dynamics of social and generational fusion. He worked together with Samuel Bowles to create *The Myriopticon: A Toy Panorama of the Rebellion*, which brought the Civil War into the domestic space of storytelling and parlor theater: children sold tiny accompanying tickets and read from an at times humorous script that was paired with scrolling scenes from the war, wondrously backlit courtesy of a candle.[38] *The Contraband Gymnast* was a flipping acrobat toy that invited the contentious political status of southern African Americans into the homes of many white Northerners even as it—however problematically—suggested the continuity of the black body with the idea of America (the gymnast himself doubles as a fluttering American flag). *My Grandfather's Games* and the only slightly later *Games of 1776* used the multigame innovation, undoubtedly grounded in some degree of cost savings, to create a platform through which people of a different era might understand their own past. As a generation struggling to sustain a sense of history and national belonging, the "1776" of Bradley's compilation was metonymic for a supposed moment when Thomas Paine's "common sense" seemed to exist in a way that now felt impossible.[39]

By linking these two games explicitly to history (both national and more broadly familial), Bradley suggested that playing could be a way to relive the past, to feel and understand important things about how the revolutionary generation had *lived through* rather than *conceived of* "the social." While *Boy's Own* books nostalgically flattened the past in order to produce an aggregate reference to the present, Bradley's backward-looking offerings showed him thinking of games explicitly as theoretical objects, as models of a differential historical imagination. This reflected a sophisticated awareness of the role that media could play in the negotiation of a culture, as he used games and toys to reinvigorate feelings of both intellectual and physical intimacy after the traumatic losses and separations of the war. *The Checkered Game of Life*, after all, was subject to cross-gender and cross-generational marketing, played by both soldiers and civilians in dramatically differing contexts. Yet as soldiers returned from the conflict in the spring of 1865, it's not difficult to imagine the simple comfort of playing a game that all involved had suddenly become familiar with—an unlikely point of social connection between the fractured domestic space and the horrors of the battlefield. As these families rediscovered how to coexist and enjoy one another's company, what better shared activity than a game about judgment and the decisions one *could* control, as well as the public identifications one should and shouldn't make? This particular emphasis on individual but socialized decision was a key operational distinction between *Life* and previous games in the American market.

Before the mid-century, most U.S. games were imports or slightly varied copies of popular British games.[40] Many of these were newly published versions of very old games: checkers and draughts; chess; the Indian game of *Pachisi*; and, of course, numbered card games. Notably, in these games there is either no representation of the player outside of the players themselves (as in poker) or else the representation of the player is dispersed across multiple pieces. This may speak to the simulation these games were meant to invoke: a view from on high of war, of military command, and of monarchal authority. For instance, in a game of checkers or chess, the moves happen one at a time, but the movements are divided among a range of player-controlled pieces. As a result, losing a piece or facing a setback may be a disappointment but, depending on the value of the piece, may not require large-scale adjustments to player strategy. The disappointment of losing a piece in checkers is more akin to the death of a character in a third-person narrative than to the abrupt end of a first-person narration. In the first instance, the focus of the story may shift, but the fundamental perspective does not change. In the second instance, barring the introduction of a secondary narrator (or tricky science fiction), the story is over.

By contrast, *Life* situates the player as the manager of a single actor within the gamespace; in this way, the marker is not a representation of others under the control of the user but a representation closer to that of the user controlling himself or herself. In a sense, this marker delineates a tactile *you* position that can then be inhabited as an *I*, a formal and visual second person that becomes the ludic first person. Many traditional games opt against employing this type of unitary player representation, but it alone does not make Bradley's game unique. Instead, it reveals the ancestral link between *Life* and an earlier form of board game known commonly as a *race game*. In race games—widely popularized in Western contexts as *The Royal Game of Goose* and *The Game of Snake*—players compete to be the first to reach a finish line (or square) by accumulating die rolls on a linear track.[41]

The first amusement of this type known to be manufactured in continental America was the 1822 *Traveller's Tour through the United States*.[42] Essentially a map of the eastern United States, the game board is crisscrossed with a serpentine line stopping at 139 different points, corresponding to different American cities. Each of the cities on the game map has a listing in the key enclosed with the game (cross-referenced by the number listed at the indicated point) that includes some brief trivia about the city and its population. Boston, for example, is described as "the largest city in New England [and] situated on a peninsula at the bottom of Massachusetts bay. It has a fine capacious harbour, and is extensively engaged in commerce."[43] After spinning the teetotum to see who takes the first turn (highest roll leads), players start off the board and continue to spin to see how far they travel, alternating turns and reading the city information aloud as they move along.[44]

The operations of game play in this sort of game are a function of basic arithmetic: take the number of the space you are on, add to it the number you have spun, and then record the new sum by moving your piece to the corresponding number. Reflecting this, the typical term for a player's game piece in this era was a *counter*.[45] In *Traveller's* and other games of its ilk, this counting terminology underlines the fact that the visualization enabled by the game board and player piece is primarily a way of spatializing accounting procedures. Additive arithmetic on a linear game board (*Traveller's* does not allow backward moves) constitutes the algorithm, or the discrete input-output structure, of the game. The spinning teetotum produces inputs, and the rules of arithmetic produce consistent outputs that determine the player's in-game outcomes.

This ties race games like *Traveller's* indirectly to the history of the term "algorithm," which was "a corruption of the name of the Persian mathematician al-Kwārizmī."[46] Laying the foundations of modern algebra, al-Kwārizmī's work introduced the Western world to the convenience and accuracy of performing arithmetic with Hindu-Arabic numerals. In its first instances, an algorithm was a symbolistic replacement for the spatial counting operations traditionally handled by the abacus. A game like *Traveller's* combines these operations by allowing the marker and board to act either as a counting device (one can imagine younger players counting out each individual number they pass) or as an *ac*counting device through which players represent the arithmetic totals they have calculated (placing their piece directly at the total).

In *Life*, this counting is displaced from the central playing field. The player piece, which Bradley still refers to as a "counter," does not represent an accounting of progress but rather figures an object allegory of a self defined and located by mobilizing decisions.[47] Here, by contrast to *Traveller's*, the game board is a *freeform* grid consisting of sixty-four squares—a format putting pressure on the visualized counting terminology native to other period games. Starting in the bottom left corner at "Infancy," a player spins the teetotum and coordinates his or her rolls (one through six) with instructions for movement written on the bottom of "record-dials" that remain separate from the field of play. These dials take the place of the game board visualization required by race games like *Traveller's* and record how many points a player has scored toward the hundred-point goal (via a small brass swiveling arm that points to an arc of numbers like the minute hand of a clock). This adjustment leaves the board open to new functional interpretations. If the counting operations of the game have now been moved to the periphery—a subroutine to the central focus of game play—then we must now look to the supplementary algorithm that this displacement allows to take place on the board. Put another way, if the game board isn't a visualization of the *counting* going on, what exactly *is* it visualizing? The answer suggests Bradley's innovation: to make the "exercise of judgment" the primary focus of the game.[48]

Combining chance and choice, *Life* foregrounds decision making. Rolling a one through three allows the player to move one square: either "up or down" for a one, "right or left" for a two, and "Diagonally in either Direction" for a three; rolling a four through six duplicates these options, adding the ability to move "one or two squares" in either of the aforementioned directions. Players alternate turns, decide their directions, and follow the instructions listed on the square upon which they land, which usually lists either a point value (to be added to the record-dial) or another square to which the player should move his or her piece. Point-value squares are more sparsely portioned than one might imagine; more often than not players are simply moving about the board in the effort to get near the squares that will notch the record-dial ever closer to the win.

Already we can note a strain in the terminology of Bradley's patent: the movable piece he calls a counter is less a token marking a precise accumulation of points than an indicator of *position* amid a field of choices imbued with a relative value not transparently related to the game-board square. Accordingly, Bradley warns that reaching "Happy old age" (the square most distant from "Infancy" and worth a game-changing fifty points) is not necessarily a foolproof strategy for winning the game. He writes, "As 'Happy old age' is surrounded by many difficulties, fifty [points] may oftentimes be gained as

soon by a succession of smaller numbers as by striving for 'Happy old age.' "[49]
The manipulation of the counter in the field of choices and the presumed, if
simple, relationship between player and counter were precisely the aspects of
the game Bradley hoped would allow it be a teaching tool—not just of *information* relating to virtues but also of smart and virtuous *habits* of decision
making. This is because the results of the game are dictated by player judgment rather than random number generation alone.

Here it is important to keep in mind that both the actions of the players
and the limitations bounding them determine the outcome of the game, as
with any algorithm. Algorithmic media requires interactivity at some point in
its decision tree in order to produce a result. It is what McKenzie Wark calls "a
finite set of instructions for accomplishing some task, which transforms an
initial starting condition into a recognizable end condition."[50] In *Life*, the algorithms of the game rules govern things like: the starting position of the
counters, the possibilities afforded players upon spinning a given number, the
results of inhabiting a given space, and the end conditions for declaring victory. None of these rules, however, *does* anything without the players supplying the inputs that give starting values. So while there is a very real sense in
which the player's outcomes are bound and determined by the structure of
Bradley's algorithms, the regular iteration of decision points in the game ensures that the outcome is never wholly out of the players' hands.[51] Every slide
and scrape of the counter materializes a choice, yoking movement and visual
representation to intellectual purpose in the vein of Bradley's later work with
the tactile pedagogy of Friedrich Froebel's kindergarten gift blocks. Grasping
Life as an experiment in decision making and character rehearsal, it becomes
relevant to ask what kinds of decisions it requires its players to make.

To open such an analysis, we might look at restrictive positions on the
board, such as edges and corners. In these positions, a player's counter is
against the boundaries of the game board, suggesting a back-against-the-wall
feeling that Bradley may have intended to generate among gamers who landed
on these squares. This reading is supported by the content of the backline
squares—"Prison," "Jail," and "Disgrace," and at other edge squares like "Poverty," "Gambling," and "Ruin." Further, even the positively valued squares at
the edges of the board are risky places to be: "Fat Office" is surrounded by
"Ruin," "Prison," and the game-ending "Suicide."[52] Yet "Suicide," that most
aggressively bleak inclusion from a twenty-first-century perspective, is nearly
impossible to land on, as there is only one lonely place—"the red square between Ruin and Fat Office," as Jill Lepore notes—and one roll from that place

that can force you onto the sad image of the hanging man.[53] As I contemplate this operational figure of sympathy for the compulsion to self-harm, I am further arrested by the fact that Bradley builds a kind of haunting into the insistent visual index of the game: one cannot play *Life* without acknowledging the way that some people feel forced into death. Even if you never land on it, the image remains. Finally, since there isn't much reason to cross this square, "Suicide" remains one of the most legible icons even on aggressively played game boards—as *Life* ages, its potential pitfalls stand in high contrast to safer routes. Closely played, the game reveals a complicated sensibility regarding the limit point of its core theme.

Moving to locations even more restrictive than the edges, all of the game's *corners* allow only six options for player movement, contrasting the sixteen available at central locations on the board. Unless you are just starting or finishing *Life* it is never a good idea to be in a corner. Correspondingly, "Infancy" and "Happy old age" are the only themed squares occupying these positions. And to further discourage those who would dart across the board directly to "Happy old age," this pinned position is surrounded by negatively themed squares that effectively rob the player of a turn ("Gambling," "Intemperance," and "Idleness"). Functionally, this means that if you were to land on "Happy old age" and not win the game in the same move, you would have only a slight chance (one in six) of attaining any points in the following turn. Moreover, you would have a 50 percent chance of having to wait at least two more turns before another scoring opportunity—a deterrent against living fast and retiring early. For Bradley, even the positive elements of *Life* require a keen sense of situational strategy and timing.

A further case in point, Bradley's use of "Truth" may be the most suggestive combination of content and operation in the game. In play, the "Truth" square has no value of its own, but it puts you within striking distance of beneficial squares, such as "Wealth," "Matrimony," "Happiness," "Politics," "Cupid," "Perseverance," and "Congress," with the only negative single-turn outcome being "Crime."[54] In other words, assuming the position of "Truth" is *strategically* smart: to seek out "Truth" is to have the potential for happiness or love and to forestall the possibility of "Ruin." On the flip side, "Truth" is not automatically valuable. "Truth" alone is ambiguous; it requires judgment and is not an end in itself.[55] Here again, *Life*'s operational approach conveys a considerable amount about how its inventor hoped to influence players' senses of practical morality.

Yet Bradley's game was not alone in its focus on virtue and vice. Earlier

board games of moral instruction "mirror[ed] popular notions of the successful Christian life" by schematizing visualizations of virtue's positive effects and
vice's negative outcomes. An important representative of the genre, William
and Stephen Bradshaw Ives's 1843 *The Mansion of Happiness* was a race game
like *Traveller's* with strong thematic parallels to *Life*. Indeed, it is almost always grouped in with *Life* as a kind of predecessor in histories of American
board games. In *Mansion*, players traverse an inwardly spiraling path of sixty-
seven squares culminating in "The Mansion of Happiness," all while navigating a gauntlet of Christian morality.[56] If players land on a space relating to one
of the virtues, they jet forward on the path toward the center. On the other
hand, if a player lands on a vice, say "Passion" on the fourteenth space, that
player will have to return to the sixth space, "Water," for as the rules caution,
"Whoever gets in a Passion must be taken to the Water and have a ducking to
cool him"; similarly, a "Sabbath Breaker [square twenty-eight] was 'taken to
the Whipping Post [square twenty-two] and whipt.'"[57] In application, the
goal of the game was to avoid vices (which lead to backward moves), amass
virtues (which lead to forward moves), and achieve a counting score of sixty-
seven as quickly as possible, similar to Bradley's hundred-point goal.

The differences, however, are what shift the emphasis from *informing* the
player to *re-forming* (changing) the player. In Bradley's game, the progression
one makes toward the score of one hundred is neither linear nor wholly left to
chance. As opposed to the forward motion of *Mansion*, players of *Life* are
persistently given choices regarding the direction they would rather take in
the pursuit of a game-winning final score. This means that the player's role is
changed from one of spinning the teetotum and watching the results—
perhaps forming positive or negative associations with different spots on the
board, perhaps not—to one in which he or she might choose to weather a
certain degree of vice on the road to greater virtue. The addition of judgment-
based decision points in Bradley's game imparts a stronger sense of player actions (rather than chance alone) determining the outcome. Players must
formulate a personal navigation strategy, making their relationship to the
game more interactive and connected to habit-oriented forms of social
training.

The dominant manner of thinking through such training in the mid-
nineteenth century was through the figure of "character." Karen Halttunen
writes: "Within prevailing Lockean psychology, the youth's character was like
a lump of soft wax, completely susceptible to any impressions stamped upon
him. . . . The term *character*, in fact, could apply not to the lump of wax itself

but to the impression made upon it."[58] The image of "soft wax" becomes an opportunity for figuring character as Locke's famous tabula rasa, a blank slate upon which the sensational world acts. The character of an individual is, Locke argues, "acquired . . . imprinted by external things, with which infants have earliest to do, which make the most frequent impressions on their senses."[59] "Ideas," he continues, fill the "empty cabinet" of the mind and make the person who he or she is, yielding a passive perspective on character that is the result of factors largely out of a person's control.[60]

This information-based view of character impression is clearly present in both the instructional goals and the mechanics of a game like *Mansion*. Here, players come across spaces, as in *Life*, such as "Generosity," "Ruin," and "[Becoming] A Drunkard."[61] The consequence for landing on these spaces, which is wholly the result of the teetotum roll, is demarcated in a key that comes with the game, admonishing: "Whoever possess Audacity, Cruelty, Immodesty, or Ingratitude, must return to his former situation . . . and not even *think* of Happiness, much less partake of it."[62] In this game, the player is informed that the presence of a vice in the mind precludes the presence of virtues, and thus prevents a happy result. It is as if the cabinet to which Locke refers has only room enough for one set of ideas or the other. Accordingly, the goal for the players is to educate themselves as to what these positive ideas are, and to have a properly arranged stockpile (the visual analogy being a perfect accumulation of sixty-seven points, the endpoint of the game). Emphasizing this, the instructional passage lingers notably on a static and scenic depiction of the player's mental state: the player "possess[es]" the vices (rather than acting them out) and as a consequence is prohibited from moving on. This situates game play wholly in the realm of forming either negative or positive associations with specific moral ideas, "Audacity, Cruelty, Immodesty, or Ingratitude" against "Charity, Humanity, or Generosity."[63] Accordingly, the characterological goal of a game like *Mansion* runs parallel to its operational goal: a player accumulating points is, at the same time, accumulating associational impressions, ideas of moral value.

Bradley shares this focus upon impressions in the patent for *Life*, asserting that "it is intended to forcibly impress upon the minds of youth the great moral principles of virtue and vice."[64] However, though the language of impression follows the Lockean precedent, the nature of these impressions is distinct from that in *Mansion*. In *Life*, impressions are made on a player by facilitating the active repeatability of decision making (re-forming the player through *iterations* of judgment) in addition to the possession of ideas. This operative addition is the central reform mechanism of the game. Bradley writes, "As the player . . . oftentimes has the choice of several different moves, the game becomes very interesting, the more so from the fact that the chance of the die is so connected with the frequent choice of moves involving the exercise of judgment."[65] While in *Mansion* it is enough to *possess* "Prudence . . . [to move] toward the Mansion of Happiness,"[66] in Bradley's amusement that good judgment must be "exercise[d]"—a use-it-or-lose-it approach to the same principles.

It is worth clarifying that in *Mansion* there *are* undoubtedly moments at which inputs must be given to the rule system in order to produce forward movement. Player involvement at these decision points, however, is essentially that of a random number generator. At the onset of a turn, the player spins the teetotum and counts his or her piece forward the number of spaces rolled. There is no arguing with the die: if you're on square 24, roll a one, and notice that one space forward will land you on "Immodesty," you cannot instead move one space backward to "Truth," or across the board to the adjoining square 52, "Humanity." Unfortunately, it's "Immodesty" or bust.[67] In this case, even though players technically interact with the algorithms of the game, the mode of their interaction is limited to the physical act of spinning the teetotum. If there is a tactile mnemonic at play it is this: touch things at your own risk.

In the current climate of video games, *Mansion*'s mode of activity might not be called *interactivity* at all, given that interactivity is typically associated with a real sense of *agency* (that is, a real give and take between the decision process of the algorithm and the decision process of the player). Addressing this issue, Janet Murray writes, "Activity alone is not agency. For instance, in a tabletop game of chance, players may be kept very busy spinning dials, moving game pieces, and exchanging money, but they may not have any true agency. The players' actions have effects, but the actions are not chosen and the effects are not related to the players' intentions."[68] On the other hand, as previously noted, players of *Life* are given ample opportunities to take an agential role in the game, to, as Bradley puts it, "exercise [their] judgment."[69] In this way, Bradley's player/counter/game dynamic is more akin to Meadows's definition of avatar discussed earlier: an "interactive social representation of a user." It is interactive, in that the decision-making process is two-sided (at least), involving the input-output system of the game rules *and* the player's activity of judgment within this system. And it is social, in that the decisions of the players are represented visually on the board by a small piece of wood with which they associate themselves, for the benefit of other players. These players, in turn, can formulate their own strategies, as well as expressive conceptions of their playmates, through this token and its movements. It is, however, also important to linger on the double meaning of "exercise" in tying this back to the nineteenth-century goal of "character" formation.

Insofar as Bradley's counter is more avatar-like than in previous American games, one can see the game as profoundly interested in representing a self *controlled* by the best judgments of the player. A *counter*, by this rubric, was more like a puppet manipulated by the player than a sum of numbers. This emphasis on self-control was directly related to what Steven Mintz identifies as one of the core goals of mid-century reformers: "The traits associated with a firm character had a strongly moral dimension; they included personal integrity . . . a capacity for hard work, and self-control . . . For early-nineteenth-century child-rearing experts, the primary goal of socialization . . . was to implant a strong will, a capacity for self-discipline, and sense of duty deep within the individual character."[70] By playing at such "self-control" in Bradley's game, players were, at each turn, habituated to the notion of *judgment* being a contributing factor to good character development. Possessing good ideas, as in *Mansion*, was not enough; one had to use these ideas to generate active solutions to an ever-changing gameplay situation. This is at the core of the game's reform goals: at every turn, players form and iterate (re-form) a strategy for negotiating the board, representing their "will" and reinforcing their "capacity" for self-control. The repetitive nature of decision in a turn-based game like *Life* meant that one "exercised" the faculty of judgment by playing. Rather than a self that is impressed upon by the outside forces of the game/world, this self "forcibly impress[es]" its avatar (that is, develops procedural strategies) as a way of shaping the options that the world rains upon it. And instead of an accumulation of static ideas, player "character" materializes in the iterated assemblage of these local instances of strategy over time—the slowly engraved directional grooves that link one square to another in a forensic indicator of strategy that can be read years later. The emphasis shifts to a visualization of *how* you react rather than *what* you know.

As a Massachusetts contemporary of Bradley, Ralph Waldo Emerson offers a gloss on this process-minded reimagining of the Lockean wax metaphor, asserting in "The Transcendentalist," "You think me the child of my circumstances: I make my circumstances. Let any thought or motive of mine be different from that they are, the difference will transform my condition and economy. I—this thought which is called I—is the mould into which the world is poured like melted wax. The mould is invisible, but the world betrays the shape of the mould."[71] Where the earlier depiction of character situated the self as a malleable piece of wax and the world as composite agential force doing the impressing (lending itself to analogies of the divine), here Emerson turns this on its head, suggesting that the world itself is wax and the self is a sculpting force that impresses a shape upon the raw materials provided. This inverted metaphorical figure has two consequences significant to the parsing of character's relationship to self and agency. First, while it still gives some ground to the outside world's ability to affect the product of the impression process (one can imagine different mixtures, colors, and consistencies of wax), Emerson's metaphor gives the final public configuration of agency to the self. Differences of "motive," which one might reasonably link to habituated strategies of judgment developed in Bradley's game, have a direct effect on the "shape of the mould." As a result, the aggregate force of a person's own active judgments has a direct effect on the self that is realized in the public world.

Moreover, Emerson's image evokes a transposability not present in the earlier metaphor. By thinking of the self as a mold, one is encouraged to imagine multiple wax productions yielded from the same basic structure, each one slightly different in terms of the raw material furnished (the "circumstances" the world presents) but proximately linked via the mold's underlying shape. Here one might think of the ever-changing states presented by a moderately open-ended game like *Life*: each turn instances a new circumstance, new raw materials for testing the desirability of the current expressive strategy or mold. Bradley hoped these habits of judgment would not only be "forcibly impressed" on the character of the game's players *within* the game but also capable of being ported to a real-world perspective on self.[72]

Taking an alternative slant, we might adjust this sense of character by thinking of it not through Emerson's familiar reworking of the wax metaphor but rather through the lens of Bradley's own experience as a draftsman and lithographer. Though he did less and less of the manual labor involved in presswork as time went on, in the early years Bradley was the primary trainer for his crew and often had to step in to complete jobs when his pressmen went missing (sometimes to the chagrin of his customers).[73] To make a reproducible image, he would use a special *wax* crayon to draw on a limestone plate, rendering the plate water-resistant in all of the areas he had drawn upon. Then, using a chemical wash containing gum arabic, he would wipe down the stone to produce an opposite effect in the whitespace of the drawing. When he poured a combination of ink and water over the stone, the plate would retain ink precisely in the form of the wax drawing, and from here the image could be *impressed* upon sheets of cardstock or paper. It could be trying work, intensified by the idiosyncrasies of the technology: "The drawing surface of the stone had to be kept absolutely clean; one drop of perspiration on it reproduced smudges on the finished print."[74] For a two-color print like the red and black *Checkered Game of Life*, this impression was doubly complicated by the need to pull the first print, dry it, and then accurately line it up with a separate inking for the second color—a process even further developed in the case of the full-color chromolithographs I discuss later, in Chapter 5. Appreciating this process and its centrality to Bradley's business, it is not unproductive to imagine that when Bradley says a game will "forcibly impress upon the minds of youth the great moral principles of virtue and vice," his controlling metaphor is not wax molding but wax drafting and lithographic reproduction.

Pursuing this, one might think of the movements of players as akin to the drawing of wax upon the limestone (rather than pouring the wax into a preestablished mold). At this point, far from the relative permanence of engraving or etching, adjustments can be made, just as in any given game a player's strategy might change or adjust. Through the habituation of certain types of decision making at iterated turns in the game, however, one might imagine that these momentary tactics or inspirations will begin to be inked—linked to positive strategic outcomes that the player wants to reproduce, in the game of course but perhaps in real life as well (since this distinction is specifically rendered ambivalent by the content of *Life*). Once the players' habits are "inked" they can then be reproduced and transposed into different situations, as different individual documents. In the case of printmaking, each individual document maintains the idiosyncrasies of the medium and the pressing (how might an errant drop of sweat gradually change the picture over the course of many impressions?), while still maintaining a proximate genetic similarity that can read as a single text. In the case of *character*, this text is a person's public identity or avatar. Much as the lithographic press "forcibly impress[es]" its prints upon the many leaves of paper and cardboard that make up an edition run, the player now has a sense of repeatable, but nevertheless potentially mutable, character. And even if this reading requires a few logical leaps, a bit of calculated risk in this regard may be warranted. Because even allowing for some amount of analogic fuzziness, it seems to me ultimately imperative to consider the degree to which extant technologies of reproducibility—the resources, tools, and mechanisms that were the *everyday associates* of media producers in this era—must have had bearing on the figures that these media producers deployed to imagine collective life. It is unlikely that the specific affordances of material reproducibility had no bearing on models of social and personal reproduction. Discussed further in the next chapter, metaphors of self are nearly always drawn from those models most ready at hand (often literally).

For now, suffice to say that the idea of social reproducibility reminds us that Bradley's game participated in an emerging discourse, one insisting that the relationship between selfhood and society or selfhood and history was not passive.[75] *Life* supplements and contrasts itself to earlier figurations of Romantic-era selfhood, aptly visualized by the counter of a game like *Mansion*. In these previous figures the self is a cipher, or in Locke's language an "empty cabinet" through which the events of life pass. If these events happen to be virtuous, the vessel gains value. A poem prefacing *Mansion* explains that the game "gives to those their proper *due*, / Who various paths of vice pursue, / And shows (while vice destruction brings) / That good from every virtue springs."[76] Unlike in *Life*, where a virtue like truth is framed as a strategic position and may not "spring" positive results, *Mansion* both thematically and operationally asserts that one's choices have very little to do with outcomes. Agency is the ability of the individual to *know* rather than the ability to *decide*. This perspective can be summed up by William Wordsworth's position in "Expostulation and Reply," first published in the 1798 *Lyrical Ballads*:

> The eye it cannot choose but see,
> We cannot bid the ear be still;
> Our bodies feel, where'er they be,
> Against, or with our will.

> Nor less I deem that there are powers,
> Which of themselves our minds impress,
> That we can feed this mind of ours,
> In a wise passiveness.[77]

Here we are given the image of a "passive" self "impress[ed]" upon by the circumstances of the world—much in line with the Lockean metaphor to which Emerson found himself responding in "The Transcendentalist." Will is subordinate to the hungry mind that fills itself with sights and sounds, and the player's role is, again, one of accounting rather than accountability.

This ideology of "wise passiveness" is reflected in the American literary context by a poet like William Cullen Bryant. Taking the torch of Wordsworth's wise cipher, Bryant's speaker in "The Prairies" (1832) collapses history and nature into a justification for the transcendent self of the present. Bryant writes:

> The Prairies. I behold them for the first,
> And my heart swells, while the dilated sight
> Takes in the encircling vastness. Lo! they stretch
> In airy undulations, far away,
> As if the ocean, in his gentlest swell,
> Stood still, with all his rounded billows fixed,
> And motionless for ever.[78]

The viewer "Takes in the encircling vastness," transforming the immensity and incorrigibility of the natural world into a "sight" that locates the speaker who has mastered it, much as a Claude glass frames an image and points an optic line from the scene to the eyes of its viewer. Moreover, in this instance, "tak[ing] in" amounts to a similar accounting to that found in *The Mansion of Happiness*, where the player who takes in the most virtues is given his or her "due" in the form of forward movement toward the endpoint of the game. The ebb and flow of accounting is reflected in Bryant's teleological perspective later in the poem: "Thus change the forms of being. Thus arise / Races of living things, glorious in strength, / And perish, as the quickening breath of God / Fills them, or is withdrawn."[79] The player who stands at the endpoint of history, at the top of the game, occupies that position because the "breath of God"—or the roll of the teetotum—has made it that way. Within a naturalized Protestant ethic of grace and election, those who have experienced withdrawals of this "breath," who have moved backward on the board, have only gotten what was due to them all along.

Yet if informed passivity is a virtue linking *Mansion* to early Romantic modes of privileged self-awareness, then we find an analogue for the interactive self of *Life* in Whitman's "Song of Myself." While both Wordsworth's and Bryant's speakers appear to yearn for a perfect passivity within the game of life that allows them a certain amount of subjective interior transcendence, Whitman's "gigantic and generous treatment" never quite leaves the active and exterior parts of this game behind. As an attempt at both prompting and rendering social life within the constraints of paper media, Whitman's textual subject is always, as he writes, "both in and out of the game."[80] Accordingly,

his use of the second person and repetition in the poem shows him determined to leave the reader with a strong sense of implication, responsibility,
and material embeddedness within the world he demarcates.[81] Tracing the
medial continuities between Bradley and Whitman enables a reading of "Song
of Myself" that moves beyond the apparent categorical emptiness of its "I"
and toward a more active understanding of the poem's potentials and sensual
interventions.

Walt Whitman and the Puzzle of Puzzles

A curious thing happens if you squint a bit at the title page and frontispiece of
the first edition of Whitman's *Leaves of Grass* (Figure 6). Though the image of
an author on the verso (that is, the left side of the binding crease) was a typical
accompaniment to recto titling (on the right side), the proportion of image to
text feels playfully conceived. A tiny (yet full-bodied save for the lower legs)
Whitman gazes at you ambiguously, self-composed, leaning against one hip;
you can barely make out the eyes, but it is certain that he looks in your
direction—a challenge, an invitation? Glancing away from the intensity of
this miniature man, you scan to the recto and are accosted by a massive bit of
interposing signage, a constellation of font sizes that produces a near shouting
effect: Leaves! of (this time even bigger) Grass! Below you note, in a more
subdued font, the place and year of publication, "Brooklyn, New York: 1855."
In the context of the kind of public banners and billboards that historian
David Henkin has so vividly recovered as part of our urban model of mid-
nineteenth-century New York City, it's almost as if the title itself were a sign
hanging in the air, one much closer to you than the provoking man staring
from across the way—as close, indeed, as this little green book, where even
the cover evokes the grass just outside your door or under your feet as you
read. This book—the book bent open in the reader's hands, paper arching out
against the fingers on either side—is nothing if not a "medium," a center
point of exchange between the body of the reader and the distant body of
Whitman himself, whether figured on the verso or out loafing in the grass
somewhere.[82] This codex is the place where, if you feel the literal tension of
those pages against the edge of your thumbs, you share a *feeling* as well as a set
of terms with someone else through the mediation of something that is neither of you, although it is now and for this moment intimately associated with
both at once. This shared association, a tactile dislocation of self relocated in

Figure 6. *Leaves of Grass*. Brooklyn: Walter Whitman, 1855.
Courtesy of Library Company of Philadelphia.

the instant of readerly interaction, might be the starting point for a conception of the collection's entry-point poem, "Song of Myself," that takes a second look at its seemingly private, engulfing, lyric "I." The book, and that "I," are, in this view, less markers of some secret world to which we have stolen access, and more the markers and playfield for a staging of the type of association Milton Bradley would materialize five years later on the pasteboard grid of *Life*.

After the celebratory opening of "Song of Myself," the speaker declares, "what I assume, you shall assume / for every atom belonging to me as good as belongs to you."[83] Here, as with the interactive counters of *Life*, Whitman establishes an early interface between the first and second person as recursively connected positions, a structured place from which to understand circumstance and shape it accordingly: "You shall listen to all sides and filter them from yourself."[84] As a result, the imperious "I" of the speaker's effusion is inaugurated with a gesture that is equal parts ego and radical formal empathy:

we are the same because we shall occupy the same grammatical *place* in the text, a place where "all sides" are "filter[ed]." The speaker's use of "assume" in these opening lines reinforces this by playing on both a locating sense— "assume the position!"—and an informational sense—"here are the facts that can be assumed." This multivocality of "assumption" foregrounds Whitman's equivocation between locating the reader in a *place* and giving a *range* of data possibilities that he or she may work with at that location. As in *Life*, the position a marker assumes has an intimate relationship with the options available to it (the assumptions it may make).

These possibilities are enumerated throughout the poem as various character types, locations, and affections that radiate outward in a flurry of inclusive disjunction—"or"s that do not preclude the possibility of "both." We see one of the most explicit statements of this in Whitman's characterization of the grass that forms the poem's central metaphor: "Or I guess it must be the flag of my disposition, out of hopeful green stuff woven. / Or I guess it is the handkerchief of the Lord . . . / Or I guess the grass is itself a child."[85] This series of disjunctions never excludes any of the others; they are consistently additive, although only one may be read at a time. Each option maintains a singular quality both in terms of textual space and in terms of the temporal mechanics of reading. In this way, the repetitive syntax, while yielding a synchronic sense to the poem that many have noted, also acts as a textual metronome repeating a familiar beat that ensures the discrete separation of each possibility.[86]

Moreover, in terms of format, there is the suggestion of the kind of newspaper printing work that had informed much of Whitman's life. From the dense two-column arrangement of the preface to the irregular clustering of lines that distinguish his poetry throughout, Whitman cues the movement of the eye across discrete morsels held together and split apart by the cognitive gravity of the page and its whitespace. In both form and format, his collection figures both synchrony and diachrony. Being an American is being *this* or *this*, or all of these things, but only as time allows, only as one lingers or returns to a given option in an ever-growing list.

Demonstrating a strategically flickering interplay between the liminal and the discrete, Whitman uses the phrase "I am the" to reinforce this effect. In one short passage, he writes: "I am the hounded slave," "I am the mashed fireman with breastbone broken," "I am the clock myself," and "I am an old artillerist, and tell of some fort's bombardment / . . . . and am there again."[87] Here, analogous syntax reinforces the connection between each of these disparate narrative characters, linking them in an inclusive "I am," notably in the present tense. Yet it also invokes the metronomic quality discussed above, acting as a reminder of those that have previously passed: the slave transforms into the fireman, and the fireman into the ticking clock. As a reader scans the disparate activity of these lines, they either say or think an "I am" that becomes, in Elizabeth Maddock Dillon's useful diptych, a "mimetic" script for subjecthood accompanying the "ontic" act of holding, sitting, standing, or lying down.[88] There is a strangeness to the inclusive disjunction of the language that I would argue mirrors the uncanny feelings of physical difference and relatedness in the poem. Here the flesh itself becomes a messy but nonetheless legible-in-flashes kind of poetry along with the text. "Read these leaves in the open air every season of every year of your life," Whitman stresses in the preface, "and your very flesh shall be a great poem and have the richest fluency not only in its words but in the silent lines of its lips and face and between the lashes of your eyes and in every motion and joint of your body."[89]

Equally suggestive in a more conventional mode, the concreteness of each incarnation, the ability of the I/writer and linked you/reader to place themselves in the role that follows the "I am," is specifically coupled to the passage of time. The "old artillerist" has a place ("[I] am there again") just as he begins to "tell of some fort's bombardment." Telling a story takes time; it requires the teller to move in one narrative direction over another, to make choices. This interaction of temporal movement and identity reminds us of *Life*'s synchronic grid, where "Wealth" is always present, but players only enact its benefit in the right moment, in time, using the position they have assumed on the board. As a player's eyes must drift across the possible positions available and settle upon the one that they would like to make, so must a reader (the "I" or "you" of Whitman's poem) give attention to one thing at a time, even as they might remember the total assemblage. And as with Bradley's counter, what holds Whitman's ambivalent first/second person together is its unity as a place of decision making, along with its persistence as a thing that remains even after one has moved one's hands away.

Apprehending the self as a possibility locus coincident with a body may account for Whitman's declaration that the poem should be seen not as something one reads but rather as "someone."[90] This term, "someone," acts as a personal cipher or marker, only fully intelligible in the action of choosing to linger on one or the other of the character choices imagined by the transcendent speaker. One cannot understand who "someone" *is* in the abstract; the pronoun simply stands as a mathematical variable might, a formal placeholder, unable to produce an output on its own. Yet one might understand this someone as a specific person if supplied with information about either the person's actions or the framework in which those actions were carried out. "Song of Myself" is at pains to produce the latter, but it makes appeals to the reader to provide the activity that will make this framework productive of a concrete self (rather than an abstract someone). "Not I," Whitman writes, "not any one else can travel that road for you, / You must travel it for yourself."[91] The "you" of Whitman's song gains its constitutive definition by making decisions of focus from within the possibilities enunciated by the poem, similar to Bradley's algorithm.[92] This "you" is a strategy for visualizing an inhabitable marker, for allowing any number of readers to imagine themselves as a part of the world Whitman creates. In other words, it is defined as an avatar: in and through its situational *use*. In the patent for *Life*, the usefulness of the game lies its capacity to "exercise . . . judgment"; in the original 1855 preface to *Leaves of Grass*, Whitman echoes this focus, claiming that the poet "is no arguer . . . he is judgment. . . . If he does not expose superior models and prove himself by every step he takes he is not what is wanted."[93]

By 1856, Whitman was developing this figure in a specifically national mold, drawing again on the discourse of character that was so important to Bradley and other reformers. He writes to Emerson: "There is being fused a determined character, fit for the broadest use for the freewomen and freemen of The States . . . each indeed free, each idiomatic, as becomes live states and men, but each adhering to one enclosing general form of politics, manners, talk, [and] personal style."[94] Here, again, Whitman defines the "fit[ness]" of this figure by its capacity for broad "use"; it is not a model to aspire to but a facilitator of any number of future models, a figuring figure. In this way, what Whitman refers to as "character" is, in its formal sense, less like the "character" described in Halttunen's work and more akin to the avatar figure Bradley would develop in *Life*: a tool for *developing* a self *as* aggregated judgments, a formal index through which the "free" and "idiomatic" might be expressed and habituated. Because of this, we might say that Whitman's "determined character" is the lithographic press itself—or the "forme" of the printing press, a wooden frame that held movable type in place during the printing process—rather than the iterated impressions made from it.

Coming to a similar conclusion, Wai Chee Dimock has argued that the self at the center of Whitman's poem is "turned into a categoric idea, so that it can remain structurally inviolate even as it undergoes many substantive variations, even as it entertains an infinite number of contingent terms."[95] Whitman does this, she claims, to eliminate the role of chance in the ethics of democracy. In short, the formal democratic subject must be vacated of luck, of the contingent, in order to guarantee the categorical equality of all human actors in general and all democratic U.S. citizens in particular. In order for there to be a universal and unified notion of justice, chance cannot play a role in its validity: "[Whitman's is] a noncontingent poetics, which . . . *in effect* eliminates luck by eliminating the invidious distinctions it fosters. . . . The objects of Whitman's attention are admitted as strict equals, guaranteed equals, by virtue of both the minimal universal "Me" they all have in common, and of a poetic syntax which greets each of them in exactly the same way, as a grammatical unit, equivalently functioning and structurally interchangeable."[96] For justice to be equally applicable, from the slave to the auctioneer, the structure of subjectivity must be seen as strictly equivalent across the board.

What Dimock highlights here dovetails with the general ethic of fair play that, in important ways, acts as a limit to the actions and potentials of the avatar figure as discussed. In gaming terms, the price one must pay for playing a game is to accept its rules, as well as its form, format, and medium. These limitations rule out certain possibilities, both strategic and otherwise. For instance, we saw earlier that the rules of *Mansion* insisted on purely linear motion. Because this structured the possibility of the player's counter, it forced the player to move to "Immodesty" when a less linear rule system might have allowed a move to "Truth" or "Humanity" instead. Through this, the game guaranteed a structural interchangeability, a kind of justice, for all the players; it produced a discrete output for any input the chance roll of the die might impose. This is not to say that luck does not play a role, but *from the perspective of the player* its role is strictly determined by rules of the game. The self cannot take advantage of its own luck one way or another, and so the concept of luck as we understand it can be said to disappear. Contingency may exist in the spin of the teetotum, but *in effect* (to borrow Dimock's phrase) it looks as much like determinism as anything else—it looks, in fact, a lot like the "breath of God" that Bryant imagines—because all players are forced into an "equivalently functioning" agency.[97] Accordingly, *Mansion* produces a selfhood that is akin to the self Dimock reads into "Song of Myself, "a self that is beyond luck [and correspondingly] is . . . *barred* from the contingent."[98] The present analysis of *Life*, however, offers an alternative perspective on Whitman's poem, one that is developed through an understanding of the operational differences between *Life* and *Mansion*.

While the rules of *Life* do adjudicate certain core conditions of winning and losing, contingency is built into the role of the players—even beyond their unruly interactions around the game board—via a foregrounding of the tactical roles they might take within the algorithm at any given turn. Whitman's use of the second-person perspective and inclusive disjunction shows him employing a similar mechanism, despite the syntactic and categorical concessions he makes to enable it. While the text itself may be notably "silent about those objects that, for us, are not categoric, not interchangeable or substitutable,"[99] it is only as silent as a game board without players. Whitman invokes this in one of his most pointed passages, calling to mind both the symbolism of gaming amusement and the chaotic role of interpersonal sensation. He writes:

> Let up again to feel the puzzle of puzzles,
> And that we call Being.
>
> To be in any form, what is that?
> If nothing lay more developed the quahaug and its callous shell
>   were enough.
>
> Mine is no callous shell,
> I have instant conductors all over me whether I pass or stop,
> They seize every object and lead it harmlessly through me.
>
> I merely stir, press, feel with my fingers, and am happy,
> To touch my person to some one else's is about as much as I can
>   stand.
>
> Is this then a touch? . . . . quivering me to a new identity.[100]

Indeed, via a purely formal analysis the poem appears "callous." But one cannot determine "callous[ness]" simply by appearance; one must be willing to "touch" or interact with the object in question, and it is precisely on the issue of interaction (a central aspect of the avatar figure) that Whitman lingers in this passage. Here, he is at pains to force the poetic medium to reach out, despite the coldness of the textual space, to develop a relationship with its readers. If, as he has written earlier, "you shall assume" the same position as the "I" of the poem, then the sensational image of "stir[ring], press[ing], [and] feel[ing]" serves to draw you into the ontic materiality of holding a book, of touching that book with your fingers and restlessly moving about in your seat. And, tellingly, what you are touching in this moment is the material document of this poem, a poem Whitman described in his notebooks as "someone," just as he does here in the moment of touch: "To touch [your?] person to some one else's is about as much as [you?] can stand."

Again, this "someone" is a variable in need of substantiation; and this substantiation requires a nonabstract agent such as the reader. What of yourself will you begin to associate with the book, the ideas, the time spent in reading, the place that surrounded you, and this thing that kept you there? How will these associations change *both you and the book*? With these questions in mind, it is not surprising that Whitman seizes the moment of touch to foreground the "instant[aneity]" and disruptiveness of this sensational connection to the poem as a path to "new identit[ies]," stable points of focus in the undecided algorithm that makes up the poem. One might see here a correspondence between the "callous shell" and the game marker, and the noncallous shell that such a marker becomes when it is touched by the player—moved in ways that "quiver" it to a new position of possibility on the board, a potential "new identity." If Whitman's text is silent in these moments, it is because interactivity takes place across the interface of the book, between the text and the reader, between the player and the avatar. Again, "Not I, not any one else can travel that road for you, / You must travel it for yourself."[101] An avatar, in one sense, may be a figure of formal representation, but its fundamental value for Whitman lies in its ability to mediate between a productive simulation and the user's reality. "Folks expect of the poet to indicate more than the beauty and dignity which always attach to dumb real objects," he claims in the preface, "They expect him to indicate the path between reality and their souls."[102]

The power he ascribes to poetry is in the way it reminds one of the unfathomable excesses within "things"—that which goes beyond their conceptual "reality" as "dumb real objects." The body itself would be just such a "dumb real object," a "callous shell," if it weren't constantly interposed with associative sensations that prompt it to "talk wildly," to adopt new models or playfully turn "traitor" to its typical habits of behavior, framed by a static concept of self. Instead, "Being" is found, Whitman says later, in a "villain touch" that extends beyond any concept, and that suggests a certain bodily liberty over conceptual models of self: "All truths wait in all things. . . . What is less or more than a touch?"[103] What you see represented in Whitman's poem is a manifold or categorical person, but what you feel and experience in the seeing of this "person" is an act of touching, a contraction of feeling and thinking that is part of the radical potential figured by the piece. As in Bradley's *Life*, Whitman's avatar figure can be viewed as an attempt at achieving a legible and outward-directed view of freedom within the increasingly restrictive context of "reformist interiority and middle-class institutionalism."[104] The cost of this legibility is implication in a system of possibilities that is not, strictly speaking, *free* in the most powerful sense of the word. "Both in and out of the game," the avatar is a figure that exists avowedly with one foot in the rule systems or ideologies of its moment: in this case, the interiorization of culturally dictated identity categories, outward character as the representation of self, and a general drive toward human proceduralization that corresponded to specific forms of technological growth and engagement in the middle nineteenth century.[105]

Yet, as we have seen, both Bradley and Whitman's representative interventions use these ideological poles as tools to leverage the agential, using *legibility* to imagine a parallel and tactically unpredictable *ability*. In Bradley's game, players were encouraged to see matrices of traditional values as opportunities for crafting an accountable and publicly materialized individual agency. This agency was undoubtedly bounded by the underlying algorithms of the game, but these algorithms became the basis for strategic habituations that a player could transpose into a mathematically complex number of recombinations suited to different situations. Similarly, Whitman's "Song of Myself" used ambivalent pronouns, repetitive syntax, and complex lists of "American" character traits to visualize the poetic speaker as a model for a self, an avatar that could legibly incarnate—"celebrate" itself even—and fully interact with the world around it without an assumed divide between thought and feeling. In Whitman, the recombination of known quantities, achieved by putting atemporal representations in contact with temporal realities, forms a basis for thinking through how a "someone" becomes an agent, how a "you" becomes an "I," as well as how this process is both figured and given matter on the page—not just for writers but for readers as well. To read game and poem together is to disallow certain all-too-easy erasures of dimension, to remain focused on elements of media interaction that were a part of everyday life, and to take seriously the idea that authors and readers were aware of these dimensions. The construction of self and avatar was indebted not only to conceptual or grammatical innovations but also to the cognitive environments that gave a body to these innovations.

Before developing these embodiments further in the chapter that follows, it's worth reinforcing that Bradley and Whitman, examined in parallel, give us considerable insight into the specific range of resources being employed to reimagine agency in the mid-century moment: fixations on the graphic affordances of visual media, attempts to materialize the potentials and limitations of categorical forms, and deployments of interactivity used as a way to constitute social bodies both *near* and *on* paper. In both Bradley and Whitman, it is clear that the important value may not be whether you win or lose but how you play the game. Yet in both it is equally apparent that no matter how we may wish it, we never play alone—the question of "how you play" is given shape by materials outstripping any individual. Teasing out the implications of this operative social agency, an "individualism" conditioned and incarnated, if not fully dictated, by nonindividual interactions, requires a move into the less celebratory, more darkly lit territory of confidence men and transformation games.

CHAPTER 2

A Fresh and Liberal Construction

State Machines, Transformation Games, and Algorithms of the Interior

Well, I see it's good to out with one's private thoughts now and then.
Somehow, I don't know why, a certain misty suspiciousness seems
inseparable from most of one's private notions about some men and
some things; but once out with these misty notions, and their mere
contact with other men's soon dissipates, or, at least, modifies them.
—Herman Melville, *The Confidence-Man* (1857)

Anything but a private man, the bumbling Peter Coddle is the star of a most enigmatic nineteenth-century narrative—a misty lack of information characterizes his every turn in the text. Succumbing to fatigue midway through his journey from fictitious rural Hogginsville to New York City, he returns to his carriage for some rest and recuperation: "I put my quizzing glass away, laid back in my seat, and took a good snooze, with a cup of coffee for a pillow."[1] Alternatively, "I put my quizzing glass away, laid back in my seat, and took a good snooze, with a quart of caterpillars for a pillow." Moreover, there is some doubt whether it *was* "a quart of caterpillars"; the pillow could have been "an Irishman" as well. Or "a Dutch farmer." Or "half a dozen doughnuts."[2]

These variations are not the result of printer's error or editorial dispute over final authorial intention. They are, in fact, an integral part of the story; any one of them (and many others) might be correctly substituted. This is because *Peter Coddle's Trip to New York* (1858) is both a short narrative and a self-described "Game of Transformations," the nineteenth-century equivalent of what we today are most familiar with as *Mad Libs* (Figure 7).[3] Using pre-made cards containing various article-noun combinations, players would fill in the blanks to produce readable (if absurd) sentences, creating a slightly different story every time they played. In this game, William Simonds—a Boston-area newspaperman and printer who moved into the children's-book trade under the pseudonym "Walter Aimwell"—had produced a "Literary Puzzle" that conceived of the text as a kind of equation, with words in the place of numerical constants and syntactic blanks in the place of algebraic variables. The "misty notion" of a narrative outlined by this form was made concrete in the manifold moments of player "contact" that made up the game—literalizing the nearly systematic interplay of anxious absence and confident social contact that is equally essential to Herman Melville's notorious "problem novel," *The Confidence-Man: His Masquerade* (1857). Making no pretensions to high literary art, Simonds's game nonetheless provides an important technical perspective on the operations and operators at the core of

Figure 7. *Peter Coddle's Trip to New York*. Boston: Gould & Lincoln, 1858.
Courtesy of The Strong, Rochester, New York.

Melville's text, with its patchwork of dubious characters, like undefined algorithms, "modifie[d]" by a revolving door of masquerading avatars and accompanying arguments.

Initially embedded within the youth-targeted novel *Jessie; or, Trying to Be
Somebody*, the reading game of *Peter Coddle's Trip* crystallized a functional perspective on story making and character that suffused the work, as well as the
mind, of its author. William Simonds (born in 1822) took a procedural approach to nearly everything he did, informed by a consumptive immersion in
the hardware of writing and publishing for most of his short life. He began his
career as an apprentice at a lucrative Boston printing office, taking over as sole
editor of the *Boston Saturday Rambler* at twenty-three. Like many upwardly
mobile young men in the period, he persistently used a journal to quantify his
accomplishments in year-end "Summar[ies]" that tallied the number of events
attended, books read, dollars accumulated, and even, in an obsessively reflexive turn, the sum of notebook pages occupied by each of these entries.[4] As a
teenager, he invented code languages and established a set of self-governing
rules that closed with the instruction to "ask [himself] each day a set of questions to be answered in writing."[5] Discussed at greater depth in what follows,
this fill-in-the-blanks ethos was pervasive in Simonds's professional practice,
present both in his assessments of self-advancement upon taking over the *Boston Saturday Rambler* ("I have been looking forward to just such a situation as
the one I am now to fill") and in his draft sketches for book titles, which all
follow a common form: "Ettie; _____ _____," "Ronald; or, the Adopted
Son," "Annie _____ _____."[6] Though he may not have originated the mechanism that drove the story of his most enduring character, there is no doubt
that he found it an incredibly useful compositional principle, weaving it
deeply into the fabric of his literary labors.[7]

As the final novel Simonds would complete before succumbing to a
chronic lung hemorrhage in July 1859, *Jessie* provokes an expansion and diver-
sification of my argument about nineteenth-century character into less individually centered territory—into the realm of "contact" and *interplay*
suggested by the epigraph to this chapter.[8] Like many children's authors of the
time, Simonds frequently engaged in metanarrational play, using the conge-
nial voice of "Aimwell" to explain answers to riddles, gesture at the physicality
of the book, and generally break the fourth wall in order to address his young
readers. Though such asides were hardly a rare practice in the novel genre,
Simonds-as-Aimwell often pushed beyond the simple performance of con-
spiratorial intimacy and into moments that broke down a neat division of

textual insides and readerly outsides: to "read" these books is not to lose one-self in the reading but to persistently have the threshold of inside and outside put at issue.[9] Even beyond directly pedagogical asides in a Christian reformist mode, narrative inventions like the protagonist Jessie Hapley and the narrato-rial Walter Aimwell offer detailed outlines of games that can be played by readers—sometimes presented through dialogue, sometimes in letters, and sometimes via other intranarrative media stagings (Figure 8). They then demonstrate the playing of these games in ways that become part of the nar-rative world, as rules and speculative play scenarios unfold in tandem.

For a game to be both explained and played within the textual scene was a notable departure from the traditional instructive mode of *Boy's Own* an-thologies, likely prompting readers to try out games they might have skipped in a more procedural guidebook. Accordingly, the reality of these books could become startlingly present for readers, as they did not simply *see* what the

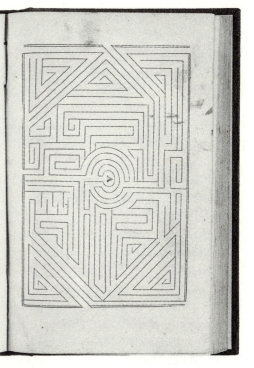

Figure 8. From Walter Aimwell, *Ella; or, Turning Over a New Leaf.* Boston: Gould & Lincoln, 1855. Courtesy of American Antiquarian Society.

characters did but were also given the means to run through iterations of a complex ludic performance for themselves—offering the foundation for even deeper associations with characters who shared parallel tastes and gameplay sensibilities. It's as if one were expected to take a number of sips of fortified wine, throw on a jingling motley hat, and descend a catacomb midway through "The Cask of Amontillado." As if Poe were to pause suddenly and inform the reader in the particulars of stone masonry, asking them to try building a small wall before continuing the textual journey. (Perhaps some associations are better left on the page.) Reading, in the children's metagenre adopted by Simonds, was as much about *doing* as it was about *imagining*. It was an approach grounded in an operative rejection of the idea that books were instruments of passive narrative absorption.

Even before the introduction of *Peter Coddle's Trip to New York*—a game demanding both a social ensemble and extratextual action—*Jessie's* game activities specifically revolve around the type of scriptive practices that allow one to attain positive social character: creating and distributing home newspapers, reconfiguring cut-up lines of existing poetry to create original pieces, and, most centrally, keeping a diary. After a pictorial insert replicating the title page of Jessie's journal, Aimwell turns to his audience to observe that "the motto which Jessie inscribed upon her title-page"—the phrase "Try to be Somebody" in a flourish of quasi-medieval font—"will strike some minds as being both too ambitious and too indefinite."[10] In a maneuver that recalls Melville's own metanarrative reflections on "originality" in *The Confidence-Man*, Aimwell ponders the potential for variable meaning in his terminology—and prompts his readers to do the same—lingering on the ambiguity of "somebody" as a vague placeholder versus *a* "somebody" as a substantial success. Attaining this end—filling in the void of character invoked by the equivocal "somebody"—involves quite a bit of game playing, both among and upon the pages that circumscribe Jessie's life.[11] And Simonds isn't especially sly about the connection: Jessie Hapley escapes the ominous and stereotypically catastrophic future imprinted upon her by an alcoholic father by joining the "Page" household at the opening of the novel.

Together with Mrs. Page's twelve-year-old son, Ronald, Jessie directs the majority of the paper play that constitutes the primary action of the book, attending a school where a gamified system of advancement honors students with the "Grade of Fidelity" for all who "paid a decent respect to the rules."[12] Ronald puts this acquired attention to rule systems into action and "invents" *Peter Coddle's Trip*, "A New Pleasure" that Jessie publicizes in the Page household newspaper.[13] The form of the game replicates the thematics and operational imperatives of the text. Fidelity to the rules of *Peter Coddle's Trip* produces the pages of a moral narrative; fidelity to the rules of good character, in turn, produces the moral "somebody" that Jessie becomes—a part of a family, a "Page." In this view, the entire book is recast as an abstract machine devoted to the copious production of well-formed "pages": a synecdoche for Simonds's lifelong work on the printing press, itself an input-output device that ensures consistent textual legibility on the level of form, if not content.

This notion of identity was, of course, a familiar trope of mid-century functional views regarding selfhood in a literary vein, analogous to the mechanisms and medial awareness that were tracked via Walt Whitman and the avatar figure in the previous chapter. By encouraging readers to fill out the details or focal points of their own "I" or "self" in "Song of Myself," Whitman's work was an invitation, if not an imperative, to transform the categorical "someone"—figured by the algorithmic grammar of the work—into a "somebody," an avatar agent capable of acting legibly in the American social sphere, seizing the immediate creative potentials of both formal and forensic interactions. Evoking a parallel sensibility, Jessie's "indefinite" pronoun is indeed shown, by the end of her story, to earn its more substantive honorific sense, as the young protagonist's actions literally fill in her developing character for readers. And though her writing—and in particular her use of a diary to attain this goal—may lead us to suspect this is a deeply private enterprise, Jessie's transformation illustrates a debt to the social dimensions of this "private" form, where journaling is simply another facet of media play in the novel, a social medium with all the appearance of individual interiority.

The preceding chapter concluded with a bit of a turn by positing that we never actually play alone; *Jessie*'s functional approach to media's role in self-production helps to further reinforce why. Even when we play games or read books in ways that are solitary, these media unavoidably incorporate elements of social agency: documentary regulatory systems like Whitman's categorical grammar—or physically constructed materials like the codex pages of *Leaves of Grass*—carry on the phantom lives of social forces and social agencies. It is worth remembering that objects maintain these constitutively associative agencies even in the near absence of subjects.[14] Yet even as we try to maintain this understanding, the rhetorical tendency in writing about "self" and "character" in nineteenth-century literature pulls insistently toward the individual perspective—a touchstone of the liberal humanist picture of subjectivity that prevailed in the period. This perspective exerts such a conceptual gravity that even a strangely computational view of self (like that evoked by Bradley's game, Whitman's poem, or Simonds's book) begins to seem an exercise in insularity—as if "character" in all its varied medial incarnations could be played alone, as if it *were* being played, essentially, alone. This is not because the description is wrong so much as because it is partial, slanted in the direction of the individual subjects we ordinarily prefer to apprehend via the terminology of the "I." The light cast from this "I" can appear to be cast solely "inside" or indeed upon nothing at all, as if the "I" were a black hole and the subject its event horizon, revealing interior contours but illuminating nothing beyond.

Having pursued this description through the first-person conceits of "avatar," we can now pivot in a different direction. If the firmly coordinated individual perspective on agency led us to imagine nineteenth-century character through the lens of avatar, then a more wobbly view—a skeptical, critical, perhaps Melvillian view of embodied social action as an illumination "raying away from itself all round it"—must grapple with the fact that the workings of everyday agency, however operative and interactive, are not entirely self-chosen.[15] Instead, they are elastically dictated—for good or ill—by and through other bodies and other media. This view takes us into territory where we might make contact with prehistories of the posthuman or cybernetic self that is, for the most part, treated as a twentieth-century invention.[16] Beyond introducing an alternative way to read Melville, a coincident aim of this chapter is to think about how certain importations of game-like perspectives acted as bridging figures that linked nineteenth-century ideas of character to later articulations of the relationship between self and social texture. To understand this evolution, we must shift our model subtly to view algorithmic character not just as a judgment-created avatar but as a more ego-neutral "state machine."

Drawing on computer science, critical game theorist Jesper Juul defines a state machine as "a machine that has an *initial state*, accepts a specific amount of *input events*, changes state in response to inputs using a *state transition function* (i.e., rules) and produces specific outputs."[17] And while Juul uses the language of machinery, state machines can be abstract as well as hardware-based—a properly used multiplication table and a grandfather clock are state machines on different orders of complexity. So it goes with the simple linguistic gaming of *Peter Coddle's Trip*. An initial state (legible but gap-laden prose) accepts a discrete set of input events (the word cards), and then basic rules effect the transition to a new state (read the uppermost card to fill the gap), producing an output (the resulting sentences). Nested within the narrative of *Jessie*,

Simonds's game makes an operative argument for a pervasive idea within antebellum reform literature, highlighting the growing instrumentality of characterological legibility, of becoming "somebody."[18] As *character* was conceived of to allow privately willed decisions that might be publicly legible and discretely managed, what could be considered "state machine subjectivity" arose as a figural mechanism of self-invention.

Despite their centrality in the twenty-first century, state machines are not commonly considered as meaningful features of literary history prior to the invention of the computer.[19] Yet when characterizing the difficulty of Melville's *The Confidence-Man*, published in the same year Simonds was composing *Jessie* and also centrally concerned with ideas of characterological "fidelity," critics sometimes rely on oblique invocations of this figure to make their point: portraying Melville's final novel as "an algebraic equation with too many variables in plot, character, and narrative voice to allow for a definitive solution," registering the way it "gives ontological priority to the Question over the Answer," and noting that the book's characters "seem more like representations of functions than like representations of persons."[20] Situating this work in the context of machine metaphors and the nascent philosophy of computational thought in the mid-nineteenth century, I contend that these insights may amount to more than the clever figural deployment of numerical or logical images. Instead, these glancing critical depictions of Melville's nearly programmatic prose hint at a significant but underdeveloped aspect of what Wai Chee Dimock might call a "domain of cultural inscription" native to the nineteenth-century United States, with its influx of machines—both real and abstract—expanding, codifying, restricting, and enabling new forms of imagination, action, and selfhood. Fixating on the compound political, mechanical, and computational significance of the state machine reveals meaningful continuities between the rhetorical and material domains that shaped models of self in the nineteenth-century United States, in literature and beyond. At the same time, this inquiry educes a threshold vocabulary that facilitates broader perspectives on the conceptual schema that continue to focalize thought in the twenty-first century—the "digital" imaginary that configures many foundational assumptions about communication and identity in the present.

Beginning with Simonds's literary amusement (and the practices that led him to it), in this chapter I develop a method for engaging with the state machine as a model for a specific cultural logic. This allows *Peter Coddle's Trip* to inflect a close reading, perhaps a close playing, of *The Confidence-Man* that is sensitive to the dislocating ironies of both its narrative *and* its style. Deemed "unstable," "unreadable" even, because of its flat characterizations and elliptical narrative structure, Melville's novel, I argue, uses figures of machine-like substitution and transformation to probe the mechanisms of antebellum public character less equivocally "celebrated" in coincident work.[21] If the book is unreadable, it may be because reading (of a certain sort) is the wrong lens through which to view Melville's writing; this misapprehension is, in fact, the core thematic of a textual scene that is filled with characters who suffer themselves to be "read," while others use this reading to play a different sort of game: "A fresh and liberal construction," contends one, "would teach us to regard [the whole cabin-full of players] . . . as playing at games in which every player plays fair, and not a *player* but shall win."[22] Taking such a statement seriously prompts us to ask: why are the nonplayers of Melville's text so invested in a readerly consistency that forecloses play and, like clockwork throughout this Mississippi masquerade, leaves them open to manipulation? Paradoxically, the Confidence-Man's victims see consistency as the only legible means for change—but this consistency seems to require them to unsee their capacity to play with (and within) the systems of conversation and characterological exchange that define them. The consequence of that unseeing is that they themselves are played like games.

Darkly twisting Johan Huizinga's famous characterization of "man the player," Melville's Confidence-Man indeed plays people, temporarily empowering them to reinvent themselves in ways that provide him with an income. A widow becomes a charitable woman. A young student becomes a businessman. And a sick man becomes a recovering patient. Melville's antihero systematically exploits each character's desire for a single consistent interiority, rendering the characters as transformation games of a sort: state machines. While the input that springs them to life is merely his carefully chosen words—"little argument[s]," as he calls them—the outcome is a physical exchange: money in his pocket.[23] William Simonds was free in his role as a game maker to highlight mechanisms of exchange between text and media in practice and within his writing—free to ask his youthful readers to think of their reading and writing habits, essentially, as functional and interventional models rather than passive practices of absorption and assessment. Yet it may be that, even beyond Melville's growing reputation as an author not to be read, resistance to *The Confidence-Man* indexed an adult reading public not prepared to be taught how to read "literary" books anew. Despite his much commented on metanarrative critique—in fourth-wall breaking asides that lambast readerly expectations of consistency—Melville, unlike Simonds, could not compel readers to adopt the playerly sensibility of a game that was sold in the same storefronts as his ill-fated book.[24] As in the previous chapter, I attempt here to recover specific dimensions of this sensibility as a way to allow metacritical reflection on those elements of historical reading practice that tend to evaporate when focusing on a book as a narrative and descriptive exercise, rather than a site of socially sustaining media interaction.

Pages, Presses, and Scattered Types; or, the Case of William Simonds

It's hardly contentious to say that textual modularity defined the ethos of printing in the antebellum United States. Often enough, "the only variability," to repurpose Melville's provocative turn of phrase, "[was] in expression, not feature."[25] Newspapers cribbed liberally from other newspapers—repackaging content under differing mastheads and in differing contexts for differing communities of taste—much like the digital "feed aggregators" of our own time.[26] Authors, from Edgar Allan Poe and Harriet Beecher Stowe to William Wells Brown and Hannah Crafts, adapted and creatively lifted whole passages of content (some of it their own) to mobilize existing copy toward differing and at times ironic ends.[27] And a subcurrent (really a flood) of blank books, forms, and accounting ledgers facilitated a new professional revolution predicated on data management and recordkeeping that could maintain common shapes for information even as it traversed vastly different networks of use.[28] A tireless antebellum printer whose work ethic likely contributed to his early death, Simonds was no exception to the rule of adaptive reuse, and he dove into his configurative labors with something of an artistic flair.[29]

As a well-liked member of the Boston Mechanic Apprentice's Library Association during his adolescence, Simonds volunteered anthemic poetry for the organization's Fourth of July celebration—a piece commemorated in the annual literary chapbook that was shared affectionately among the association's members.[30] In July 1846, he took over editorial duties at the *Boston Saturday Rambler*, working with his brother Charles, first at 141 Washington and then around the corner at 12 School Street. Here, in the heart of the Boston printing and paper goods establishment, he developed the connections and practices that would condition his later literary output. Scanning the nearly three-by-four-foot "enlarged sheet" of the *Saturday Rambler* during Simonds's editorship and looking past specific content, one can see the challenge of his week as the work of filling diachronically persistent sections, at times explicitly figured as containers, surfaces, or knottings: "The Ladies' Budget" (a "budget" was a wallet), "The Youth Casket," "The Altar" (marriage announcements), "The Urn" (obituaries), "Gatherings of Fact," and "The Editorial Melange." The relentless schedule of the popular press combined with the demand to populate typographically dense columns of page space meant that many newspaper editors took a capaciously interchangeable approach to content. This was simply the easiest means to keep paper moving out the door: the page, in a practical view, was an irregular grid of elongated rectangles to fill with whatever relevant material one could find, like a puzzle in curated chunks of political narrative and bite-sized fragments of "useful and amusing" knowledge. For Simonds, the effort to fill these discrete sectional bins with impressed type—a volumetric approach to writing—must have had a certain intellectual resonance. Here was a career printer who had cut his teeth arranging lead matrix type from literal upper and lower "cases" into the standard printing press "formes" that held the contents of a page together for inking and impression. Rapidly filling materially constrained formes with modular content wasn't a game; it was a pervasive and practiced labor operation linked to everyday survival.

Moreover, the ambitious Simonds did not think of form filling and interchangeability as a purely physical or mechanistic practice—at times it could be employed in playfully critical ways as well. Showing his links to the information networks of the American Tract Society and abolitionist newspapers like Boston's *Emancipator*, a notable front-page article from January 1847, subtitled "OUTRAGEOUS ASSAULT ON AMERICAN CITIZENS," relates the following: "We learn from a Hayti paper, just received, that a most diabolical outrage has been perpetuated on several of our own free citizens, in consequence of a judge of one of the courts having decided that none but free colored persons could enjoy any of the rights of citizenship in that republic. One of the county courts has had five white men and *two white women*, professing or claiming to be free, *whipped and sent out of the city;* and the editor thinks that if this course is followed up, the court will soon free the city from the *nuisance!*"[31] After cautioning the reader not to be "alarmed," Simonds goes on to reveal that, in fact, he has changed the names and places of the story, leaving its fundamental form—an article in the *St. Louis Republican* from the previous month—unchanged while swapping the race (it was black men and women) and place (this happened in Missouri, not Haiti). He doubles back, printing the original story farther down the page in a successive sequence, essentially forcing his readers to reread, with altered associations. The swap allows him to redirect the ostensive outrage of his readership toward the "glorious exploits of our own free and happy land." "Strange," he meditates, "how essentially 'circumstances alter cases!'"[32] If the "case," in the most literal gloss of Simonds's declaration, could be a state of affairs, it could also be a container filled with alternative "circumstances." Here, Simonds conspicuously uses a kind of fill-in-the-blanks operation to create a moment of editorial intimacy and cognitive dissonance, inviting a simple but powerful comparative interplay of types (both literal and sociological) upon the page. Creating habits of rereading and doubling back was also a way, in the profusion of paper media that constituted his audience and market, to ensure certain levels of habituated investment in his particular paper over others. And it was in the youth sections of the paper that similar tactics could be profitably employed to create iterative attachments even without explicitly social content.

Enigmas, anagrams, and puzzles of varying kinds—like the crossword puzzles of our own moment—prompted repeat visits, as solutions were offered only in subsequent editions. This was a savvy means of guaranteeing that children getting hold of the *Saturday Rambler* would get into their parents' ears about securing a regular copy. Devoid of the political and current events interest of the front page, these sections were nevertheless a way to create cross-edition devotion to a paper that often had trouble collecting subscription payments, despite a relatively broad circulation base.[33] Yet the demand for quality content was no less acute than in the political arenas, and it was likely here that Simonds benefited from his many active neighbors in the game and puzzle markets.

At 133 Washington Street, a few doors down from Simonds's print shop, the firm of Saxton and Kelts sold games and *Boy's Own* books during the holiday season—and was favorably written up in the *Saturday Rambler* in anticipation of 1847 New Year's sales.[34] Munroe and Francis, another publisher of *Boy's Own* books, was just around the corner at the intersection of Devonshire and Water (having recently moved from 128 Washington).[35] Though it is difficult to establish a definitive connection, simply strolling down the block would have introduced Simonds to new games he might use in the growing "Youth Casket" and "Fireside Recreation" sections of his paper. And given that *Boy's Own* books were themselves compilations drawing upon many sources—as we saw in the last chapter—there would have been even fewer than usual moral qualms about repurposing their content. Simonds's

continued effort to diversify the original material in the paper and to expand
its media interest through the introduction of regular pictures and city views
was further accompanied by a persistent commitment to the unit-moving sections devoted to games and puzzles—which conspicuously remain in the
same location (back page, second column) throughout the entirety of his editorial tenure. Four years after Herman Melville's Tommo had used knowledge
from a "Young Man's Own Book" to build popguns that delighted the al-
legedly cannibal "Typees" of Nuku Hiva, Simonds was drawing from coincident books to survive among his own life-consuming types.[36] These games
were a structural element of his practical writing practice, not an afterthought
or occasional bit of fluff. And the strategy of rambling the proximate urban
byways, using what one finds to survive, clearly made an impression on Simonds, both in terms of the eventual storyline of *Peter Coddle* and in his first
book, *The Boy's Own Guide* (1853), where he imagines his advice occupying a
similar metropolitan topography: "If you please, you may consider my hum-
ble counsels as 'street-signs,' put up at corners, to guide the young stranger
into the right path."[37]

Working with another of his advertisers from the *Saturday Rambler*—a
small Congregationalist and scientific publishing firm called Gould and Lincoln at 144 Washington—gave Simonds plenty of opportunity to return to
the fertile intertextual production territory of his newspaper days. On one of
these walks in early 1857, in the midst of composing *Jessie*, it is probable that
he came across a game called *A Trip to Paris*, made by an elusive pair named
Mudge and Spooner working at 251 Washington.[38] *A Trip to Paris* was a dynamic social game that satirized the object culture beginning to dominate the
lives of urban New Yorkers in the 1850s. Yet this satire—given the geography
of the "trip" in play—was at one remove. *A Trip to Paris* was avowedly *not* a
game intended to "reform" or gesture at such reform in any way; it was instead
a strikingly political tale poking fun at the differences between the United
States and France by lampooning French political, artistic, and metropolitan
culture. Told in the third person, it centered on the travels of one Jothan
Podd, a cosmopolitan New Yorker who declares at the opening of the narrative that he must expand his horizons by travelling to Paris, to "return the
personification of ———."[39] It was designed as an ensemble game on a number of levels, in which a variety of characters—Podd, Slim, Puff, and a French
cavalry general, among others—take the lead at various points of the story.
This replicates the rotating procedures of the players, who, each given cards
with objects on them, are directed to flip and read them as the storyteller

reaches blanks in the narrative: "It is desirable that the cards be not looked over by the person holding them, and that no selection be made, but that each be taken as it appears."[40] In this way, the shock of absurdity in *A Trip to Paris* is, in effect, directed at the confusions of cultural immersion. "Jothan thought it a strange country," the narrator remarks while skirting close to explaining the joke, "where such things were used for such a purpose."[41]

Appropriating the mechanism of *Trip*, Simonds's *Peter Coddle* domesticates the alienation of "things"—shifting the motivating circumstance of the story to an intranational journey to New York City. Further, he centers these feelings of ludicrous estrangement in a single subject, Peter Coddle, who narrates his own tale to the rural listeners of his native Hogginsville. As with Whitman and Bradley, Simonds's professional practice had been at least partially defined by the things around him, and by the suggestions and inventions offered to him by a particularly vital collective of media makers. This makes it all the more interesting that his most enduring creation was a fill-in-the-blanks story where the main character is defined by a random assortment of things and people. These associates and associations are summoned into the narrative via a circle of players—explicitly indebting it to a circulating geography of interchangeable things that defined an individual via a set of community utterances.[42] The blanks to be filled in, the terms spoken by the circle of people playing the game, are all *things*—not grammatical substitutions, as in the later *Mad Libs*, but nouns and substantives. On another level, each thing is itself inscribed upon a card, not called forth from the mind of the player but revealed and read before being set aside. Thus the narrative of *Peter Coddle*, even before one had produced it through gameplay, was already burdened with a gravity of associations about community, speaking, objecthood, personhood, and modularity.[43]

It also conspicuously features a suave urban confidence man. After leaving his rural home in search of "a larger field in which to . . . make his fortune," Coddle arrives in New York City sometime after sundown.[44] He naively meanders the streets until he catches "the eye of a well-dressed gentleman" who takes a portentous interest in his safety: "'I suppose you wish to find . . . . . of the right sort. I suppose you've heard,' says he, 'about the rascally tricks that are played off here upon strangers. . . . That's the reason I took you aside. If you want a good cosy home,' says he, 'where you will be out of the reach of these sharks, and where you can have anything you call for, from . . . . . to . . . . . or . . . . . , just come along with me to my boarding-house.'"[45] Later, Coddle will wake up robbed and hungover, a victim of his erstwhile friend, but for now he is drawn in by the kindness, a kindness whose magnetism is indebted to objects drawn and interposed by the players. Using a long list of stock phrases provided on cards at the end of the narrative, players fill in the elliptical blanks by either selecting at random (the "Game of Transformations"), arguing with others over appropriate substitutions (the "Game of Literary Patchwork"), or trying to determine the precise non-absurd locations of every given phrase (the "Literary Puzzle").

Through these omissions, the game forces players to take an active role in determining the shape of Coddle's character by constructing the content of his desire—what Coddle "wish[es] to find" is conspicuously absent from the dialogue, as well as the things he might "call for" at the boardinghouse. In one iteration, he might have a weakness for good food, convinced by the con man's depiction of "a heap of pancakes," "a stick of candy," and "a basket of chips."[46] On the other hand, he might be more inclined to luxury, lured in by "a velvet sofa," "twenty-three dollars," and "a mint of gold."[47] In the formal terms of the game, the players determine the very objects that act as the basis of Coddle's confidence in the well-dressed gentleman, excitedly seizing their moment as the caller looks to them for the completion of a line.[48] These determinations, moreover, are precisely what the successful confidence man must make in order to render Coddle a mark: he identifies appropriate items to fill in the gaps in his fabricated narrative (regarding what he has at his boarding house) and as a result succeeds in *his* game.

In an unexpected turn, the player and the con man have more in common than Simonds may have intended. At the very least, the game creates an atmosphere of anticipation revolving around well-timed interjections that produce a kind of social satisfaction in a story that both is and is not one's own. Both the player and the confidence man are able to work a system to their benefit by providing substance to a formally consistent set of blanks: What kinds of things will make Peter Coddle comfortable enough to return to the boardinghouse? What nouns will dispel the grammatical discomfort of a story riddled with blanks? The answers to both of these questions require an agency willing to cooperate with a preexisting structure. Registering this on the level of operative style, Simonds's "Game of Transformations" implies that anyone who can appropriately work the lacunae of a system—who can identify the structural inputs and play the game accordingly—is bound to laugh last. The puzzling invention of a story becomes the basis for a humor of absurd social wholes.

Put another way, the pleasure of playing is in creating a temporary narrative unity out of a figure of raw (but structured) indeterminacy. Aimwell clarifies, "Of course the story will read differently every time the game is tried, for the transformations it is capable of are infinite. No, not exactly infinite, which means without limits; but it would take many lines of figures to express the precise number."[49] The finite amount of included cards/phrases renders the game's narrative possibility a question of finite playerly permutation, rather than "infinite" writerly freedom. Yet even if one were to expand the set to an infinite array, the player's freedom would still be discretely bound. Structural boundaries produce the consistent framework necessary to communicate the identity of the story, regardless of the differences between its subsequent iterations. Because of this, players could feel a certain amount of confidence that, despite their most absurd efforts, something resembling a story (and therefore funny as opposed to utterly nonsensical or opaque) would be the result of their play.

Puzzled People in *The Confidence-Man*

Even beyond the material saturation of printing machines and their literal formes, the playful interest in formalized linguistic transformations that characterizes Simonds's game had surprising parallels to the logical system being developed across the Atlantic by a theoretical forefather of computer science, George Boole.[50] In his 1854 publication, *An Investigation of the Laws of Thought*, Boole puzzles over "the grounds of that confidence with which [scientific truth] claims to be received"; that is, he wonders how general truths of the world might be agreed upon despite the fact that they are "never [exemplified] with perfect fidelity, in a world of changeful phenomena."[51] Supposing that this "confidence" is largely the result of the consistency of our formal expressions with regard to these truths, Boole makes a strong (and historically revelatory) connection between logic and algebra, concluding, "The laws of thought, in all its processes of conception and of reasoning, in all those operations of which language is the expression or instrument, are of the same kind as are the laws of the acknowledged processes of Mathematics."[52] The fruit of this idea is the development of a new propositional logic, moving away from the basic syllogistic system of Aristotle to a symbolic math of the mind by turning logical *operators* like "and," "or," "is," and "not" into an algebraic form (that is, $\times$, $+$, $=$, $-$) and representing logical predicates with "letters [like x, y, and z] as in mathematical analysis."[53] By formalizing the grammars of logic, one could pursue deductive conclusions, telling new stories about the relations of things while remaining assured in the validity of a result. Form, as in Simonds's word game, *is* the very confidence that enables productive play and variability. And within this schema it is plain to see that "operators" are at a privileged core of any kind of transformation—a terminological coincidence that allows us to pivot to related questions in the social calculus of Melville's most functionally driven book.

The Confidence-Man is a novel that does not have a plot so much as a series of functional social situations arranged in sequence and held together by a conditioned formal bias—that is, by the fact that events happen in the same book and, in narrative terms, on the same boat. It waggishly opens on April Fools' Day, the occasion of many a complex procedural prank, and after roving through a number of conversations between different characters, closes as the cabin of the steamboat descends into an ominous and ambiguous darkness. From classroom experience, I can say that this book actively *angers* even twenty-first-century readers (specifically, undergraduates) looking for a narrative that would *do something to them* rather than a richly populated and structured stage upon which something might be done. Going back to the critics referenced at the opening of this chapter, Melville's novel is kind of antistory that emphatically stages the question of how stories are used: their function and functionality in the world, and the work that readers do, whether consciously or not, to produce consistent meanings in the act of reading. It is a book to be *used* more than *read*, persistently playing as it does upon the notion of documentary "forms" in the bureaucratic sense.

Throughout *The Confidence-Man*, culture, tradition, and narrative or characterological structure provide quasi-mathematical forms of sociality that evoke both Boolean logic and *Peter Coddle* gameplay, while accommodating a variegated range of individual personalities. Strangers move among strangers, yet consistent assumptions about ethics, custom, and law ensure the spectrum of baseline reactions. Melville gives expression to this dichotomy early in the novel, using the symbolism of the river upon which the narrative takes place, as he writes: "Here reigned the dashing and all-fusing spirit of the West, whose type is the Mississippi itself, which, uniting the streams of the most distant and opposite zones, pours them along, helter-skelter, in one cosmopolitan and confident tide."[54] Insofar as the Mississippi has a certain assurance of identity, this is guaranteed not entirely by its content (which is always in transition) so much as by its form, by its topography and geographical consistency. The banks of the river and the depth and incline of its bed might be said to structure the basis of its formal identity, much as the skeleton narrative of *Peter Coddle* gives a foundation to its identity as a legible story.[55] In the language of mathematics, the *form* of the Mississippi River could be considered a "function," such as $f(x) = x + 2$. Here, "$x + 2$" defines the boundaries of the function abstractly without giving specific details about the value of x. One might usefully understand this as the banks of the Mississippi. In order to produce a particular shape, however, the actual instances of x—what are called the "arguments" of a function—must be defined as well. In the case of the Mississippi, this is where the "streams of the most distant and opposite zones" come in, providing various and "helter-skelter" inputs that, when combined with the topology of the banks, produce what Melville calls the "cosmopolitan and confident tide" of the river.

In the same passage, Melville telescopes this figure toward the direct setting of the novel, the steamboat *Fidèle*,[56] fusing the image of a fluidly changing natural phenomenon directly to the world of human machines. He writes, "Though always full of strangers, [the steamboat] continually, in some degree, adds to, or replaces them with strangers still more strange; like Rio Janeiro fountain, fed from the Corcovado mountains, which is ever overflowing with stranger waters, but never with the same strange particles in every part."[57] Melville encourages us to imagine the *Fidèle* as a formal system of transition by linking the imagery of the river and the riverboat—variable things with "never . . . the same strange particles in every part"—emphasizing that they nevertheless answer to consistent names. Flipping the image on its head and using Melville's metaphor to return to the concept of the state machine introduced earlier, we might think of the x's in a functional equation as "strangers," perhaps following the Greek *xenos*. These "strangers" have a place in the machine—it doesn't *do* anything without them—but their precise role is to be determined by what they bring to the system (their "argument"): the boat does not operate without a crew and passengers.[58]

Disguised as an austere and silent deaf person, the Confidence-Man emerges from this already pregnant scene, "in the extremest sense of the word," Melville writes, "a stranger."[59] With his clothing evoking the collage aesthetic of the boat population at large, he blends into the mass of passengers and eventually stops in front of a placard (ironically) warning passengers to be on the lookout for a wanted "impostor." Pausing briefly, he scribbles the phrase "Charity thinketh no evil" onto a small slate and holds it before him.[60] He follows this up with a litany of variations on this theme, increasingly

annoying his audience: "Charity suffereth long, and is kind," "Charity en-
dureth all things," "Charity believeth all things," and "Charity never faileth."[61]
Through all of this, Melville writes, "the word charity, as originally traced, remained throughout uneffaced, not unlike the left-hand numeral of a printed
date, otherwise left for convenience in blank."[62] This structural continuity between each of these phrases suggests that the man in cream colors is playing a
bit of a *Peter Coddle* game with himself, although the effective outcome of this
game is hardly antisocial.[63] Indeed, as he rests below "a ladder . . . leading to a
deck above," passengers begin to treat him as an elliptical blank in their own
interpretive transformation game.[64]

Transposing himself against an obvious symbol of transition, the
Confidence-Man becomes an ambiguous part of any movement between
decks, a variable in the ladder's transitional function. And the crowd wastes
no time in assigning him values, submitting arguments that they hope will
define his character to their fellow onlookers. Perched on a "cross-wise bal-
cony" (evoking both biblical allegory and the standard variable "x" mentioned
above), they refer to him alternatively as:

"Odd fish!"
"Poor fellow!"
"Humbug!"
"Singular innocence."
"Means something."
"Spirit-rapper."[65]

These declarations, typographically presented as a long column of substantives, conspicuously echo the layout of the "Phrases to supply the blanks" that
close *Peter Coddle* (themselves "arguments" to be placed into a functional
narrative):

A humbug.
A new idea.
This, that, and the other.
A bureau drawer.
A dancing-master.[66]

By foregrounding a structurally placed variable, a "blank" with a clear call for
contextual meaning, both Melville's and Simonds's narratives figure the type

of variable consistency that is the hallmark of the "state machine" as a formal structure reinforced by the pervasive paper media of accounting previously discussed. Both efforts represent a general fixation on transformations of this sort in the popular mind. The emphasis is on form and interaction, in persistently iterative attempts to produce a meaning—a new output state—by supplying an "argument" to a "function."

Some historical exploration of the term "state" can shed light on this preoccupation. In earliest usage, "state" connoted both the general condition of a person or thing and the politics of estate management.[67] Historically, the latter had less to do with our modern conception of "state" as a self-fashioned governing *system*—as Eric Slauter has written, "the state as a work of art" that temporally "emerge[d] from the manners, customs, tastes, and genius of the people being constituted"[68]—than it did with the state as a politically necessary stalemate binding individual landed estates and their owners. The "state" was a result of political or economic exigency, a contingently given combination of individual estates, an associative figure rather than a definitional concept. As the corollary of a ritualized and caste-based aristocracy, it was not much affected by time or institutional progress.

At the onset of the nineteenth century, as James Chandler suggests, the term "state" had taken on genuine configurative and temporal meanings, both of which converged in the literary genre of the "state." "By the end of the [eighteenth] century," he writes, "successive volumes published under the genre-marking title 'The State of X' tend to be cast as part of a series of volumes with annual dates featured in their titles."[69] Annualization materialized a diachronic chain of states into an apparent causal continuum, while synchronic hierarchies of value supported a comparative notion of cultural progress. Chandler continues:

> The crucial element in this new Scottish-Enlightenment sense of history . . . is a dialectical sense of periodization in which particular "societies" or "nations" . . . are recognized as existing in states that belong at once to two different, and to some extent competing, orders of temporality. On the one hand, each society is theorized as moving stepwise through a series of stages sequenced in an order that is more-or-less autonomous and stable. . . . On the other hand, this same historiographical discourse always implies a second temporality, one in which these different national times can be correlated and calendrically dated in respect to each other.[70]

By the end of the eighteenth century, "state" had come to signify the current arrangement and condition of an entity understood both as progressive sequence and as the unified features by which it might be weighed against others. An insistence on formal unity, despite stepwise changes of state through time, required a new intellectual focus on the procedures by which a changing entity might retain its identity. The exchange and maintenance of state documents—and of the document itself as a reflection of "state(s)" in what Lisa Gitelman has called a "know-show" function—became a way to link permanence and comparativity to material practice.[71] And while the rhetoric of "nation" had a place in this, using the power of the press to inspire a representational idea of "print-nationalism,"[72] Christopher Castiglia observes: "One finds, in the writing of antebellum political theories . . . less talk of *nationalism* than of the *state* as a network of civil institutions."[73] Nationalistic media itself drew on mechanisms of "state" change that were being deployed to facilitate a wider ranging set of material practices linked to legible social action.

One can clarify this by thinking through the ontology of Simonds's language game. *Peter Coddle* is defined by the structure it gives to the gaps in its narrative: you may place a noun here and not there, syntax and verbs persist without recourse. Although any given iteration of the game might read entirely differently—might embody a wholly different output *state*—the structure of the game, the thing one is inclined to call *Peter Coddle*, remains steadfast—just like the characterizing format Simonds had given readers of the *Boston Saturday Rambler* through the forme regularization of the masthead, page sequencing, and column configuration. Shifting the figure to a political register: in a democracy based on written ideas, it is the settlement of those very ideas through documents that comes to define the *character* of the state, if not its particular unspoken priorities at any given time. A discursively instantiated set of conditions held in place—whether laws, rights, or more simply social rules—render the state as a state machine, and ensure confidence in its identity. If things are to change, documents must be *edited, appended to, and put into proximate conversation* with an ever-growing mass of media that visualizes—like the patent models of the nineteenth-century U.S. Patent Office—what the democracy "is." The logic of a social object as a machine offering series of "blanks" to be adjusted, filled, and manipulated in the pursuit of the next state, though a difficult abstraction on the face of it, is made concrete on nearly every level of media production and invention in the mid-nineteenth-century United States. Expanding technologies of printing facilitated both broader access to and deeper saturation of bureaucratic documentation with its attendant officializing "forms." Moreover, the wide-scale growth of these technologies placed more and more of Europe and America into contact with the "formes" and interchangeable practices of publishing. Within this set of associations, Boole's notion of language itself as a field of functional form and configuration—as a series of interoperable state machines—was not only thinkable but incredibly cogent.

As the document-driven institutions that composed the operation of this state machine grew, so did the scope of this particular figure. Materialized reform was pursued not only in the external political world but in the "interior" world of habits and self-control as well—as we saw, for example, with Jessie's desire to "be somebody" through the production of visible pages. Building on this, Castiglia argues that the reform dictates of the state were firmly (if conflictedly) relocated in the "interior" of American citizens, yielding a kind of institutional consciousness that he calls an "interior state." This interior was, in Castiglia's phrase, a "virtual arena" in which individual citizens mediated between their own ambivalent bodily wants and the myriad identity categories materialized by a rising tide of pamphlets, books, and graphic media: drunkards, masturbators, and gamblers; but also gentlemen, teetotalers, and abolitionists.[74] And lest we amble into somewhat ghostly notions of the operations at play here, it must be reinforced that these affective and discursive performances of "interiority" were undergirded by an iteratively provoking *mediation of inscribed types* that was an everyday reality of social being in this moment.

Following our analysis of the historical dimensions of "state," each of the identities listed above might be seen as a potential output of the citizen as state machine.[75] Changing one's habits, reformers believed, was akin to adjusting the strategy by which one played one's own interior game. Advocates of reform assembled a ready stockpile of character "types" that corresponded to specific strategies of self-management: follow the right strategy and you could be assured of an appropriately legible outcome, your body itself a page to be read by others who could recognize your social genre. Growing institutional demands on one's interior led, however, to a corresponding multiplication of potential outputs, putting an impossible strain on the "citizens possessed of [these] riven interiorities."[76] Reform institutions demanded adherence to strict rules of "good" character, while lived experience demanded a constant (and changing) mediation among these rules. The resulting conflict between differences of circumstance and habit and the drive to materialize type—both *in* type and through modes of legible exchange—meant that any person's capacity to embody a particular identity was more a function of the person's desire to appear that way in a given context than it was a real depiction of a stable sense of "interiority."

In *The Confidence-Man*, Melville uses the trope of "puzzlement" to express the intense desire to cease this feeling of interior volatility.[77] The Man with the Weed in His Hat accuses a merchant of not remembering him as an old friend; in response, "the good merchant look[s] puzzled," frustrated that he cannot fulfill the role of the genial gentleman.[78] The Man uses this "forgotten" acquaintance role to throw himself upon the merchant's sympathies and walks away with money. The Man in Gray listens as a young clergyman confesses his lack of faith in the identity of Black Guinea, an early incarnation of the Confidence-Man as a disabled beggar. The minister declares, "I confess, this [lack of faith] puzzles me."[79] The Man in Gray takes on the role of interlocutor, allowing the clergyman to absolve him of his guilt by accepting a trust on behalf of Guinea. Later in the narrative, the Cosmopolitan patiently waits in front of an old watchman with a Bible in the main sleeping quarters, until "the old man . . . look[s] up puzzled at him a moment."[80] He proceeds to use their religious connection to gather the old man's trust, escorting him out of the room and leaving the sleeping passengers to "the sad consequences which might, upon occasion, ensue from the cabin being left in darkness."[81] Even the stoic Missourian succumbs to puzzlement: "He revolves the crafty process of sociable chat, by which, as he fancies, the man with the brass-plate wormed into him. . . . Before his mental vision the person of that threadbare Talleyrand [the Confidence-Man] . . . passes now in puzzled review."[82] While being puzzled is a variety of interior bewilderment, it also holds the promise of being solved, of one's confounding anxiety being resolved. As Wai Chee Dimock persuasively puts it, "What the confidence man sells to most of his victims is in fact a promising version of the victim's own self."[83] Conspicuously, most of these transactions involve movements of paper: the exchange of cash, the signing of contracts, the taking down of names, and the reading of handbills. What the con man sells his victims is not just a "promising version" but, in a sense, a promise *note*, a materialization of self—in the voice of another and in writing—that would otherwise be left as an abstract feeling of social anxiety.

Despite, or perhaps because of, the demands that institutions of reform placed on citizens, the feelings of anxiety associated with a chaotic and competitive interiority were regulated in part by imagining the self as a consistent decision algorithm, a state machine with which one could tinker to produce repeatable results over time. Melville suggests that a suturing continuity was achieved, despite changes of circumstance, by both *imagining* and *documenting* oneself a consistent output system, a personal Mississippi "uniting the streams" in a "cosmopolitan and confident tide."[84] Being an abolitionist, therefore, was a function of determined outputs, ideally (if not actually) corresponding to a consistent interior. In order to buy into the apparent guarantee of such a regulated interior, a person would have to engage in specifically legible expressive and affective responses, talking in specified ways about slavery and race, and perhaps to donating to abolitionist institutions. If one acted according to these rules, one might not only call oneself an abolitionist but would also have the security of identity that went along with other people recognizing one as "an abolitionist." Moreover, since the only indication of a person's success was the output state (Do people recognize you as an abolitionist? Is that in fact the Mississippi?), an after-effect of interiority was a somewhat paradoxical realization of codependence.

To be recognized as what one wanted to be was to have *confidence* (literally, "together faith") that one had successfully regulated one's interior state machine. This required others to provide both opportunities for demonstration and validations of effect. "Puzzling" rhetoric conveys deep irony in Melville's novel, representing both lack and form; it figures bewilderment with the lack of a singular self-defining character position as well as the opportunity to discretely correct this performative failure—again, often through material transaction.[85] A case in point, the clergyman is committed to embodying a charitable disposition of trust, which is unsettled by a skeptical customhouse officer. Unable to unilaterally apply charitable trust to Black Guinea because of this seed of doubt, the clergyman feels an intense anxiety at losing the functional basis of his character. If character must be realized in the iteration of consistent visible states—the public application of trust, for instance—then a failure to repeat the desired results is a failure to actualize character.[86] Yet more than this, Melville's characters feel puzzled when sensing that their public display (the output) is *mismatched* with their imagined interior state machine. To feel a specific mismatch, the clergyman must formulate an algorithm of potential "correct" action (in this case vocalized by the Man in Gray): "We should shut our ears to distrust."[87] Notably, this takes the form of generalized instructions, like those typical of both game and reform manuals of the time. This formalization produces the conditions by which an anxiety resulting from failure becomes, in addition, an anxiousness for resolution. Consequently, being "puzzled" in Melville's writing is both to be shaken in one's facile sense of character and to be ready to enact a desired public self; it is to be configured as a state machine awaiting an appropriately formed argument. The clergyman and the Man in Gray continue:

> "How shall I be sure that my present exemption from [doubt's] ef-
>   fects will be lasting?"
> "You cannot be sure, but you can strive against it."
> "How?"
> "By strangling the least symptom of distrust, of any sort, which
>   hereafter, upon whatever provocation, may arise in you."
> "I will do so."[88]

The language of potential at the close of this passage registers the clergyman's desire to reaffirm the consistency of his character. As a result, he is all too happy to oblige the Man in Gray's request for charity on behalf of the Seminole Widow and Orphan Asylum. Because he cannot fully resolve his "puzzlement" without a public act of confirmation, "puzzling" becomes an opportunity for the Confidence-Man to act as an argument does within an algorithm, transforming formal potential into an expressed public reality. Identifying the "need" of his marks, the Confidence-Man can set his own values (both in terms of how much money they should give and in terms of its supposed purpose) and therefore exert a game player's control over his mark's expressive outcome.

At the opening of the narrative, we saw the Confidence-Man as a speechless deaf man navigating the crowd and constructing a basic state machine with his chalk slate. The formal continuity of this small state machine was the phrase "Charity . . . ," and the inputs were a series of phrases that he scribbled in the proceeding space, producing different output phrases and, correspondingly, different reactions from his fellow shipmates. In the later chapter, "A Charitable Lady," this character is immediately recalled. A well-dressed widow loafs on a sofa, pondering the Bible: "Half-relinquished, she holds the book in reverie, her finger inserted at the xiii. of 1st Corinthians [the well-known passage on charity], to which chapter possibly her attention might have recently been turned, by witnessing the scene of the monitory mute and his slate."[89] Upon examination the narrator hints, "If she have any weak point, it must be anything rather than her excellent heart."[90] The irony is that her "weak point" (in terms of her capacity for being puzzled) is precisely this: her "heart," or her desire to be a "Charitable Lady."

As a supposed advocate for the Seminole Widow and Orphan Asylum, the Confidence-Man does not aim for a weak point so much as this self-perceived *strongest point*, which will be basis of their confidence. Sliding beside the Charitable Lady, he asks for her "confidence," and she blurts out: "Why—really—you—" and "Really, sir—why, sir—really—I—."[91] These fragmented reactions might be seen as a cycling-through of unresolved subjectivities, a demonstration of a state machine without an appropriate input. Significantly, her outbursts end short of *defining* the role that either she or the Confidence-Man will take, trailing off at the very moment where some substantial definition would need to be given. And her first full sentence confirms the variability that she reads in the Confidence-Man, answering his question with a confused, "Really, sir—as much—I mean, as one may wisely put in a—a—stranger, an entire stranger, I had almost said."[92] When he pushes her on the issue of confidence anew, she is again reduced to sputtering: "But I—I have—at least to that degree—I mean that—," "Believe me, I—yes, yes—I may say—that—that—." Finally, "She sat in a sort of restless torment, knowing not which way to turn. She began twenty different sentences, and left off at the first syllable of each."[93] Here she has become like the deaf man's sign in between its various substantiations, a state machine formalizing a presentation of self but incapable of producing outcomes without input. Each elliptical sentence that she utters, one might well imagine, would correspond to a different known quantity—to a different value of x in her undefined equation, or to a different identity she would like to claim for herself. Yet without an argument, she is effectively unable to produce characterological statements.

The charitable widow is a model of interior "puzzlement" in both senses of the term: she is confused, but she is also desperate to be given some kind of stable value around which to frame her public identity. Dizzy, she looks to the Confidence-Man for reassurance: "At last, in desperation, she hurried out, 'Tell me, sir, for what you want the twenty dollars?'"[94] After he reveals that he is an advocate for the Seminole Widow and Orphan Asylum, the woman gives him money, and he proclaims that she has "confidence."[95] In other words, she has resolved the conditionals, the "ifs" of her state machine, into a steady singular output. By giving her a charity to which she can donate, the Confidence-Man allows her to actualize the interior she so intensely wants. Before his intervention, she could not be sure that her documented character would correspond to this desire; however, much as adding a value to an equation allows one to plot a graphic point (an actuality that realizes the potential of the abstract function), the Confidence-Man's willingness to go from a "stranger" to an agent of the Asylum allows the widow to plot *herself.* The singular legibility of her story—the small narrative plot of a woman giving to a charity—affirms the consistency of her interior and averts, for the moment, the shuttling anxiety that begins the chapter.

In a parallel scene, the Confidence-Man takes advantage of a young collegian, playing on his desire for apparent maturity. Under the guise of the Man with the Weed in His Hat (a symbol of mourning), the Confidence-Man begins by seizing upon the youth's "weak point." He lectures the boy on reading the pessimistic Roman historian, Tacitus, each time addressing him with a reminder of his age, calling him alternately, "my young friend" (four times), "dear young sir," "my dear young friend," and "my dear young sir." With this he reduces the young man to a stammer, just as with the puzzled widow: " 'Sir, sir,' stammered the other," "Sir, sir, I—I—," "Sir, I—, I—," "Really, sir—I—," and finally, "Upon my word, I—I—."[96] The Man with the Weed closes this preparatory work with a speech calling to mind the real-life story of the "original" confidence man: " 'Did you never observe how little, very little confidence, there is? I mean between man and man—more particularly between stranger and stranger. . . . Confidence! I have sometimes almost thought that confidence is fled; that confidence is the New Astrea—emigrated—vanished—gone.' Then softly sliding nearer, with the softest air, quivering down and looking up, he continued: 'Could you now, my dear young sir, under such circumstances, by way of experiment, simply have confidence in *me?*' "[97] Hearing this, the youth silently flees the scene. Yet although the scheme does not yield a profit in this first instance, the Man with the Weed has set the stage for taking advantage of him later on. He has "puzzled" the collegian such that the youth is desperate to prove that he is not defined by his age—and he will take the first available opportunity to materialize his mental state to an outside audience. His opportunity comes moments after the Seminole Orphan advocate leaves the side of the charitable woman. The Black Coal Rapids stockholder (again, the Confidence-Man in disguise) enters in the chapter that follows, entitled "Two Business Men Conduct a Little Business."[98] In this role, the Confidence-Man exclusively refers to the collegian in mature terms: "Pray, *sir,* have you seen a gentleman with a weed hereabouts, rather saddish gentleman?" "Have you seen him, *sir?*" and "Really, you are quite a business *man.* Positively, I feel afraid of you."[99] When he reveals that he has stocks on him, the youth demands to see a statement of the condition of his company while the stockholder tries to deflect with talk of the Man with the Weed. But the young man will hear nothing of it: " 'Let the unfortunate man relieve himself.

—Hand me the statement.' 'Well, you are such a business-man, I can hardly deny you. Here,' handing a small, printed pamphlet. The youth turned it over sagely. 'I hate a suspicious man,' said the other, observing him, 'but I must say I like to see a cautious one.' "[100] In a wry comic turn, the stockholder begins to refer to the boy's age *the moment* the business side of their transaction has finished: "Business transacted, the two came forth, and walked the deck. 'Now tell me, sir,' said he with the book, 'how comes it that a young gentleman like you, a sedate student at the first appearance, should dabble in stocks and that sort of thing?' "[101] The collegian does not buy another stock.

In each of these instances, "puzzling" is an opportunity for the Confidence-Man to play the *Fidèle* passengers as if they were a discrete game.[102] And this game is a familiar game, a recognizable game—not an experiment in characterological genre but the repetition of an extant form. When puzzled the passengers are under the impression that, in order to be understood as what they desire to be, they *must* embody a kind of interior consistency that can only be enacted (and validated) by cooperating with the Confidence-Man. While performing the role of the "monitory mute," the Confidence-Man figured himself as a structural variable to which passersby might attribute a value, meaning, or argument; later he reverses the operation, insinuating himself into the interior equation of social constants produced by the passengers. By shifting the associations linked to certain core words and concepts, the subtle wordplay that accompanies nearly every interaction in the text, he shifts even the "operators" by which his marks process his "arguments." This allows him to set his own value and to control the expressive outcome of the passengers such that it yields an income for himself, while remaining true to the form they wish to realize.

The Cosmopolitan of the novel's second half reveals the nature of this operation when relating his encounter with Pitch the Missourian: "I seized a chance, when, owing to indignation against some wrong, he laid himself a little open; I seized that lucky chance."[103] To do this, it is imperative that he first identify a gap or equivocal space in the functional character of his mark, illustrated in the conversation between the Missourian and the agent of the "Philosophical Intelligence Office": "The man with the brass-plate wormed into him . . . persuad[ing] him to waive, in his exceptional case, the general law of distrust he systematically applied to the race."[104] At this moment, the form of the gap is noted as a "conditional confidence" that Pitch has in the stranger's understanding of human nature.[105] He then implores the Confidence-Man for input: "Do you think now, candidly, that—I say

candidly—candidly—could I have some small, limited—some faint, conditional degree of confidence in that boy? . . . You have suggested some rather
new views of boys, and men, too. Upon those views in the concrete I at present decline to determine."[106] Here the agent seizes the opportunity that Pitch
has given him in structuring his perspective as a conditional, an if-then statement requiring a "candid" argument from the Confidence-Man. And the argument (or answer to his question), unsurprisingly, is that yes, yes, the
Confidence-Man *does* believe that "candidly, [Pitch] could" trust that the boy
would be different from all the rest.[107]

By providing this argument, the outcome is secured, and the "ifs" of the
Missourian's conditional confidence are determined much as they were in the
case of the widow and the young businessman. Papers, in the form of money
and addressing information, are then produced to render the operation concrete. And the P.I.O. agent reinforces the notion that the document is the
discrete finale of a process, rather than a new site of ambiguity, saying to
Pitch, "Respected sir, never willingly do I handle money not with perfect willingness, nay, with a certain alacrity, paid. Either tell me that you have a perfect
and unquestioning confidence in me . . . or permit me respectfully to return
these bills."[108] The Confidence-Man eliminates the conditionals of interiority
by acting as the value that enables their material expression, echoing his earlier declaration to an old miser: "No ifs. Downright confidence, or none."[109]
Playing on a character's desire to become an eternally self-consistent state machine, a game or puzzle, the Confidence-Man becomes the very embodiment
of systematic variability—of the "lucky chance" he seizes in Pitch. By the time
Frank Goodman approaches him, the misanthropic Missourian has wearied
of such interactivity: "No you don't. No more little arguments for me. Had
too many little arguments to-day."[110]

Yet in spite of this rejection, and its implication of continuity between
Goodman and the other avatars of the Confidence-Man, the Cosmopolitan of
the second half of the book seems to shift the perspective slightly.[111] In these
later chapters, we move from a relentless portrayal of the ways that the social
necessities of "confidence" lead to potential victimization, to a demonstration
of how one might fight fire with fire, variability with flexibility and structured
perseverance. John Bryant notes that Goodman is "a different order of operator, a 'new kind of monster,' a victim who fights back," adding that the Cosmopolitan's purpose is "to inculcate in readers an appreciation of the
suppleness, not the rigidity, of Goodman's mind, to have readers experience
the tense repose of his perpetual questioning that necessarily swings from one

certainty to its opposite."[112] We might think of this as a kind of "playerliness" native to the iterative social practices embodied by the repetitive enunciations of *Peter Coddle* gameplay—a provisionally absurd, iteratively ironical playerliness "worth the consideration of those to whom it may prove worth considering" that was not the mode of reading privileged by the critical establishment that shipwrecked Melville's career as a popular writer.[113] Though the Cosmopolitan closes the narrative on the sinister note of leaving the ship's cabin in darkness, it is surely an ambiguous signal—one that, to repurpose William Spanos's more skeptical argument, invites the reader to "think the positive possibilities" of confidence, to maintain "an alternative comportment to being that acknowledges its contingency, its nothingness."[114] In a world where legible subjectivity is imagined as a state machine, Melville's "evil" protagonist may be part of a troubled utopian figure, a gesture of agency and invention in a world seemingly doomed to being played.

Utopic Operators and Drummond Lights

Louis Marin argues that the fundamental work of any utopia lies in its ability to act as a "neutral" to ideological structures, ironizing the differences or binaries of a given discourse: "The neutral must be grasped as the transitory and passing term that allows movement from one contrary to another."[115] By this definition, the "Mississippi operator" might be considered as a proximate neutral in his marks' various utopic gestures toward consistency of character, an ambiguous associate that enables the marks to modify their "misty notions" through social "contact" (to return to the quotation that opened this chapter). Yet while all of his marks manage to change themselves according to their will, this change is rendered deeply ambivalent by the fact that this will is both conditioned and enacted by outside forces. As a result, the character positions they believe they have embodied lose credibility as self-determinations in the eyes of the reader. The Confidence-Man stands in for the ambiguity of personal reform in an ideological context that seems to rob citizens of the very things that would make such reform personal. Melville's novel indicates that if individual action is to be constrained by the emerging figure of the state machine, then it becomes an imperative of agency for one to avoid becoming so intently wrapped up in the management of the machine as to allow outside forces wholly to dictate its function. An agent must become an operator who shifts the core functions of a characterological form at the risk of becoming a puzzle; a statically institutionalized interior leaves no room for direct social reinvention. The agency at play—one tied up not just in the delivery of arguments that fill in blanks but also in the varied shifts of meaning that these arguments attach to even static forms—places a special burden on the transitions that are enacted through altered sets of associations with the same documented figures of speech. Marin argues that utopics tend to set the stage whereby previously unspeakable topics might become intelligible, "anticipating, but blindly" the transition from one mode of culture to another.[116] If this is the case in *The Confidence-Man*, we might understand Melville's lead character as a utopic study in the requirements of agency during the age of state machine subjectivity, anticipating the role of playful reassociation in the settling and unsettling of social character. In the chapters that follow, the specific materializations and procedures of this focal and associational play are tracked by a set of mid-century games more directly engaged with configurative and scopic practices than *Peter Coddle* or *The Checkered Game of Life*.

But as a prelude to these discussions, we should now simply note that the Confidence-Man represents a special type of nineteenth-century utopic figure: that of the agent as inventor.[117] To "invent" is to "devise first [or] originate" and derives from the Latin root "invenire" meaning "to come into or upon."[118] The Confidence-Man, as we have seen, uses perceived gaps in the interiority of his marks as opportunities to insinuate himself into their imagined state machines, filling in the blanks as in a game of *Peter Coddle* and interacting with them to produce a legible public output. Through his success, he represents the importance of the momentary, the variable, and the associative as interactive (and critical) supplements to the structures of state and consistency that dominated U.S. reform discourse of the mid-nineteenth century. As institutionalism sought to flatten time in a manner that would ensure a consistent and ostensibly well-formed future, *The Confidence-Man* reconfigures focus onto the differential moments when character is or might be invented anew. If agency is effectively displaced in these moments, it is because the marks are unwilling to use the codes of consistency as a tool or starting point—recapitulation becomes an end in itself, "the universal application of a temporary feeling or opinion" lamented in Melville's letters to Nathaniel Hawthorne.[119] Consequently, they cede their originality and their capacity for invention to the Confidence-Man. Seizing on the phrase "quite an original," Melville explains:

> What is popularly held to entitle a character in fiction to being
> deemed original, is but something personal—confined to itself. The

character sheds not its characteristic on its surroundings, whereas, the original character . . . is like a revolving Drummond light, raying away from itself all round it—everything is lit by it, everything starts up to it . . . , so that, in certain minds, there follows upon the adequate conception of such a character, an effect, in its way, akin to that which in Genesis attends upon the beginning of things . . . to produce but one original character, he must have had much luck.[120]

For Melville, the truly original character must be willing to interface with the codes that surround and locate it. It is not separate from its contexts but decidedly uses its position to create subtle (or not so subtle) shifts of focus. Turning on a light, for example, may not rearrange the furniture, but it does change the kinds of things one might think to do in a room. The light alters function by altering associations, emphasizing or creating apparent connection between preexisting structures in ways that reinvent a space. It is, more properly, an infrastructure, not a structure in itself—not the furniture or the city upon which the Drummond light shines. To become this light, to be an inventor of "original character," Melville insists that "luck" must be involved, and this returns us to the importance of the momentary in the character of the Confidence-Man. One is not timelessly lucky but instead must find luck in time, like the skillful player of a game. Indeed, Melville's equivocal protagonist—with his willingness to reconstruct social meaning in local and contingent improvisations, to seize and to make his own "lucky chance[s]"— gestures toward a world where the shape-shifting Confidence-Man looks to be more hero than villain, for some at least. It gestures at a world where gaming and associational "playerliness" may be the most relevant form of agency available, a means of fungible intervention that we ignore at our own risk. And that world may very well be our own.

CHAPTER 3

The Power to Promote

Configuration Culture in the Age of Barnum

I apprehend that there is no sort of object which men seek to attain, whether secular, moral or religious, in which humbug is not very often an instrumentality.

—P. T. Barnum, *Humbugs of the World* (1865)

A wooden square is dissected with surgical precision. A diagonal bisects the center, and a cut parallel to this divides the upper remaining triangle into a smaller triangle and a long trapezoid. From the center of this trapezoid two cuts are made: one perpendicular, splitting the shape clean in half and persisting to bisect the lower triangle in two; another at a forty-five-degree angle, creating a right triangle and leaving a small parallelogram as its remainder. A careful final cut severs the other side of the trapezoid in half, leaving a right triangle, the twin of the previous, and a smaller square, the child of the original untouched wooden piece. These seven "tans"—a square, a parallelogram, two small right triangles, one medium triangle, and two large triangles— become the instruments of a rich pictorial language. From seven come many: amoebas, plants, animals, human bodies in all kinds of activity, and human faces in a range of form and countenance. The player's capacity to imagine small changes in the arrangement of these wooden bricks is the only limit to the figures he or she can create. And in trying to re-create the puzzles of others, one must be willing slowly and methodically to move the pieces into and out of a variety of different positions, touching, testing, pondering, and evolving the mass of shapes from one figure to another until the desired effect is achieved. Success is a kind of communication: "Out of a set of raw materials, you made a shape I understood. Out of the same materials, I made many figures, but settled on yours."

The mechanical configuration puzzle now commonly known as a tangram was a timeless Chinese invention passed down through generations, "at least four thousand years old." Or so the story went.[1] In fact, tangrams were not so antique. Drawing on a tradition of modular table sets called butterfly-wing tables, the tangram was invented in late eighteenth-century China and brought to both America and Europe by maritime traders in 1816.[2] A short but intense fad for the game swept France and England in 1817 and 1818, complete with cautionary tales of people driven to life-threatening distraction by "puzzle madness." In one satirical caricature (cut with panels evoking the seven tans), a man ignores his wife's advances, a lawyer misses a public hearing, a mother neglects her child, and children set aside their homework—all to focus their efforts instead on the simple puzzle (Figure 9).[3] The fervor in Europe died down after 1818, but interest smoldered in the United States, with pirated European editions supplementing consistent domestic showings throughout the middle part of the nineteenth century.[4] Twenty-two years after the first American collection was copyrighted by James Coaxe, Winshang Punqua's *The Chinese Puzzler, Designed to Strengthen and Amuse the Mind* (which came with a set of carved ivory pieces) went into its second edition in 1839 "due to the rapid sale of the first edition"; and in 1844, C. C. Chapman published a boxed set of 329 tangram problems with pieces under the title *Scientific Amusements; for the Old and Young, the Grave and the Gay*; it went through six editions due to high demand.[5]

By the mid-century, tangrams, and configuration puzzles more generally, were seen as important educational guides, a popular training tool for a manner of abstract thinking and invention that was firmly of its moment.[6] The mid-nineteenth-century United States was a world lived in pieces, from the content "bins" of Simonds's newspaper and discrete chunks of data aggregated by bureaucratic forms, to the large-scale labeling of urban signage differentiating block from block and gridding up places like Manhattan. Machines, writing, and amusements were increasingly subject to media modeling practices that took a granular and geometric approach. Maps, trains, and even faces were split into interchangeable pieces for newly invented puzzle adaptations; and in kindergarten blocks, basic shapes were put into relation with each other as ways of understanding the piecemeal composition of figural complexity (Figure 10). The tangram was only the simplest and perhaps most graceful

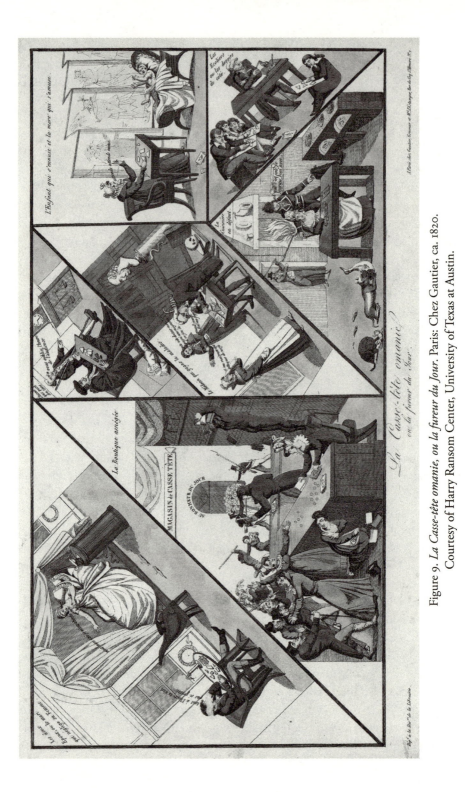

Figure 9. *La Casse-tête omanie, ou la fureur du Jour*. Paris: Chez Gautier, ca. 1820. Courtesy of Harry Ransom Center, University of Texas at Austin.

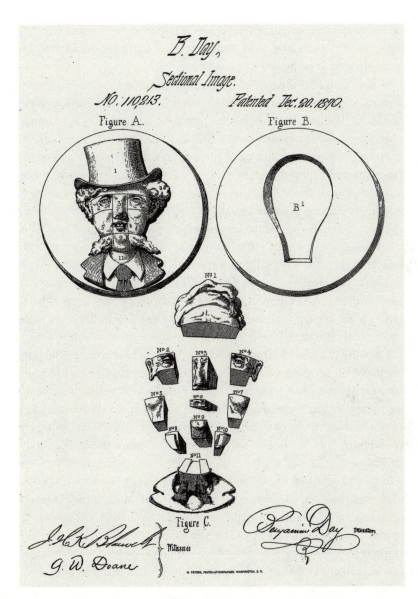

Figure 10. Benjamin Day. Grotesque Sectional Puzzle. U.S. Patent 110,213. 20 December 1870. Source: United States Patent and Trademark Office, www.uspto.gov.

variation of an amusement *style* that was conspicuously ubiquitous. Its persistence was not a measure of its antiquity—it was a game very much *of* and *for* the culture that embraced it.[7]

Where, then, did the romantic claims of tangram timelessness originate? In a word, they were a humbug: a term the self-proclaimed "Prince of Humbugs," P. T. Barnum, once defined as "putting on glittering appearances—outside show—novel expedients, by which to suddenly arrest public attention, and attract the public eye and ear."[8] In contrast to a swindle, which cheats its audience by promising something and offering nothing in return, a Barnumesque humbug fulfills its promise of entertainment by creating a context for something of value—however literally disingenuous. The false history of tangrams was devised by one of the foremost U.S. puzzlists, a onetime civil engineer named Samuel Loyd. After publishing a small collection of tangram figures in 1875, Loyd took it upon himself to revive interest in the puzzle in 1903 with a book called *The 8th Book of Tan*. Using tangram forms to tell a story of human evolution, and claiming that his work was simply the transcription of an ancient Chinese creation narrative given to him by a fictional expert named "Professor Challenor," Loyd spun a yarn in which the tangram "out-Darwins Darwin, the progress of the human race being traced though seven stages of development up to a mysterious spiritual stage which is too lunatic for serious consideration."[9] Loyd's hoax fueled public interest in the game by playing on techniques of humbuggery that would have made Barnum proud, combining entertaining novelty (Loyd introduced 438 newly invented figures in the book) and a vogue for both the exotic and the historical.

In fact, Loyd owed some part of his later success to a partnership formed with the infamous showman early in his career. After turning away from engineering to start an editorial column on chess, Loyd devised a three-piece configuration puzzle commonly called the "Trick Donkeys." Here, players attempted to arrange two downtrodden donkeys, printed on thin strips of paper, in such a way that the addition of a third strip, with two mirrored riders printed on it, would give the appearance that the men were riding the animals. (It was substantially harder than it sounds, and correspondingly satisfying to solve.) In 1871, Barnum noted public interest in the puzzle and offered Loyd a massive licensing fee of ten thousand dollars to begin officially calling it *Barnum's Trick Mules*. Loyd accepted. Soon millions of copies were distributed around the country, making it one of the most recognized and beloved puzzles of the nineteenth century.[10] The "Prince of Puzzles," as Loyd was once affectionately called, and the "Prince of Humbugs" thus formed a relationship based on a complex form of mutual association: Barnum's name would help bring attention to Loyd's puzzle, and Loyd's puzzle would ensure that players so engaged couldn't help but associate its entertainment value with Barnum's name.[11]

In this chapter, I suggest that the link between nineteenth-century configuration puzzles and Barnum's success in business was not limited to the marketing partnership formed by Barnum and Loyd. Instead, the popularity and durability of configuration puzzles (with tangrams being an especially pervasive example) can shed light on the modus operandi of Barnum's career—on the mechanisms of association and social engineering at the core of his "original" genius. Providing a specific and historically native model of pictorial meaning making, tangrams miniaturize, materialize, and codify the practices native to the configurative agency that closed the previous chapter. But, of course, the term "configuration" has wide application in games. Moving pieces according the rules of Bradley's *Life* can be considered a configuration of its algorithms, as can the placement of nouns in the gap-laden narrative of *Peter Coddle*. Yet in tangrams the term attains a direct clarity: to succeed in the game is to shape (figure) together (con) the seven pieces according to a given diagram.

A secondary configuration was frequently necessary to drive interest in the game, to render these shapes legible and satisfying. Because the images created by tangrams were so abstract, puzzle books often provided additional details that contextualized the underlying figures—similar shapes were sequenced near each other to draw attention to slight differences requiring difficult rearrangements, figures were filled in with a face or clothing, and images were connected to ongoing narratives (of which each tangram was a panel) (Figure 11). To return to Barnum's earlier definition, these extra materials were not a swindle but a humbug or "outside show." Ludic paratexts were crucial to the game's entertainment value, integral to the player's sense of purpose in playing because they forged a communicative connection between the player's arrangement of the pieces and the puzzle inventor's figural vision.[12] In this way, the player of the tangram engages with configuration on two levels, as both a shaping together of the blocks in a common space and a mutual and communicative "together shaping"—becoming a part of the shaping process by trying to see as the inventor saw, letting a joint imagination create the legibility and corresponding enjoyment of the figure.

Set this alongside Barnum's 1842 exhibition of the so-called Feejee

Figure 11. *The Chinese Puzzle*. New York: McLoughlin Brothers, ca. 1870.
Courtesy of Lilly Library, Indiana University, Bloomington.

mermaid, and meaningful parallels emerge. The mermaid itself is a reconfiguration of known elements, executed so as to obscure the artifice of the arrangement—and determining how this combination might be accomplished was part of the game: "The monkey and fish were so nicely conjoined that no human eye could detect where the junction was formed . . . it was a most remarkable specimen of ingenuity and untiring patience."[13] Yet the "ingenuity" of this anatomical configuration was not enough to sell the public on the piece; indeed, the traveling sailor who supposedly brought the piece back from a South Asian expedition in 1817 "did not realize his [monetary] expectations."[14]

Barnum relied on a secondary configuration that mirrors that of the tangram books, themselves hitting American shores just a year before. He surrounded the exhibition of the Feejee mermaid (both in newspapers and on the exterior of the American Museum) with woodcuts and transparencies of traditionally attractive mermaids, meant to train the eye of the audience on what they were about to see and to allow them to bring their own desires into the imaginative play: desire for the fantastical made real, for the triumph of science, and, obviously, for an eroticized female form. And as in tangrams, Barnum created stories that situated the mermaid composition, displaying it "with other animals forming connecting links in the great chain of Animated Nature."[15] To fully realize the exhibitionary potential of the Feejee mermaid, Barnum relies on paratexts, literally "texts alongside," or again as he calls it in his definition of humbug, "outside show."

The simplified configurative protocols of tangrams thus shed light on a set of practices performed and visualized throughout Barnum's first autobiography, *The Life of P. T. Barnum, Written by Himself* (1855), drawing attention to the emerging relationship between objects, communication, and legible agency that would come to define action in the new urban economy. As people from all walks of life came to the cities of the northeastern United States, the desire for personal and technological reinvention—both readily available democratic avenues to success—demanded a particular sort of strategic social engagement. And this engagement was built on an understanding that a person's associations literally made the person. Discussing the associationist philosophy that was the "dominant orthodoxy" in schools of the early national period, Christopher Looby writes, "[Association] is the characteristic term [David] Hume used to describe how a succession of distinct perceptions or sensations are put into a *relation* or *connection* with one another (which nevertheless are still distinct), but then are artificially *confounded* with one another due to our natural propensity to posit identity or sameness where it does not truly exist."[16] Here, the merely related attains a *feeling* of necessary connection or logic through the repeated coincidence of distinct things, experiences, or terms.

For nineteenth-century Americans, character could not only be defined via the apparently direct logic of documentary *types* but also settled and unsettled through more sidelong operations that allowed proximity to suggest meaning—a "confound[ing]" of sometimes contingent social or spatial placements that effected powerful metaphoric and metonymic operations. As we began to consider by way of Melville's notion of "original character" in the previous chapter, a thing might change meaningfully simply by virtue of its surroundings—its proximities and associative affordances—even as it remains substantially the same. Of course, awareness of this phenomenon is essential to advertising practice in our own time. Yet in Barnum's moment, the messy configurative deployment of the proximate seems to have been born of certain inevitable juxtapositions that were native to the antebellum city, the street, the newspaper, and the specific requirements of media more broadly.

Though I have started at some distance from Barnum, using the tangram to begin building a model of meaningfulness in specific kinds of proximate configuration, in what follows I aim to understand Barnum by looking at his work as fundamentally configurative, and by examining it in playfully configurative ways. This perspective illuminates a continuity of method throughout the showman's career, yielding additional insight into the distinctive species of social agency that was facilitated and expressed in both the textual space of his autobiography and the physical space of the American Museum. To follow up on the *sense* of connection employed here, and reflect on its potential for historiographic significance in studying the power of proximate, I have arranged this chapter itself as a series of "alongsides"—performing the way that materials at a slant might impact meaning, not just in marketing or autobiographical writing (or in the controlled chaos of a museum of disparate things), but also in ways of understanding history. Although it is subject to the varying degrees of harmony that are inevitable to such layered arrangements, my aim is to gesture at the potentials indicated by distinct narrative and material resonances that become confounded and flattened over time. By foregrounding and returning to the tangram as a concrete and historically native representative of specific communicative practices involving human/thing proximities, I fixate on what Lauren Berlant has recently termed "infrastructures" of association. Even as it is undoubtedly more abstract than either *The Checkered Game of Life* or *Peter Coddle*, the tangram also tangibly models a world in miniature, a set of "protocols or practices that hold the world up" in Barnum's time, suggesting different ways of seeing social invention in the work of both literary and spatial exhibition.[17]

Critics have argued that Barnum's mode of exhibition (and related success) was characterized by his talent for creating spaces where spectators could define themselves in relatively direct and differential ways. Rosemarie Garland Thomson contends that Barnum's physical curiosities helped viewers confirm their own normality by making "the physical particularity of the freak into a hypervisible text against which the viewer's indistinguishable body fades into a seemingly neutral, tractable, and invulnerable instrument of the autonomous will."[18] The exhibition is not so much *used* as *used up* in the process of visualizing a neutral subject. Similarly, in *Humbug: The Art of P. T. Barnum*, Neil Harris sees these displays as opportunities to amass information in the service of determining the reality or hoax of a given exhibition, reinforcing one's own ingenuity: "Barnum's elaborate hoaxes . . . trained Americans to absorb knowledge. This was an aesthetic of the operational, a delight in observing process and examining for literal truth. . . . Barnum's exhibitions concentrated on information and the problem of deception."[19] I want to expand on these views by showing that Barnum's success is not only a measure of his dexterity in pandering to particular formations of "normality," nor is it solely in his ability to engage people's appetite for procedural exposé. Both these views, though crucial to an understanding of spectacle in the moment, do not take full consideration of the way that Barnum's exhibits use "outside show" or paratexts to implicate and embed the viewer, configuring the spectator as a part of the exhibit rather than fundamentally distant.[20] Barnum accomplishes this by remaining close to the same configurative practices that made tangrams a continued presence in households throughout the country.

Interpolating the Little D

Convincing his parents to let him ride along with a cattle dealer traveling through his hometown of Bethel, Connecticut, the adolescent Barnum makes his first trip to the bustling metropolis of New York City when he is eleven years old. Alone in the city, he spends the bulk of the allowance provided by his mother (one dollar)—as well as trade credit from two handkerchiefs and a pair of stockings he "was sure [he] should never need"—to purchase molasses candy.[21] From this sugar-rush bliss, Barnum accompanies another, older youth to a local market on the docks, where, among the incredible stores of meats, he witnesses a minor act of vandalism that makes a lasting impression. He recalls:

> I think I shall never forget an inscription which I saw painted on a
> small square piece of board and fastened to a post on the dock at
> the rear of the market. It was a corporation warning, and read here
> as presented.
>
> FIVE DOLLARS FINE FOR
> THROWING any kind of DAMD
> aged meat or fish into
> the Public Docks.[22]

Failing to scan the split second and third lines as "damaged" (and the "D" as a wry addition), Barnum "was astonished at the profanity of the public authorities, and wondered why they could not have said simply, 'aged meat or fish,' without prefixing the offensive adjective." He laments the "deplorable state of public morals" until his friend explains that some "wicked wag . . . had interpolated the little 'D,' and thus made the word 'damaged' express its own true meaning."[23] The revised sign thus straddles the line between the obscene and acceptable (a line Barnum himself would frequently trouble) and in so doing, at least in the eyes of his friend, the inscription comes closer to a truthful expression of public anger with the meat dealers. It solidifies an irony that may very well have been intended in the original scan of the sign—hinted at by the sporadic use of capital lettering—explicitly linking a punitive approach (the public fine) with the frustration that undoubtedly underwrote the punishment.

The story of the little "D," so indelible in Barnum's memory, evokes a theme with which I closed the previous chapter: the etymological parsing of invention as a "coming into" (from the Latin *invenire*). In Melville's novel *The Confidence-Man*, the titular character reconfigures the interior state machine of his marks by exploiting a perceived "gap" in the confident expression of their identity. Likewise, by "interpolat[ing] the little 'D'" at an opportune space on the public sign, the "wicked wag" reconfigures its physical significance (while leaving the preexisting text intact)—intervening and so reinventing, however slightly, its original meaning. Thought of in this way, it becomes highly suggestive that the episode would make such an impression on the mind of Barnum. Here was a man who would make his fortune artfully arranging and rearranging both curiosities and the stories that surrounded them, interpolating new details where it could increase the novelty or ambiguity of a given attraction. In his autobiographies, he was constantly fine-tuning, rewriting, and even splicing new chapters into existing editions, "tacking them on" to add additional color or nuance to his public image.[24] Meaning was made in the tangram-like contact of proximate, but nevertheless distinct, things—creating interest in the torque and interplay of significance as much as in the direct suggestion of a relationship or explanation.

Barnum's exhibition of the elderly slave Joice Heth provides a more complicated example, showing Barnum using both physical and narrative reconfigurations to ensure the persistent interest of a fickle public. After purchasing Heth from her previous owner, he first presents her as a biohistorical curiosity because of her advanced age and supposed role as George Washington's caretaker and nurse. He displays her at Niblo's Garden, where, as an article in the *New York Evening Star* puts it, there is an atmosphere of unfailing "genius for the invention of novelty."[25] This atmosphere of invention permeates every aspect of Heth's presentation. "Rigg[ing] her up for a show" entails positioning her beside "a well-smoked and antique bill of sale," as well as placing two large backlit transparencies on either side of the exhibition alcove that announce "JOICE HETH 161 YEARS OLD."[26] Physically nesting her within the confines of the story he wishes to tell, Barnum uses striking visual cues to secure a specific reading. (Interestingly, the inline text with which these transparencies are presented in his *Life of P. T. Barnum* mirrors that of the dock sign, which is the only other sign depicted this way in the text.) Later, when audiences begin to dwindle, Barnum capitalizes on the popularity of Maelzel's chess automaton, revising the public narrative of Heth (via an anonymous newspaper letter) to suggest that the woman was not a biological anomaly but a mechanism, "a curiously constructed automaton, made up of whalebone, india-rubber and numberless springs."[27] Barnum made a life and career out of "interpolat[ing] the little 'D'"; his dominant professional mode was always that of the businessman as inventor, happy as he was to tinker with a display to make it resonate with the body public.[28]

Can a Person Be a Scriptive Thing?

Yet even as this makes sense—theatrical performances of all sorts rely on well-considered stage configurations to situate viewers and immerse them in a visual world of suspended disbelief—surely we have reached an uneasy moment. Because while it's all well and good to open a discussion of Barnum's configurative practices on the level of movable letters, signs, and paragraphs, there is a meaningful discomfort that arises when we begin to imagine that a flesh-and-blood woman, an elderly and nearly paralyzed one at that, can be arranged to the same effect. This discomfiture is partially indebted to the sense that there must be *something more* to Heth's exhibition than merely the control of narrative through arrangement—something beyond mastery and forcible submission—and that this something more, especially in the context of slavery undergirding Barnum's display of Heth, must be addressed. Though it's not explicitly the aim of this chapter to think through the various stagings of race and possession in the antebellum United States, some reflection may help us to keep hold of the ways that the ludic configurative practices that

follow have bearing on a number of less amusing or technologically productive circumstances.[29] The arrangements of words and things that animated
practices of social configuration were, after all, always caught up in a relation
to actual bodies, even when those bodies were unequivocally less encumbered
than Heth's. It is precisely the poisonousness of Heth's relation that can help
to track the power of small adjustments to shift an overall scene, and I'd like
to zero in on that.

Within the limited range of motion available to her both physically and
socially, the agency Heth had was not, and could not be, agency of the variety
imagined by Walt Whitman or Milton Bradley. Nor was it the "full play" desired by Barnum himself.[30] In his extended treatment of Heth's exhibition and
legacy, Benjamin Reiss reminds us, "[Heth] was at all times doing a slave's
work. This work entailed not only literal servitude to a white man but a figurative public servitude to the northern whites who visited her and followed
her story. Audiences reacted to her in ways that reveal much about their own
conceptions of what it meant to be white, to be black, to own oneself, to own
another, and to be owned."[31] Accordingly, the particular entrapments of
Heth's situation do not lend themselves to a conceptual agency that we can
easily plot as such, the type of agency that allows one to play the same game as
everyone else, the agency that looks a bit like privilege or social enabling, perhaps "confidence." There is a differential between performer and audience
that exceeds even that typical of the theater. However, although "the American past [Heth] ostensibly embodied was itself an imaginary mimesis," as Uri
McMillan points out, there was nevertheless an ontic reality of bodies in a
room—a room typically described as crowded—that outstripped her performative representation.[32] Lingering here, on the overflow of breathing, sweat-
ing, coughing, and touching entities arranged in her presence, one might
usefully observe something of the avatar and something of the *thing* in the
stories told about Heth.[33]

I should stress that when I employ the term "thing" with regard to Heth,
I am emphatically attempting not to diminish but to expand her humanity, to
expand the sense of her effect on others to include at least as much disruptive
potential as we would allow to nonhuman material things of all sorts—signs,
portraits, and all kinds of other "alongsides" to a lived experience in shared
space.[34] All too often representations of people are rendered through a nearly
objective subjectivity that imagines the bounds of "subject" through a tightly
circumscribed lens, a lens that has its own racial legacies. In this view, the
subject is a grammatical position, an "I" or "mind" that can select in the

manner of Whitman's avatar self. As we saw with Whitman, however, the touchiness of being in a body is something that can destabilize and resituate a "subjective" view, revealing its potentials for movement, its implication in social and associative worlds that exceed the concept of a singular self. These are the moments in "Song of Myself" when self becomes less an "object" than a "thing," a thing that somehow, to adjust Robin Bernstein's phrase, invites *itself* to dance. If we pause to consider it, the basic act of respiration—inhalations and exhalations that are unseen and unchosen—can remind us of the ways in which our own subject always "conspires" with something that exceeds its self-image. Where a failure of respiration can bring the messy complexities of the body rushing back into consciousness, a particular "breath of fresh air" can similarly "inspire" one to modes to thought that hadn't occurred before. The body is a *thing* in every moment, and the bodies of others can conspire with our own in ways that exceed the simple visual or ideological dynamics of a social scene. Getting at alternative nuances of the complex associations at play with Joice Heth, we might entertain the idea of each body in the room—in the alcoves of Niblo's or in the "small ball-room" of a Boston concert hall—as a "thing," or, at the very least, an object with a number of implicit objections.

Speaking to this, one of the most arresting moments in Bernstein's *Racial Innocence* comes when Bernstein depicts a young Frances Hodgson Burnett whipping a black rubber doll in a reenactment of the lashing scene between Uncle Tom and Simon Legree. Noting that this scene is in some manner enabled by the resilient "materiality of the doll itself," she concludes that the interaction acts as a form of somatic conditioning for the role-player, "configur[ing] blackness as an elastic form of subjectivity that can withstand blows without breaking."[35] Heth was not a rubber doll, though some may have desired to think of her in that way as they imagined her skin to be a kind of "india rubber." But neither, of course, was she only the "object" of analysis that Barnum "rigged" her up to be. Many others have focused on the various disruptive or ironic dimensions at play in her performance, notably Reiss's identification of the potential for a "pasquinade" of signifyin(g) in her storytelling or McMillan's analysis of her punctuated "sonic of dissent."[36] By using these preoccupying "punctums" to supplement writing about Heth's social scene, historians and critics have layered significant human dimensions upon an inhuman situation.[37]

To this I would interpolate an element that is considerably more minor: her smoking. "Joice," Barnum begins a short anecdote on this characteristic, "was an inveterate smoker."[38] He continues to develop this trait by reprinting Grant Thorburn's account from the *Evening Star*, emphasizing the particular intensity of the habit: "I find that with all her other rare qualities, she is *a profound smoker*. Her attendants are obliged to abridge this luxury, else the pipe would never be out of her mouth. . . . So, if smoking be a poison, it is, in her case at least, a very slow poison."[39] Similarly, David Claypoole Johnston, providing a caricature of Heth to illustrate "vitativeness, or a propensity to live," sketches her reclining with her pipe prominently in hand.[40] Smoking might not have been an element of Barnum's particular objectification of her race or history, but it can often feel as though it was deeply linked to her person—a way Heth found "to live" beyond the compulsion of her performance. The fact of her attendants seeking to "abridge" the activity, moreover, gestures at something of its excess to the social picture that Barnum and his associates sought to produce for their audience.

Seeing this through, if the scripting of Burnett's doll was transmitted through the material tolerances of rubber (suggesting rough play with the African American body), the script conveyed by Heth's body in motion, a perpetually smoking body, was one of suffocation, watery eyes, and a scent that would stick to you—a scent you could walk through but not exactly ignore. Though the atmospheric world of the nineteenth century was hardly one of smokeless rooms and air purity, there is something potentially moving in the image of a black woman smoking heavily within an enclosed space, crowded among a variety of dehumanizing and patronizing white guests. While this may indeed have been a scene reflecting the "collective ingestion of an icon of black motherhood," as McMillan argues, it was also simultaneously a scene of a more literally toxic ingestion.[41] We might see Heth's smoke itself as Barnum's "little 'D'"—an interposition and interpolation that introduces a productively wicked irony to the situation. The viewing body breathing these exhalations could never completely "[fade] into a seemingly neutral, tractable, and invulnerable instrument."[42] Instead Heth positions herself, despite her paralysis, as an aggressively poisonous puzzle piece, blowing smoke at a public that reads her according to its own foggy notions of raced personhood and national myth. Like a tangram piece dropped in something unpleasant and reused, composite shapes can continue to be made, but these new shapes cannot be neutrally detached from the associations attached to individual pieces. The faces or figures made will always carry a trace of disgust, a trace of something that exceeds their current use.

Alternatively, if we were to imagine "race" as a biological genre that

Northern audiences were learning to read within these cramped spaces, then we might see Heth's action as a parallel to the images used to illustrate tangram figures in their accompanying documentation. Here, her respiration itself could be viewed as the intervention of a survivor leaving a lasting though invisible impact on her associates—a secondhand "shaping force" wielded meaningfully as an indirect consequence of the close proximity that was required by the "scientific" examinations of the exhibition.[43] We are left with an implicit figure of racial toxicity that might not be narrated but was undoubtedly felt in the lungs and smelled on the clothes. If Barnum's signage could bring the humanity of Heth into conversation with national history, then her pipe added an even more literally sticky and suffocating set of associations—a differently sensible "picture" held next to the puzzling configuration of race in antebellum New England.

Of course, Heth's smoking might just be a habit that no one ever really flinched at, and I'm not arguing that secondhand smoke won the day. But I think it's valuable to think about the ways in which even incredibly small tonal shifts, including slight shifts of atmosphere and surrounding, might change the overall effect of a scene. (One recalls the control of "atmospherical medium" that Hawthorne attributes to the romancer in the preface to *The House of the Seven Gables*, an overlap we will return to in the next chapter.) Though I double back to establish the technological contexts of Barnum's promotional ethos in what follows, we might bear in mind Heth's example of the smoky boundary crossings that occur between "objects" and "things," crossings that give a somewhat unruly creative power to the configurations at play. Invention was the guiding ethos of the mid-nineteenth century, but there were always pieces that didn't fit or that might have fit differently. And it was precisely this potential for something to fit differently—to look as expected but *feel* different in meaningful ways—that the most successful inventors of the moment seized upon with special verve.

Doubtless Valuable: The Business of Artful Arrangements

Born on 5 July 1810, P. T. Barnum was undeniably a man of his time, coming of age in an era that placed particular emphasis on the role of inventors, both literal and figurative, in the social and economic life of the country. Between 1790 and 1809, the U.S. government granted a total of 1,179 patents, averaging fifty-nine new cataloged inventions a year. Contrasted to this, by the time

Barnum published his first autobiography in December 1854, the United States Patent and Trademark Office had granted 1,759 patents in that year alone, averaging 466 patents annually in the intervening period between 1810 and 1854.[44] Although patent statistics are not always a one-to-one measure of inventive activity, these numbers gesture toward a general surge in people's desire to archive and profit from "invention," as well as a growing capacity to interact with existing archives like the USPTO in order to make incremental technological advances.[45] Invention and novelty were a way of life in nineteenth-century America, and the aesthetics of configurative mechanics, often discussed by way of terms like "efficiency" (arrangements designed to increase productivities), "operationality" (structural arrangements that define use), and "comparativity" (hierarchical arrangement for the sake of progressive analysis), were applied equally to rhetorical and technological pursuits.[46] Hinting at this, in the span of a sentence, Barnum's recollection of the re-invented dock notice—that interpolated "little 'D'"—drifts into a reverie on how the shoemakers of the State Prison move "as if they had been automatons all moved by a single wire." It then closes on a more concrete technology: "I also saw a large windmill that same day, which was the first time I had ever seen the like."[47]

Some of this cultural vogue for technology was supported by innovations in U.S. patent law, a brief discussion of which will provide an important backdrop to Barnum's own activity.[48] While Barnum's genius was for promotion of a different kind, the Constitution upheld the enlightenment values of rational humanistic progress that surrounded its composition by assigning to Congress the "Power . . . To promote the Progress of Science and useful Arts, by securing for limited Times to Authors and Inventors the exclusive Right to their respective Writings and Discoveries."[49] On the heels of this mandate, the Patent Act of 1790 institutionally materialized patent authority by establishing an independent examination tribunal (composed initially of Thomas Jefferson, Henry Knox, and Edmund Randolph) to determine that the applicant was indeed "the first and true inventor" of a given invention and that the invention was "sufficiently useful and important."[50] This development alone put an inventor in the United States on more stable legal footing than in many contemporary European countries. Patent historian B. Zorina Khan notes that in both England and France there were no formal inquiries into the novelty of inventions submitted to the government; the French government went so far as to attach a legal absolution to all patent documents: "The government, in granting a patent without prior examination, does not in any manner guarantee either the priority, merit, or success of an invention."[51] In the United States, careful and documented examination was legal security for lower-income inventors, who could not afford to become embroiled in courtroom battles over inventions with no guarantee of state protection.

The subsequent Patent Act of 1836 built upon the earlier law, setting the price for patents at a more accessible thirty dollars and hiring an independent commissioner of patents to run the newly built central Patent Office.[52] Specifications and models of inventions could be sent free of postage to satellite repositories and upon arrival at the Patent Office would be "classified and arranged" in galleries, both for preservation and for "public inspection."[53] The USPTO saw its counterparts throughout nineteenth-century culture in what Tony Bennett has called an "exhibitionary complex"; in addition to inventor's fairs, dime museums, and magazines like *Scientific American*, Les Harrison expands on Bennett to include "state and custom houses, department stores, parlors, inns, ships, quarterdecks, forecastles, theaters, capitols, and [local] patent offices" as practical companions to this complex.[54] Paying oblique homage to the American Institute's Inventors' Fair that had driven so many customers to his Joice Heth exhibit (occupying a space across the Garden at Niblo's), Barnum's own American Museum was for a time dubbed the "American Museum and Perpetual Fair," explicitly linking dime-museum curiosity and engineering marvel.

It is in light of such exhibitions that the saturation of configuration puzzles within nineteenth-century culture makes sense. In *The Smashed Up Locomotive* Milton Bradley drew upon his experience as a mechanical patent draftsman to create a puzzle exhibiting the operation and configurability of that most iconic nineteenth-century invention, the steam locomotive. Presented as a "grotesque" pile of dismembered mechanical parts, Bradley's multishape puzzle pieces each label different aspects of the locomotive mechanism, such that solving the puzzle was also an exercise in learning the basic mechanics of the train.[55] Yet unlike many jigsaw puzzles, certain pieces were of identical shape, fitting into each other's native location as easily as the "correct" location.[56] Geometrically solving the puzzle didn't necessarily mean creating the blueprint for a working train. Rather, this presentation linked a distinctly exhibitionary strain of the sort delineated by Neil Harris's "operational aesthetic" with the notion that these parts might also be interchangeable, reconfigured into new and better machines once one understood how they worked.[57] By 1871, the Milton Bradley Company catalog noted, "This puzzle has had, and is still having, a greater sale than any similar thing that we have ever known."[58]

The examination of configurative novelty was therefore a developing cultural practice running alongside a specific legal structure designed to facilitate (and reward) a specific kind of imagination throughout the United States. For exhibitors, to discover a novel adjustment to publicly available text—as in the case of the "dam'd aged meat"—was a means to both material and social profit. So grew the acute American fascination with invention and novelty as democratized paths to the kind of power traditionally reserved for the propertied classes.[59] Winshang Punqua encapsulates this feeling in a lyric prefatory to his tangram collection: "*Try Again,* / That which other folks can do, / Why with patience, may not you? / *Try again.*"[60] Persistent and observant, inventors were "the intellectual heroes of the age."[61] Yet they were a distinctly practical variety of hero, a hero that did not approach invention as a spontaneous overflow of mechanical imagination. James Cook argues, "As popular entertainment entered the age of mass production, novelty *and formula* became twin pillars of the same promotional philosophy."[62] Accordingly, this hero was defined by a driving attention to local problems—the hero as editor rather than poet, tinkerer rather than god. One would examine, or take inventory of, the formulations that allowed a particular text to function (whether it be a machine, a body, or an artifact) as a means to discovering ways that this text might be reconfigured, ways the inventor could *intervene*, to obtain different uses or significances. In a sense, it did not matter whether these novel uses were improvements in machine efficiency or interesting reimaginings of a social text—either way, value could be enhanced.

Barnum's experience with the five-acre Connecticut plot dubbed "Ivy Island" again shows him grappling with these emerging social practices from an early age. As a youth, his grandfather explains to Barnum that, by birthright, he is to inherit a large stretch of property called Ivy Island. The entire village gets in on the joke, regaling the naive Barnum with the knowledge that his landownership effectively makes him "the richest child in town."[63] At twelve years old, he finally convinces his family to let him trek out to see the expanse that will one day be the source of his fabulous wealth. He remembers "scarcely [sleeping] for three nights, . . . so great was my joy to think that, like Moses of old, I should be permitted to look upon the promised land. The visions of wealth which had so long haunted me in relation to that valuable locality now became intensified, and I not only felt that it must be a land flowing with milk and honey, but caverns of emeralds, diamonds, and other precious stones, as well as mines of silver and gold, opened vividly to my mind's eye."[64] Barnum's vision is of a land filled not with abstract wealth, not with investment or collateral potential, but rather a kind of instantly gratifying wealth within the land itself. Like the molasses candy upon which he spent his allowance in New York, this "milk and honey" wealth would be immediately and individually consumable, an Eden requiring little outside assistance from the workaday world—aside from the occasional barter of "precious stones." The Ivy Island of young Barnum's fantasy would yield its owner value simply in its *possession*, with no special finesse, reorientation, or decision making necessary to render its worth. Had such a utopian plot existed, history might remember Barnum quite differently than as the quintessential self-made American entrepreneur.

As he soon finds out, however, this inheritance is a hoax: the treasured Ivy Island of his dreams is realized as a nightmarish swampland with little value. The island cannot be mined, plowed, or inhabited, nor will anyone comfortably survive on its native nectars. Ensconced in a watery birch bog, Barnum's inheritance is covered in hornets and snakes, which chase him out almost immediately after he makes landfall. The effect of his family's practical joke is both to foreground the increasing detachment of profit from a traditional calculus of use value and to blend the worth of the "commodity" with the worth of their joke. It is important to note that in this sense the island is far from worthless, though from the perspective of the young Barnum it may seem that way. Its value lies almost solely in its proximity to a compellingly reiterated social narrative, rather than in the more substantive use the child had imagined. Worth considering is the fact that had Barnum's grandfather explained the state of the land to him from the beginning, no one would have gained anything from it, amusement or otherwise; indeed, it would have been virtually without value. Instead of this outcome, the whole town takes pleasure in a real-life theatrical entertainment that employs an arranged matrix of stories, ironic bons mots, and a real stretch of land. Ivy Island is not valuable in spite of its being a humbug, it is valuable *because* it is a humbug—a lesson Barnum seems never to have forgotten.

What his family gives him here is an early education in the growing culture of invention and speculation. The only profit to be had from his grandfather's "gift" will be in using the land in an artful arrangement that, to a degree, does homage to this tough lesson in the power of reinvention and tactical value. The divide narrated by this episode, between young Barnum's sense of value as material use and the family's performance of value as configurative use, might be seen as a collision between a traditional economy of substance and place, and an emerging economy of tact and positionality. This economic transition meaningfully echoes the discursive formations of selfhood discussed in the first chapter by way of *The Mansion of Happiness* and *The Checkered Game of Life*. Within this framework, primary regard is given not to *what* one possesses but rather to *how one uses* what one possesses at the right time and in the right way to produce a social text. Representing this in minimalist terms, tangrams limit all players to the same seven pieces, yet only some arrangements attain significance by virtue of how they are configured with regard to ready-at-hand pictures and audience associations. Barnum's Ivy Island "joke" becomes a model for just such a reimagining of "use" as social arrangement.

This emphasis on associative contexts in the practice of joking may provide an explanation for the role of the practical jokes presented en masse in the opening hundred pages of Barnum's biography—far from narrative filler, the sociotemporal dynamics of jokes are crucial to establishing the foundations of Barnum's success as a businessman.[65] The relentless retelling of these jokes conditions the reader to linger on the "outsides" that lead to shared senses of meaning. And these outsides can be both spatial (for example, the people in the room) and linguistic (for example, alternative parses of words). Barnum writes, "Perhaps I should apologize for devoting so much space . . . to practical jokes. . . . [However,] I feel myself entitled to record [them] . . . because they partly explain the causes which have made me what I am."[66] Pages later, Barnum describes what he is or has become as a "speculative character . . . never content to engage in any business unless it is of such a nature that [his] profits may be greatly enhanced by an increase of energy, perseverance, attention to business, tact, etc."[67] While energy and perseverance may be traditional labor values, Barnum's inclusion of the more context-specific "tact" underscores his naturalization of the Ivy Island "joke"—it is not enough to be strong and persistent, one must also have a sense of how to finesse the details through savvy arrangements.

Accordingly, Barnum extends the idea as he grows older, directly translating his family's narrative configuration of Ivy Island into capital. He accomplishes this through a clever coup at the expense of Mr. Olmsted, an investor he hopes to court for the purpose of underwriting his purchase of the American Museum. Without unmortgaged property to act as collateral, and despite his numerous glowing recommendations, Barnum at first finds Olmsted reluctant to finance his purchase of the old Scudder Museum at Broadway and

Ann Street. Olmsted laments, "If you only had a piece of unencumbered real estate that you could offer as additional security, I think I might venture to negotiate with you."[68] At this moment, Barnum's dexterity at constructing a sympathetic narrative around Ivy Island becomes his greatest asset, as both timing and selective storytelling come into play:

> This seemed the turning-point of my fortune. Thinks I to myself,
> "It is now or never," and memory rapidly ran over my small posses-
> sions in search of the coveted bit of land. *Ivy Island*, in all the beauty
> in which my youthful imagination had pictured it, came dancing to
> my relief. . . . I saw no particular harm in it, and after a moment's
> hesitation I replied:
>   "I have five acres of land in Connecticut which is free from all
> lien or encumbrance."
>   "Indeed! what did you pay for it?"
>   "It was a present from my late grandfather, Phineas Taylor,
> given on account of my name."
>   "Was he rich?" inquired Mr. Olmsted.
>   "He was considered well off in those parts," I answered.
>   "Very kind in him to give you the land. It is doubtless valuable.
> But I suppose you would not like to part with it, considering it was
> a present."
>   "I shall not have to part with it, if I make my payments
> punctually."[69]

Barnum uses this information opportunistically, toward the end of the nego-tiations, when Olmsted is already conditionally confident in Barnum's capac-ities ("If only you had . . ."). Had he offered up Ivy Island as collateral earlier in the discussion, there may have been further questioning, but at this point Olmsted seems only to be looking for Barnum to say the thing that can allow him to make the decision he has already determined to make. Barnum seizes this opening not by lying outright but by forging a collaborative text; instead of assigning direct value to the land, Barnum leaves the idea of its value vari-able by first distancing himself from the price ("It was a present") and then using relativistic rhetoric ("He was considered well off in those parts"). This places emphasis on the potentials of the land, arranging it such that Olmsted is free to imagine for himself what the worth might be.[70] In doing so, Olmsted becomes a crucial and agential element of Barnum's narrative, stepping into the story (or, less charitably, the con game) that has emerged in the midst of their negotiation. As with a joke that plays on what its community can be assumed to know, this negotiation relies on Olmsted's assumptions about what a "well-off" grandfather would give to his namesake. Barnum's tactfully delivered half-truths implicate the investor. Had the venture failed to succeed, Olmsted may have lamented his decision to finance the purchase, but there is no doubt that the decision was his to make, based, to a degree, on information *he himself had provided* ("It is doubtless valuable"). With this the final security in place, he makes the purchase for Barnum, and so one of the most popular and profitable institutions of the mid-nineteenth-century United States is born.

Not *In* among the Burning Ruins—but *Out* on Broadway: Barnum's Outside Show

I mentioned earlier that Barnum describes himself as a "speculative character . . . never content to engage in any business unless it is of such a nature that [his] profits may be greatly enhanced by an increase of energy, perseverance, attention to business, tact, etc."[71] Later he continues in this vein, stating a desire to find a business "opportunity where my faculties and energies could have full play, and where the amount of profits should depend entirely upon the amount of tact, perseverance and energy, which I contributed to the business."[72] In both of these reflections, "tact" plays a recurring role in Barnum's imagined success. Still later, what drives Barnum to the American Museum is his belief that "only energy, tact and liberality were needed, to give it life"; and in the same breath he is "entirely confident that [his] tact and experience . . . [will] enable [him] to make the payments when due."[73]

So what of this *tact* upon which Barnum relies so heavily? On the most basic level, tact has to do with both literal and figurative "touch," which one sees in its connection to the word "tactile." Yet tact, as Barnum uses it, clearly incorporates a temporal finesse to this touch, a kind of good timing or opportunism (like "tactics" or a musical "tact," the opening beat of a measure)—he notes that it was "now or never" in the midst of his negotiations with Olmsted right before unleashing his humbug collateral. The combination of these two elements yields the common contemporary use of tact as "skill or judgment in dealing with men or negotiating difficult or delicate situations; the faculty of saying or doing the right thing at the right time."[74] Tact is a specifically social finesse having to do not simply with an internal arrangement of words (the raw text of Barnum's Ivy Island humbug) but rather with the skillful arrangement of those words at the right moment such that another person might see them as "making sense," yielding a kind of localized empathy that can be used in a variety of ways: to diffuse tension, to begin a relationship, or, in Barnum's case, to secure capital. All of these effects stem from an astute awareness of the complementary interrelationship of textual and contextual configurations, of exhibit and "outside show."

Returning to tangrams helps to parse this further. In Chinese, the puzzle is called *Ch'i ch'iao t'u*, which means, literally, "seven skillful/timely/opportune boards."[75] The middle character, "ch'iao," might be stretched, via the above discussion, to be understood as "tactful," incorporating as it does all of the aforementioned elements of tact.[76] Each piece must be moved in a step-wise temporal arrangement such that moving one tan to one position changes the geometric opportunities available for the eventual composite shape. The temporality of this may not be obvious, but it is there: in addition to dictating the placement of the six other tans, moving the large square to a central position means that it will not be used *later* in a different position. Tact here is both the player's touch of the tan and the tan's capacity to touch other tans in a given configuration. One might, however, also add a social element of touch to the game, as it requires a skill at producing images that either convey obvious meaning given the context of their viewing or at producing a narrative around these images such that an external observer might recognize a shape that communicates some abstract form. To succeed at the game you must not only touch the pieces but "touch" other people's imagination as well. Each level of configuration is as crucial as the others. And although communicative skill might be seen as external to the game, it is in fact what allows the game to function as such—to leave out this level is to render the game simply a mathematical set of permutations, rather than a meaningful exercise in which many people throughout the nineteenth century took pleasure. Thinking of tangrams in terms of tact helps to understand the ways in which text and context have unstable boundaries, feeding significance into each other at the porous threshold of their interaction. "Tact," more than configuration alone, is a perspective on configuration that specifically makes use of this ludic threshold between its mechanical and social dimensions.

In Barnum, tact, though explicitly noted as integral to his business acumen, is often invisible, existing as it does on layered levels of narrative composition and style, rough-hewn associations where the reader, like Olmsted, must formulate his or her own notion of meaningful transition. We see the end results, but not the process. Nevertheless, on occasion Barnum gets at the operations of tact through a kind of inversion, offering up instances of configuration *without* tact. This happens most strikingly in the account of a conciliatory letter he writes for a man dubbed "John Mallett," a significant alias because of its associations with pall-mall, a predecessor of the wildly popular nineteenth-century game of croquet. In these games, the "mallet" guides the ball by making contact, touching the player's ball with its flat face and either sending it through an iron wicket or knocking other players' balls to nonstrategic positions on the field of play. By naming the lovelorn Mallett in this way, Barnum immediately draws attention to figures of touch, though, as we shall see, not necessarily tact—foregrounding the split textual and contextual implications of the term.

At the opening of Barnum's anecdote, Mallett has himself been butted from the romantic field of play and is looking to regain the advantage. After a six-month courtship, Lucretia has refused his arm at weekly church services, instead taking the hand of another young man (the unnamed son of Tom Beers). Mallett hopes to commission a well-penned letter that will "touch her feelings," but he also desires "an explanation of this unaccountable conduct, and . . . at the same time, to give her a piece of his mind."[77] For a fee, Barnum is only too happy to oblige. However, while willing to provide the words of the correspondence, he relies on Mallett for their substantive arrangement.

The result is incongruous (to say the least), stringing together genuine curiosity, insult, poetry, threat, and sentimental appeal. It demonstrates that despite all the components of the letter-writing "puzzle" being used, the contextual arrangement is self-defeating and problematic. In a word, Mallett is tactless. Following his charge's request, Barnum begins innocuously, "*Miss Lucretia:*—I write to ask an explanation of your conduct in giving me the mitten on Sunday night last," and then immediately takes a forceful tone: "If you think, madam, that you can trifle with my affections, and turn me off for every little whipper-snapper that you can pick up, you will find yourself considerably mistaken."[78] Here Barnum pauses to narrate, in medias res, as it were, Mallett's approval of these first two lines, which Mallett likes because he guesses that the distant-sounding "madam" will "hurt her feelings very much" and that calling the competition a "little whipper-snapper" will "make her feel cheap." Barnum comments that he doubts that "little whipper-snapper" was the right phrase to use, considering that Tom Beers's son was considerably taller than Mallett, but the realistic context of the situation matters less to him than the intensity of terminology used; Mallett is determined to "begin the letter in strong terms" regardless of how those terms might read to others, and how that reading might later affect his end goal.

Betraying this insular view of textual arrangement, the impassioned Mallett then instructs Barnum to "give her another dose" ("I can have the company of girls as much above you as the sun is above the earth") before "try[ing] to touch her feelings." Dutifully following orders, Barnum contrasts the letter's earlier distance ("madam") with a personal appeal, "My dear Lucretia, when I think of the many pleasant hours we have spent together, it almost breaks my heart to think of last Sunday night." Taking a cue from the mechanical aesthetics discussed earlier in this chapter, Mallett seems intent on reinventing Lucretia's love by cobbling together a series of sentiments both formulaic and personal. Content is conceived of as neutrally modular and interchangeable, as if each piece has no associations, no hint of smoky toxicity attached to it. Rather than developing a sincere follow-up to his admission of heartbreak, Mallett asks that Barnum "stick in some affecting poetry." Far from the Romantic sensibility of poetry as spontaneous and personal, Mallett's sensibility has a ramshackle procedurality to it that evokes the schematics of so many failed patent applications: the pieces that make up the writing are not organic but mechanical, things to be "st[u]ck in" wherever they seem to fit. Unable to think of anything applicable off the top of his head, Barnum makes up his own stand-alone verse: "Miserable fate, to lose you now, / And tear this bleeding heart asunder! / Will you forget your tender vow? / I can't believe it—no, by thunder!" The poem goes on to ask that Lucretia give other boys "the mitten" and return to Mallett, closing: "Do this, Lucretia, and till death / I'll love you to intense distraction; / I'll spend for you my every breath, / And we will live in satisfaction."[79]

Had the letter ended on this note, it may have hit its target, softening an initial frustration with a sentimental recollection of the couple's history and a look to the future. But Mallett cannot resist dropping the hammer, asking Barnum to "blow her up a little more" before relenting: "I guess you had better touch her feelings once more, and wind up the letter." These conflicting directives lead to a jarring textual pairing: "I shall despise you for ever if you don't change your conduct towards me, and send me a letter of apology on Monday next. I shall not go to meeting [church] to-morrow, for I would scorn to sit in the same meeting-house with you until I have an explanation. . . . If you allow any young man to go home with you to-morrow night, I shall know it, for you will be watched," is followed immediately by "My sweet girl . . . if you could but realize that I regard the world as less than nothing without you, I am certain you would pity me. A homely cot and a crust of bread with my adorable Lucretia would be a paradise, where a palace without you would be a hades." Completing the contradictions, a postscript is added to the letter: "On reflection I have concluded to go to meeting to-morrow. If all is well, hold your pocket handkerchief in your left hand as you stand up to sing with the choir." Lucretia is seen holding "her handkerchief firmly in her right hand during all the church services." Barnum only makes Mallett pay half price.[80]

Of course, the problem in terms of the letter's capacity to affect Lucretia is that her erstwhile suitor has no sense of proportion or sequence, no awareness that each of these lines will be read in proximity to each other. As a result, he seemingly has no sense of how the arrangement will read as a whole, what picture he has created of their love, and whether it does indeed read as "love"—or altogether something else. Both the context of the individual elements (the poem, the pleas, the insults) and the social context of its expected audience are ignored, with understandably disorienting results. Consequently, what Mallett has produced is analogous to a tangram shape with no referent other than his own vengeful obsession, and no reasonable narrative in which to couch this obsession. The figure he has made has no outside show to carry its disjointed message of love, jealousy, and heartbreak; it is little more than an arranged mess. Why, then, would Barnum include the story of this letter's composition in his memoir?

The simple answer is that as entertainment, the letter is highly effective, and in contrast to Mallett's purposes, entertainment *is* Barnum's goal. More importantly, the failure of Mallett's configuration game can be recognized as such precisely because Barnum emphasizes what successful, that is, tactful, configuration *does* look like throughout the autobiography—engaging as it does with both local internal consistency and social empathy. The rhetorical function of this anecdote, then, is to allow the formation of such a local empathy with *Barnum*, offering to the reader Barnum's position as bewildered but resigned typesetter. While completely ineffective as it stands, the misguided letter's humorous pleasure arises from the friction between Barnum's/the reader's assumed tact and the tactlessness of Mallett. With all of the pieces delightfully dislocated, the presentation implicitly requires Barnum's readership to imagine an editorial role, creating an enjoyable, because agential, reading experience in the interplay of dissonant ideas, the contrast of what *should have been* versus what *was*. This is a game that *The Life of P. T. Barnum*, to this point, has already been teaching its readers to play. The modularity of

Mallett's approach to language is both Mallett's weakness and Barnum's empathetic trump card. The fact that one can't imagine sending Mallett's letter turns the episode into a kind of provocation and a reason to imagine oneself a part of Barnum's dialogue, rearranging the pieces so that they might express their "true meaning"—again, to "interpolate the little 'D'" as we see fit, with the hazy confusion of the previous configuration hanging in the background.

It was this kind of implication that Barnum played on throughout his career as a showman, layering paratextual elements around his exhibitions such that viewers were compelled to practice the protocols of an exhibit's textual world even before they had fully engaged with it as an object in itself. If Mallett's letter is an exhibition of sorts, then the whole surrounding biography becomes the context for viewing it in a specific way (humorous, not serious or pathetic). Barnum need only supply a few cues, such as his wariness over Mallett's word choice, to remind the reader of how this exhibition should be conceived by association with the other "exhibitions" of the autobiography. Such associative cues were powerful mechanisms for creating an embedded sense of viewership and readership in the nineteenth century.

Discussing Romantic-era collections, Judith Pascoe notes that there was a rise in the popularity of "association objects" in the period—objects linked with famous personages, such as Napoleon, or with historical events. But more than a one-to-one connection with history, these objects also operated in complex fields of association with regard to themselves and their viewers. Pieces were played off each other in an exhibition, with more accepted collectibles proving "the somewhat dubious authenticity of other[s]"; the presence of one object could become the "outside show" that drove interest in another.[81] At the same time, the spectator engaged in an immersive association game. If the presence of other objects enhanced the feeling that any one object was closer to its purported history, being surrounded by these objects helped spectators feel a similar imaginative closeness. By interacting with these objects, Pascoe writes, "Napoleon's cloak helped [a] visitor imagine himself as the impresario of extraordinary acts, as Napoleon en route to his next conquest."[82]

Barnum undoubtedly played on similar vogues for historical connection in his own collector's space, the spectacularly baroque American Museum. Yet at the American Museum Barnum also seemed to understand that the desire for abstract kinship ran deeper than a simple affiliation with celebrity or history; it was a desire to reinforce the protocols of associative meaning making in a novelty-saturated world. This may explain the success of his notorious "Great Brick Advertisement." Here Barnum gave an eager laborer five bricks

and explicit instructions for laying each of the first four, one at a time, on each
of the four street corners surrounding the museum, such that he had one remaining in his hand. Then, marching solemnly from corner to corner ("you
must seem deaf as a post . . . answer no questions; pay no attention to anyone"), the "brick man" would pause, exchange the brick in his hand for the
one on the sidewalk, and press on, repeating the exchange with each brick he
passed.[83] Every hour, on the hour, the brick man would finish his last replacement, enter the museum, quietly examine the exhibits in every hall, and then
exit, only to begin the process all over again. Barnum recalls that within a half
an hour of beginning his work

> at least five hundred people were watching [the brick man's] myste-
> rious movements. He had assumed a military step and bearing, and,
> looking as sober as a judge, he made no response whatever to the
> constant inquiries as to the object of his singular conduct. At the
> end of the first hour, the sidewalks in the vicinity were packed with
> people, all anxious to solve the mystery. The man, as directed, then
> went into the Museum, devoting fifteen minutes to a solemn survey
> of the halls, and afterward returning to his round. This was repeated
> every hour till sundown, and whenever the man went into the Mu-
> seum a dozen or more persons would buy tickets and follow him,
> hoping to gratify their curiosity in regard to the purpose of his
> movements.[84]

Barnum here again shows his mastery of both timing and associative configurations. The man's schedule is linked to the church bell at St. Paul's and follows a series of steps designed to allow the environment itself to create the
scene. As individuals within the crowded city streets became fascinated by the
brick man, they began to form a crowd around him, questioning his activities,
but simultaneously becoming a part of the mystery at hand. It is certainly
within the realm of possibility that some in this crowd began to enjoy their
own implication within the inner circle of the brick man's activity; at each
stop the accumulation of (non-)knowledge from the previous stop became the
basis of any "authoritative" answers newcomers may have demanded (since
the brick man himself did not speak). Blanks are filled in—as they were with
Melville's deaf and silent Confidence-Man in the previous chapter—and a
collaboratively invested social story emerges from the process.
    These behaviors were then a template for the cumulative experience of

walking and discussion within the museum: people became associates in un-
raveling the mystery and, following the man into the museum, carried that
sense of mystery and exploration in with them. An inquisitive disposition,
linked to a series of ambulatory stops and starts, sticks to them like the scent
of Joice Heth's pipe, prompting them to approach the space differently than
they otherwise would have. Why would his activity be connected to a certain
exhibit? What are the links between these exhibits? Barnum piques their curiosity with his outside show and then encourages the people to see the same
connective links between the exhibits within the museum walls—for a price,
of course. While the Confidence-Man of Melville's novel generates income by
acting as a surrogate for the agency of his marks, allowing them to attain a
sense of consistency in the process, Barnum inverts this maneuver. Barnum's
customers pay for the opportunity to be agents of their own discursive amusement, safely bounded by the scenic and operational consistency between the
museum and its periphery.

To associate the mystery of the brick man, as well as the protocol of strolling and examining, with his own museum was to embed the museum in the
audience's world and to naturalize the protocols of associative focus that
helped visitors get the most out of their museum experience. Part of this experience was an implicit engagement with tact and configuration. In the brick
man episode, as with the museum in general, meaning was cumulative, rather
than simply compositional: "When?" "How many came before?" and "How
are they related?" were questions central to understanding the significance of
any stop along the way—even where there was a lack of substantive meaning.
This was a mode of practice in some ways at odds with the protocols of museum going that would come to dominate the late nineteenth century and
beyond, engaging as they did with more systematic and classificatory styles of
exhibition.[85] A critic of the American Museum, writing for the *Nation* in 1865,
exemplifies this later ideal: "The more truly one loves a good collection well
arranged, the more he will be offended by a chaotic, dusty, dishonored collection. . . . Without scientific arrangement, without a catalogue, without attendants, without even labels, in very many instances, the heterogeneous heap of
'curiosities,' valuable and worthless well mixed up together, could not attract
our students very often or detain them long."[86] Within this more modern
tradition, one seldom reads of an exhibit as an explicitly *nested* object within a
broader museum space; a review of an exhibit understands the exhibit as
somewhat insular, classified, distinct—and indeed is atmospherically encouraged to do so through rationalized room planning, wall text, and thematically

branded signage. Exploration between and among objects is guided by chronologies, genres, and other indicators of legitimized intellectual narrative. Agency is expressed by the curators, while visitor movement becomes a passive, quasi-religious experience, an attunement of self with existing modes of knowledge.[87] It is telling that in the effort to create new modes of activity in the twenty-first-century museum, many curators are resorting to various forms of digital gaming; yet even this mostly rides the rails of existing structural divisions between exhibitions.

In documenting their visits, by contrast, guests at Barnum's museum couldn't help but make their own heterogeneous associative lists, explicitly connecting any new exhibit with what surrounded it. Much of this was encouraged by Barnum's proclivity to pack the space to the brim; other absurd, contrastive, and dissonant exhibits were literally unavoidable in the path to something one wanted to see. A description of the museum's Third Room from *Barnum's American Museum Illustrated* (1850) gives a sense of the diversity at play,

> We commence with an American Flag, torn and discolored by
> age. . . . Passing from it, we are shown a Brain Stone [coral], from
> Turk's Island, a magnificent specimen, and quite equal to its far-
> famed fellow in the British Museum, London. The Sword Fish is
> distinguished by a long pointed beak. . . . The lovers of antiquity
> and those who are curious in the customs of other countries, will be
> delighted with the Roman Urns. . . . The Common Seal, or Sea
> Calf, of North America . . . is in close vicinity with the hand and
> part of the arm of a man, who also had dealings with the ocean . . .
> a notorious pirate named Tom Trouble.[88]

Far from a discretely territorialized object, the American Museum was "a wilderness of wonderful, instructive, and amusing realities."[89] Barnum's provocatively plural "realities" cues us into the epistemological promiscuity of the experience. In a variety of woodcuts that accompany the guidebook, every illustration of the interior includes some group of viewers looking in different directions from those nearby.[90] Reality in the museum was not one thing, agreed upon in totality by a group of spectators, but instead a constellation of layered and interacting perspectives, each requiring a specific form of attention and affording a very localized kind of pleasure. Each aggregate pathway was a kind of tangram composed on the fly, weighed against others, a possible ground for communication and attendant social world building.

One gets an impressionistic view of these differently prioritized worlds when examining the selective catalogs of artifacts made by journalists during the museum's lifetime. The anxious and sensational perspective of a *Democratic Review* writer who puts the exhibition of Tom Thumb beside a "five-legged calf [that] vies with the razor with which Thomas Nokes 'slit his wife's weasand [throat]'" contrasts with a *New York Tribune* reporter's naturalistic viewpoint in the context of Barnum's "What Is It?" exhibition: "A huge California Bear, weighing over 2,000 pounds, a Sea Lion, which on this occasion is not an ordinary Seal, and a nondescript, which has not as yet been named."[91] Where a journalist from the *New York Mercury* fixates on the human element (even in animals) recalling "the celebrated and mysterious Aztec Children . . . the waggish and irrepressible specimen of dubious creation known as the 'What Is It?' . . . [and] a number of rare animals, monster serpents, the 'Happy Family,' or cats, rats, dogs, rabbits, birds, monkeys, etc.; all living together in domestic bliss," another takes a diminutive stance by emphasizing the sheer size of certain exhibits: "Gazing placidly down upon the coming visitor, stood the largest elephant that the civilization of the nineteenth century has yet known. A refreshment stand enticed us to the mammoth barrel-organ. . . . In the centre of the room was an immense tank."[92]

Each of these renditions, whether consciously or not, attempts to give associative shape to the unruly mass of exhibitions, forming a provisional model of salient meaning. The worst thing to do in this place, according to Barnum, is "pass by [an exhibit] in *silent* contempt."[93] To engage with an artifact neither physically nor conversationally was to take it out of contention as an object of associative configuration, and thereby remove it from the pool of emergent socialities in play. In a sense, Barnum aims to recreate for his visitors one of the fundamental elements of his own meteoric rise, a grasp of how to engage with preexisting materials to invent a living social world. Before owning the space, he recalls in his *Life*, "My recent enterprises had not indeed been productive, and my funds were decidedly low . . . and so I repeatedly visited the Museum as a thoughtful looker-on. I saw, or believed I saw, that only energy, tact, and liberality were needed, to give it life and to put it on a profitable footing."[94] This belief could be equally applied to his philosophy of civic engagement, as Barnum aimed to profit by allowing his visitors a space to be a "thoughtful looker-on" as well.

From a critical vantage, then, his museum space must always be taken as a tactfully reconfigured object, reimagined with each visit according to the specific interests of a given audience. Without an authoritative story, traversing the collection was an exercise in imagining what one *could be*, constructing provisional alliances to render one's character in moments of fleeting co-recognition that could become new modes of meaningful association. In a sense, the museum had no genre but was instead a genre machine—a contingent stage for the emergence of new ways to recognize continuity. James Cook gets at this contingency with regard to audience credulity: "Because viewers suspected that Barnum might have embellished the physical and cultural anomalies of these curiosities, they rarely hesitated in picking and choosing which of the advertised features to accept, reject, or amend."[95] Yet I would take Cook's argument even further: in choosing to accept, reject, or amend on the level of one exhibition, visitors accumulated perspectives and conversational protocols they transposed and experimented with throughout the museum. They invented possible social selves even as they made connections between various technological and rhetorical inventions.

Through this process of selection, individual visitors became part of irregularly interlacing audiences as they had during the brick man episode. Affinities formed with others as a way of testing, through associative play, different ways of looking, talking, and interacting with each other and the exhibits.[96] Much as Barnum could make a different exhibition out of Joice Heth by changing her physical and narrative surroundings—first highlighting her age, then highlighting her supposed similarity to novel machines—museum visitors made the museum-going experience different by configuring their own associative archive out of the "heterogeneous heap." By the time a visitor reached the top of the museum, the city itself could be seen against the cumulative conversational protocols begun in the brick man's outside show: "[He] will then find himself on the roof of this immense establishment, where he can enjoy the refreshing breeze, and obtain a view of some of the most important places of business in the City, which will well repay him for his trouble. In the small room adjoining the parapet is exhibited the celebrated Drummond Light, which can be seen for more than a mile up Broadway, when illuminated in the evening."[97] While the streets of Broadway had first been the site of museum paratext, here the relation is inverted as the museum becomes a circumscribing paratext to Manhattan, shining a spotlight on the real show—a show that will "repay" Barnum's paying customers. More than anything else damaged or destroyed in the spectacular fire that leveled the American Museum on 13 July 1865, it would seem that what was really lost was an opportunistic space in all senses of the term: an opportunity to profit, yes, but also to immerse oneself in a story, to choose and train one's configurative focus as part of a social unit. "Raying away from itself all around it," in Melville's turn of phrase, Barnum's Drummond light represents the museum itself as the "original" of the city—an operator or spatial "cosmopolitan" staging the social creation of its inhabitants.

Of course, the devastating blaze became its own public spectacle, and one last chance for some patrons to make identifying choices about the objects inside. In the midst of a giant crowd, small audiences formed around what appeared to be a kangaroo jumping from the roof (it was a pair of pants) or a desperate woman repelling down the building face (it was a wax model). A man trying to save a wax effigy of Jefferson Davis hoisted the likeness out of a window, only to have the spectators below cart the figure down the street to hang it. Finally, the brick walls of the museum crashed to the boardwalk below, "The section of the front wall facing Park-row, and at a slight deviation from the parallel of Broadway, still remained, and all eyes were turned in its direction. It was a very large, high portion, reaching to the uppermost story. About five minutes later this great façade careened gracefully over and slowly fell—not *in* among the burning ruins—but *out* on Broadway."[98] With a crash, the walls between inside and outside show were now permanently broken. In a sense, this had always been the case.

In this chapter, I have argued that Barnum's literary and exhibitionary innovation was in placing focus on these contexts of enactment and on the reciprocal and embedded interface of spectator and exhibit, rather than simply on the subject-object relationship between viewer and artifact. Barnum's diverse collection of attractions and novelty is perhaps best seen not as an insular text, a collection of ontologically distant objects against which visitors weighed themselves, but as a diffusely permeable association engine. In it those who paid a quarter were invited to play a configuration game that intimately linked them to a number of histories and socialities in process. The exhibits in Barnum's American Museum were spectacles, yes, but not as unidirectionally as is sometimes suggested. This is because, more than a spectacle, Barnum's Ann Street collection was also a generative platform for any number of novel configurative texts; it was an inventor's space as much as a display case. To deny this critically is to proceed as if the central pleasure of tangrams was in marveling over the shapes of the seven tans, rather than in the *use* of those tans to make a picture.

In the previous two chapters, I sketched a framework through which the operational selfhood of the mid-nineteenth century could be understood as a kind of localizing and localized utopic; that is, a site through which a person's action, while in one sense "determining" the person, can also be seen as an interactive embedding—an equivocal assemblage in process, rather than a contained subject. This perspective is reflected in Barnum's autobiographical writings, as well as facilitated in the practiced space of Barnum's museum. Read alongside the growing use and significance of configurative play in games like tangrams, his "original character" (to return to Melville's term) is shown in the capacity Barnum gives his patrons and readers to imagine a self in process, a self as a "tactful" or "ch'iao" social constellation. This view is important because it allows us to imagine the civic actors of the mid-nineteenth century not as empty categorical subjects bound and determined by their context but rather as embedded and active constitutive elements of that context, as mediators of potentially novel associations. It allows us to imagine the self as an inventive position in the cultural field; though to see this, we must be willing to understand how it was played at, and how inventive play with arrangement and proximity became a powerful operative model for inventive living.

Working through both Barnum's playful configurative practices and those of his audiences may help us to better unpack these interactions in our own moment. And allowing analyses of specific gameplay procedures to inform literary and media theory opens us to the critical possibility that gaming is doing more than just creating ideology-laden distractions: it reveals infrastructural developments as well as more recognizable historical structures. Tangrams, for instance, in many if not most of their nineteenth-century incarnations, were linked in content to visions of the foreign—particularly in their association with skewed and stereotyped understandings of "Chineseness." The game itself was colloquially referred to as "The Chinese Puzzle," and players implicitly absorbed prejudicial notions of cultural difference from its often-insensitive supporting artwork, reinforcing ideas of the serious and the fanciful on national and ethnic scales. Yet in practice, and examined for the kinds of operational behavior the puzzle aided in modeling—behavior interleaved with this iconographic engagement with "otherness"—tangram play offers a perspective on nineteenth-century pleasure. This pleasure was found through understanding limitation as opportunity and configurative spectatorship as social rehearsal. Given the anxieties about character-experimentation that accompanied the desire for consistency discussed in the previous chapter, it is telling that a game about finding new forms of communication with strictly limited materials—echoing a set of behaviors in public space that enabled similar ways of finding affinity—would be fused to images of the "foreign." There is no doubt that this persistent representation had (and has) negative ramifications for the actual communities to which it was (and is) attached. It is nevertheless suggestive that a game about communicative leaps, about learning to see and arrange differently but meaningfully, would be accompanied by imagery suggesting an alternative social world, a world flickering into existence through the play of associations and proximities.

In *The Ambiguity of Play*, Brian Sutton-Smith argues that play may have a crucial role in preserving ways of behaving that might otherwise be lost to the always localized "commonsense" imperatives of everyday life:

> We could say that just as the brain begins in a state of high potentiality, so does play. The brain has these connections, but unless they are actualized in behavior, most of them will die off. Likewise in play, even when novel connections are actualized, they are not, at first, the same as everyday reality. Actions do not become everyday reality until there is a rhetoric of practice that accounts for their use and value. . . . In this case, [play's] function would be to save, in both brain and behavior, more of the variability that is potentially there than would otherwise be saved if there were no play.[99]

In this way, Barnum's American Museum acted less as a historical archive (as many may have wished it to be) than as an archive of potential agencies, locally enacted and temporally volatile. Seeing this alongside the operational perspective provided by configuration puzzles allows us to understand these possibilities as they were experienced in time, as fundamentally ambivalent modes of enunciation. The pleasure is not always in the knowing but often in imagining what, and how, we might one day know.

CHAPTER 4

Social Cues and Outside Pockets

Billiards, Blithedale, and Targeted Potential

> Often the given writer who first gave vigor to the equation did not, however, intend it as a "bridge" in this historical sense, as a way of abandoning one position and taking up its opposite. Rather he cherished it precisely because this midway quality itself was his position.
> —Kenneth Burke, *A Grammar of Motives* (1969)

Standing at a sturdy and handsome bagatelle table, a caricatured Abraham Lincoln leans into his shot, an intense but comfortable look of focus on his face (Figure 12).[1] Bagatelle, a near-cousin of billiards, was played with a long cue that struck several solid colored balls (one red, the others white), sending them down the table into numbered divots awarding point values.[2] Lincoln's allegorically rendered table carries a placard along the side labeling it "the union board" and contains a larger number of divots than usual, with scores from one to twenty-one, corresponding somewhat imprecisely to the number of states he would stand to win in his landslide 1864 presidential reelection. He has already landed many shots with an even-handed dexterity, the double-valued red snugly resting in the central thirteen spot (suggesting his victory in aligning himself with the core values of the original thirteen colonies). With five balls left, Lincoln lines up his next target at the same time as he kicks over the "CHICAGO PLATFORM" upon which his opponent—an impish George McClellan—perches, grasping an oversized cue. McClellan whines that his cue "is too heavy! and the 'Platform's' shakey!!" while a pipe-smoking Ulysses Grant advises him to "surrender UNCONDITIONALLY" and Copperhead

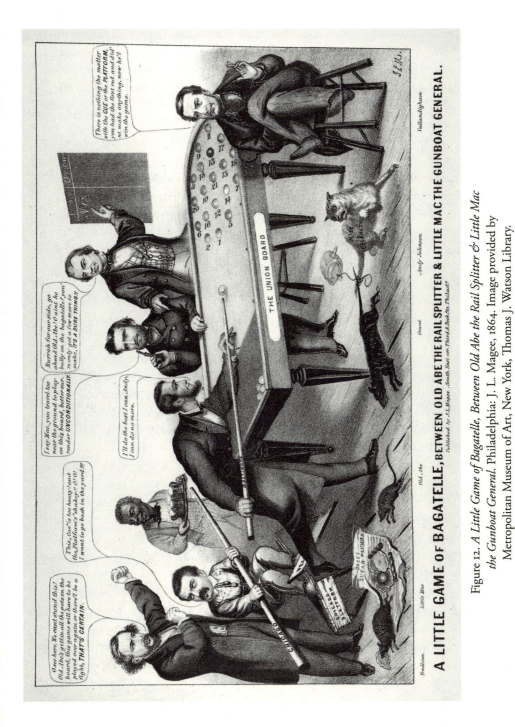

Figure 12. *A Little Game of Bagatelle, Between Old Abe the Rail Splitter & Little Mac the Gunboat General.* Philadelphia: J. L. Magee, 1864. Image provided by Metropolitan Museum of Art, New York, Thomas J. Watson Library.

Clement Vallandigham sits aloof in the corner chiding, "There is nothing the matter with the CUE or the PLATFORM, you had the first red and did'nt make anything, now he'l win the game." With "Nix" scrawled on the "Copper" side of a scorekeeping chalkboard, Vallandigham's prediction appears destined to become reality, and a smiling "Andy Johnson" cheers out, "Go ahead Old Abe!" proudly adding, "O aint he bully on the bagatelle?"

Although satirically presented here, versions of the above scene were becoming more and more typical in urban centers throughout the mid-nineteenth-century United States—and by 1864 had become common enough to merit the kind of breezy iconic reference typical of political cartooning. This wave of interest in cued targeting games like billiards and bagatelles was tracked by Michael Phelan, an Irish immigrant considered the father of American billiards, in the 1850 book *Billiards without a Master*, the first major U.S. publication on the subject. In this work, which drifts between history and rulebook, practical guide and cultural rationale, Phelan writes:

> The rapidity with which Billiard rooms and players have increased
> in this [New York] and other cities of the Union, is extraordinary.
> Within the writer's memory, the number of rooms in New York, did
> not exceed seven or eight, and perhaps not more than sixteen tables
> in all; now, there are from fifty to sixty rooms, with a number of
> tables, varying from one to sixteen in each, and amounting, on the
> whole, to something over four hundred; the number of players
> being, according to the author's computation, not less than twenty
> thousand, exclusive of strangers . . . the players of New York are
> highest on the American roll of players. New Orleans ranks next, as
> to the number of tables; though, perhaps, Philadelphia can boast of
> superior players. Boston, too, has a good number of tables.[3]

With interest in billiards expanding from a small upper-class coterie (following French fashions) to a large middle-class populace seeking entertainment and social engagement in the city, Phelan's book sought to capitalize on a developing market that had a strong desire to be seen as "bully on the bagatelle." The widespread focus on creating and controlling legible character was a central issue in the United States as it entered an era of expanding technology, urbanity, and institutionalism, creating overlap between the goals expressed in the games of the period and general cultural desires. The popularity of cued targeting games was no exception. Phelan writes, "A Billiard Room is a school where the study of human nature can be pursued to advantage," and a calm and focused demeanor reflected well on one's public character by demonstrating a mature physical self-control.[4] Yet at the same time, this personal form of "outside show" also illustrated one's capacity for a style of strategic thinking within complex and proceduralized systems—strategies of thought that were becoming recognized as crucial to success, from the presidential to the everyday.

Requiring dexterity and physical finesse to handle the cue with consistent force, billiards was (and remains), conceptually, a game largely about seeing a subset of the possible balls in play as an opportunity to create a discrete causal chain leading to a specific and controlled arrangement (for example, sending one ball to the corner pocket, leaving another near the side, avoiding unnecessary contact, and returning the cue ball to a strategic position). Put another way, the game is about the related visual operations of scoping and targeting. The relationship between these two operations can be briefly conceived in the following terms: to limit your view, or *scope out* a scene, is to have indicated an object (whether it be of analysis, aesthetic appreciation, or the like); to *target* is to put this view into contact with another narrower register, a register intended to use the wider indication in some specifically directed manner. With the cue ball in one position, the initial scoping of potential shots has to do with the operator's vision of what "object balls" fall within the range of the "cue ball"—an essential skill in nineteenth-century variants of billiards because there is no strict division between the different players' object balls (that is, no numbers), only red and white balls with different values depending on the type of shot made. *Scoping* is an important, but effectively neutral, type of gaming vision, perhaps symbolized best by the ivory cue ball itself (and the circumference of possible shots that surround it). Closely associated with scope, *targeting* reduces the scene to just one of these possibilities with a purpose in mind—the action of the cue stick—choosing a shot with a view toward changing the arrangement of the balls in a particular way.[5] Under the operative definition I'm using, targeting tracks an intentional vector between two levels of scope—the first a wide spread of possibility and the second a smaller motivated subset. Critically, this distinction will be used to prompt interpretative questions about the social and associative thresholds at play in billiards, as well as those at play in novels.[6]

The popularity of billiards in the nineteenth century signals an emerging manner of conceptualizing action and change, in games and social life in general. The sympathetic depiction of Abraham Lincoln as a savvy operator in "A

Little Game of Bagatelle" suggests a cultural respect for gamesmanship (how-ever uneasy), but also a more specific drive toward a variety of focused and delimited action forcefully represented in the figure of the billiards player. While this cartoon only explicitly addresses the wartime election, the ambiva-lence of the "Union Board" suggests a kind of utopic space in which a coolly targeted gamesmanship may have the capacity to make the United States whole again. In this chapter I argue that the social trends tracked by the bil-liards metaphor may be the reason Nathaniel Hawthorne makes playing this game an important (though oblique) character trait of one of his most frus-trating and fascinating characters, the first-person narrator of *The Blithedale Romance*, Miles Coverdale. The operative terms drawn from cued games in the nineteenth century, scope and targeting, can be productive when consid-ering the relationship of utopian thinking and literary romanticism in the same period. More than a throwaway piece of character history or simple real-ity effect, Hawthorne's nod to Coverdale's fondness for billiards speaks to a range of figural qualities that have bearing on his function as a narrator and that comment more broadly on the uses to which the book romance could be put in the mid-nineteenth-century moment. Within the developing capitalist ideologies of institutionalism and privatization, targeting was a mechanism of agency for dealing with what increasingly appeared to be a finitely limited or *reticulated* world—a world that required an embedded approach to social change. Analyzing Hawthorne's utopic-critical romance in parallel with bil-liards reveals both to be mutual conspirators in the reinforcement and appro-priation of specific targeting figures in the popular sphere.

Throughout this book, I have used games to develop various procedural logics at work in the interrelated media cultures of the nineteenth-century United States. In what follows, I deploy billiards in a similarly contrapuntal mode. Yet I begin by examining a system of figuration that is explicitly liter-ary, employing theories of utopian literature (perhaps the most game-like and spatial of literary forms) to expand our view of Hawthorne's particular variety of romanticism. With this in place, I allow the figural qualities of targeting and scope in billiards to further enrich the view. This also teases out a utopic quality present in contemporary nineteenth-century codifications of billiards, a game that was thought to have positive "dispositional" side effects. The co-operation of these two perspectives—the literary utopic and procedural ludic—continues the work of revealing the deep crossover between these two media forms while allowing us to consider frameworks of change, invention, and productive limitation that existed in American culture but are obscured by the somewhat atemporal and private model of readership provided in many literary-critical modes of analysis.[7]

Like the utopian texts it follows, however, this argument must take place via a productively refracted reading of figural qualities not wholly narrated in the works themselves, utopian theorist Louis Marin's "schema in search of a concept."[8] For Marin, the utopian work accomplishes its aims indirectly, arranging a world (or schema) such that readerly intervention is necessary to conceptualize the points of contact between the imagined world and the reader's reality; in this interactivity a set of real topics emerges that enables productive social theorizing. Approaching its politics in this indirect fashion—indeed, Hawthorne claims in the novel's preface that he does not "put forward the slightest pretensions to illustrate a theory"—*The Blithedale Romance* (1852) stages operative perspectives on possibility invention in both its form and its content, evoking a game-like and strategic view of life in the mid-nineteenth-century United States.[9] A complex functional polemic on the power of targeting to configure personal and social agencies stems from what F. O. Matthiessen notes in *American Renaissance* as "one of [Hawthorne's] most fertile resources, the device of multiple choice."[10] Though the nature of these choices is distinctly limited, I will propose that Hawthorne's text gestures at the mechanisms through which a limited imagination, such as that of the protagonist Miles Coverdale, might be the basis for an unlimited approach to an increasingly codified and commodified world. Games teach us that *limitation* need not always take the negative valence it frequently attains in critical work.

The Nail in Sisera's Brain: Utopics and Limited Imagination

On the surface, *The Blithedale Romance* tells a recognizable story of utopian failure in the face of multifaceted self-interests and romantic intrigue. Miles Coverdale, our distractible and urbane poet-narrator, tells the story of Mr. Hollingsworth, a social reformer who joins the community mainly to enlist funds for a criminal reformatory, and Zenobia, a powerful feminist orator who falls in love with Hollingsworth only to have him reject her when her inheritance is called into question. Zenobia's death, strongly suggested to be suicide, marks the bleak end to a story that begins with optimistic reorientations of intimacy and closes with a reinscription of traditional gender performance. Love and play wend toward institutional domesticity, and anything that outstrips the normative forms of male-female relationships dies or vanishes in a series of betrayals, both narrative and metanarrative. Though it ends with a declaration of love, *Blithedale* is decidedly tragic, a story of the things ruled out in the effort to fit in.

Before this heartbreak unfolds, Coverdale arrives in Blithedale with high spirits, "[shaking] hands affectionately, all round," and regaling himself and his fellow associationists with the knowledge that a world-changing "blessed state of brotherhood and sisterhood . . . might fairly be dated from this moment."[11] The central leads of the narrative are introduced to each other, and, notwithstanding a brief and eerie encounter with the wan Priscilla, a young purse maker sent to the community to escape a mysterious past, the inhabitants of Blithedale gather pleasantly around a fire to discuss possible names for their commune. (Coverdale suggests "Utopia" and is "unanimously scouted down . . . the proposer very harshly maltreated.")[12] Their conversation continues into the darker hours of the evening, and all seems off to an appropriately genial start when Coverdale suddenly falls sick. As he tosses and turns in his cold farmhouse bed, Coverdale's consciousness becomes a tempestuous medium (a lingering thematic throughout the text): "The night proved a feverish one. During the greater part of it, I was in the vilest of states when a fixed idea remains in the mind, like the nail in Sisera's brain, while innumerable other ideas go and come, and flutter to-and-fro, combining constant transition with intolerable sameness. Had I made a record of that night's half-waking dreams, it is my belief that it would have anticipated several of the chief incidents of this narrative, including a dim shadow of its catastrophe."[13] Here, a prophetic aspect arises from the fact that, within a structurally "fixed" set of ideas, iteration produces a prismatic range of possibilities, all yoked to some immutable social reality. In the biblical story, Sisera, a Canaanite commander, flees his army's defeat at the hands of Israel and stops to rest in the home of Jael. Seeming to offer hospitality, Jael waits until Sisera is fast asleep and drives a spike through his temple, killing him and ushering in forty years of peace.[14]

While in the biblical story the tent spike driven into Sisera's head was said to have effectively pinned him to the ground, Hawthorne's image of the fever dream imagines a set of ideas revolving in a circumference as if chained to that very spike, innumerable and yet discretely bound.[15] Although the ideas Coverdale has may not explicitly delineate the future for him—one would like to think that he might have prevented Zenobia's death or, on the most selfish level, done a better job of wooing Priscilla, whom he claims to love at the novel's conclusion—they do manage to show the *shape* or *shade* of things to

come, the "dim shadow of [*Blithedale*'s] catastrophe." One can imagine a series of possible outcomes, linked firmly to Coverdale's "fixed idea," forming a
kind of spherical shell around the narrative, shading it according to the peculiar alchemy of individual circumstance and nearly gravitational necessity. The
content of the fixed idea itself is less important in this moment than the figure
of the shadow cast, a perspectival effect of the relationship between the fixed
and the transitory—just as the wind blowing across a forest canopy might
create a dazzling cascade of light and darkness that changes the atmosphere of
a walk beneath the trees. To be sure, reading *The Blithedale Romance* can often
feel like trying to deduce the look of a forest scene using only the leafy panto-
mime projected on its floor.

Coverdale's name—leaving aside the fact that he spends a substantial
amount of time peering at characters from the tops of trees—suggests that his
narration plays the role of this shadow for the reader. As the sole source of
information, he provides the contours of the narrative but generally avoids
filling in certain specifics that would fully determine the story.[16] Often when
Coverdale does provide these significant details, he hangs a lantern on the artifice of his authorial license, highlighting his role in drawing together peculiar elements into a specific narrative system. Speculating that the headstrong
Zenobia had been previously married, he hedges, "There was not, and I distinctly repeat it, the slightest foundation in my knowledge for any surmise of
the kind"; recounting the foreboding dialogue of Zenobia and the mesmerist
Westervelt with respect to Priscilla, he suspects that his memory "may have
been patched together by [his] fancy"; relating Zenobia's charged legend of
the Veiled Lady, he "know[s] not whether the following version of her story
will retain any portion of its pristine character"; and when he finally relates
the crucial backstory linking Zenobia and Priscilla as half-sisters, a fact that
deeply threatens Zenobia's financial well-being, he notes that "in writing it
out, my pen has perhaps allowed itself a trifle of romantic and legendary license."[17] The end result is a pervasive narrative ambiguity that facilitates a
certain interpretative circumlocution on the part of the reader, despite (or
perhaps because of) the reader's frustration with *Blithedale*'s central character.
The utopian function of Coverdale's maddeningly partial storytelling is to
produce a kind of social Rorschach test, an ambiguous tangram, where the
critical work arises from the reader's desire to imagine what kind of object is
being represented by Coverdale's often unreliable textual configuration.[18]
Hawthorne, profuse though his prose may be in its attention to local scenic
details, uses Coverdale both to figure and to thematize the labor of discovery

and readerly invention, the unfinished business of filling in the affective and interpretative blanks.

Louis Marin discusses this operation as one of the key elements of utopic practice (as opposed to utopian generic conventions):

> That is the function of utopic practice: it is revealed by the play of "epistemological spaces" of the various discourses it activates. It renders these theoretical constructions present. It does not present them in all its *theoretical* power, however (it cannot: the utopian thinker is not a historical prophet); utopic discourse offers them as *poetic figures*. In other words, utopic practice does not construct a theoretical concept through the play of its discursive topics. Rather, it offers the setting, the space of representation. It provides the place of figurability, which is the imaginary schema and sensuous framework for it. . . . It is a schema in search of a concept, a model without a structure.[19]

Marin draws on Immanuel Kant here to illustrate a split between two important aspects of imaginative thought: the figure and the concept. The latter term corresponds to a set of associated mental objects that are linked by a discrete and cognitively necessary logic, a structural presupposition that is either fulfilled or not fulfilled by this set. For example, the concept of democracy mandates certain civic features that must be met in order for a political system to be properly named by the term ("rule by the people"). A concept is supposed to have its own strict internal logic, such that various empirical incarnations might be compared and criticized against this logic to validate the application of a given conceptual term. With his "inflexible severity of purpose," Hollingsworth might be thought to characterize the *concept* in Hawthorne's *Blithedale*, single-mindedly devoted to a criminal reform institution that was "the material type, in which his philanthropic dream strove to embody itself."[20] A "man of iron," as the spiritualist Professor Westervelt describes him, Hollingsworth allows his dream to take the form of a binary adjudication: only his precise plan will do, and only through strict adherence to this plan can one be a part of it. His declaration to Coverdale, "Be with me . . . or be against me! There is no third choice for you," neatly encapsulates his character, and provides a "conceptual" counterpoint to the largely "figural" qualities conveyed by most of the novel.[21]

On the other hand, a "figure" or "schema" is more merely incidental in its arrangement. A figure may have a historical bearing or repeat itself in ways that suggest a possible conceptualization, but its only logic is that of proximity and metonymy: one might think here of the "unsubstantial" characterization of Priscilla early in the novel. A ward of the community, Priscilla enters Blithedale as "a figure enveloped in a cloak," attaining character situationally rather than as a matter of course, a "mist of uncertainty . . . [preventing her] from taking a very decided place among creatures of flesh and blood."[22] Relating figurality to more spatial terms, Marin argues that utopic representation arranges a collection of objects from society in such a way as to inaugurate a figurally recognizable connection to the utopian writer's world while wrenching these objects from their familiarizing context (which has the weight of a social concept). This is often accomplished by strategically transposing the role of these pieces—in Thomas More's seminal *Utopia*, the conversion of gold into a kind of trash or waste—and this transposition suggests problems with the writer's society without fully conceptualizing the reintegration of its solutions. The "search for a concept" becomes the critical work that happens in the *play* between these defamiliarized social figures. As the writer and reader are forced to imagine the negative space that links the various recontextualized objects of the utopia (How might Priscilla belong in Blithedale in a way unrelated to her social belonging outside of Blithedale?), they are also imagining unspoken perspectives on their own culture, conceptual "neutrals" that are neither this place nor that place (What roles *could be* available to women like Priscilla? What modes of belonging are simply unthought?). The utopian text creates a space for critical thinking-through, an exercise in social targeting, or what Coverdale calls "an avenue between two existences; the low-arched and darksome doorway, through which [one] crept out of a life of old conventionalisms."[23]

Consequently, the sociological utopia itself (as a blueprint) is a bit of a red herring, a heuristic that sets the terms through which a new set of possibilities can be thought. The text functions to reorient affective sympathies and render conventional forms of language ironic such that terms might be recoded. With this in mind, Hawthorne's preface reads as an explicit declaration of critical utopic intent. He writes, "[The Author] does not put forward the slightest pretensions to illustrate a theory, or elicit a conclusion, favorable or otherwise, in respect to Socialism. In short, his present concern with the Socialist Community [Brook Farm] is merely to establish a theatre, a little removed from the highway of ordinary travel, where the creatures of his brain may play their phantasmagorical antics, without exposing them to too close a comparison with the actual events of real lives."[24] Like Coverdale, Hawthorne is loath to subject his romance to a direct experiential comparison; the use to which he puts Brook Farm merely parallels Coverdale's "nail in Sisera's brain" by "establish[ing] a theatre" (a fixed idea or schema) whereby transitory narrative images might be allowed a productive range of imaginary play while maintaining an embedded *feel* that refuses to alienate readers.[25] By doing so, Hawthorne can figure the possibility space of a social theory in spite of his disavowal of theory—with such a disavowal being directly in line with Marin's observation that the utopic is not a theory but a staging.[26]

This critical figuration, and the various deflective maneuvers it requires, might instead be thought of as the very "theory" of romantic fiction that Hawthorne puts forth: to stoke the imagination (and therefore represent the world as it is and as it could be at the same time) is not necessarily to give all the details to a reader but instead to suggest details in such a way as to invite theorizing as a cooperative tool building, and to invite a social perspective on reading that might lead to a more active civic life. Hawthorne theorizes the romance as a kind of *utopic* in Marin's sense: a neutral space in which the latent possibilities of the present are rendered uncanny enough to suggest critical rearrangements, or affective recodings. Marin argues that utopic texts tend to nest themselves in a network of references that "[anchor] the narrative in history. The narrative thus becomes the detached fragment of another silent narrative, exterior to the one we read. Its presence, however fragmentary in this text, grants it the authority of the pure and simple exposition of past facts. . . . This 'touch of the real,' this 'effect of reality,' here can also accomplish its opposite. It may 'de-realize' the scene . . . far from benefiting its authenticity, the one narrative may fictionalize the other, or at least . . . draw attention to its narrative qualities."[27] Compare this to Hawthorne's clarification in the preface of *The Blithedale Romance*, regarding its relationship to the historical Brook Farm, the famous Transcendentalist association where he spent the early 1840s: "The Author does not wish to deny, that he had this Community in his mind, and that . . . he has occasionally availed himself of his actual reminiscences, in the hope of giving a more lifelike tint to the fancy-sketch in the following pages. . . . The Author has ventured to make free with his old, and affectionately remembered home, at BROOK FARM, as being, certainly, the most romantic episode of his own life—essentially a day-dream, and yet a fact—and thus offering an available foothold between fiction and reality."[28] Hawthorne produces the "romantic" set piece of Blithedale by reconfiguring elements from his journals relating to the real-life Brook Farm, rearranging the fragments of his experience into a fictional environment where these characters might play through their drama. Moreover, on the level of textual reception, his reconfigured collage of entries from the "American Notebooks," while providing a specificity of detail to the scenes of *Blithedale*, also evokes a kind of ambiguity already present in the reality being narrated by the journal passages, guiding the reader into a suggestive (rather than prescriptive) engagement with the ambiguity of his or her own reality. By framing a limited array of "real life" objects as a stage for the narrative, Hawthorne reduces this reality to a few recognizable scenes, social protocols, and character types—he creates a scopic vantage of which this narrative is the diameter. Through the contact of the romance's "reduced" scopic layer and the larger layer that encompasses their lived experience, readers develop attitudes and dispositions that are then smuggled into their broader view of social realities. Targeting parts of reality in the terms of the text "de-realizes" that reality such that it becomes more available to imaginative reconceptualization.

Coverdale notes that in the shadow of his memories of Blithedale (which have constituted his first-person narration), "I have never before experienced a mood that so robbed the actual world of its solidity. It nevertheless involved a charm, on which—a devoted epicure of my own emotions—I resolved to pause, and enjoy the moral sillabub until quite dissolved away."[29] A frothy mixture of milk, sugar, and wine, a sillabub stands here as a symbol both for the airy quality of Coverdale's reflections and for his "epicure[an]" taste for mixture and variety more generally. In fact, his desire for experiential sillabubs slowly withers his resolve to stay within community—above all, it is only the contact of Blithedale's specifically limited world with the larger urban perspective of life back at his apartment that keeps his interest. Coverdale is, in many ways, the romantic narrator as utopian novel reader.

Yet while convalescing, days after his arrival at the farm, Coverdale expresses a deep yearning for the kind of variety that will eventually lead to his departure: "What, in the name of common-sense, had I to do with any better society than I had always lived in! It had satisfied me well enough. My pleasant bachelor-parlor, sunny and shadowy, curtained and carpeted, with the bed-chamber adjoining; . . . my writing-desk, with a half-finished poem in a stanza of my own contrivance . . . ; my dinner at the Albion, where I had a hundred dishes at command . . . ; my evening at the billiard-club, the concert, the theatre, or at somebody's party, if I pleased:—what could be better than all this?"[30] Coverdale's mind is drawn to the playful possibility of multiple objects of attention ("all this") and to the pleasure of constant rearrangements of priority and activity that avoid the monotony of everyday life on the farm. He begins to resemble Walt Whitman's avatar agent, an indicator of the general cultural move toward decision-making proceduralism; but at the same time, his affiliation with the "billiard-club" hints at the importance of scope and targeting within this mode, as a means to invoking a kind of fulfilling sidelong inventiveness.

Unlike the static grid of *The Checkered Game of Life*, billiards requires that a player reimagine the table and its dynamic arrangements at nearly every turn, improvisationally reevaluating the basis of his or her strategy. While the former game highlights decision making, billiards highlights the scoping operations by which one makes a decision about what to target in the first place, making a kind of metagame out of visualization and event modeling. Because the targets move, and especially because they move in relation to previous decisions on the part of the players involved, each turn in billiards might be seen as a "schema in search of a concept"—a Priscilla-like figural mystery with any number of productive conceptualizations.

A Ridiculous Piece of Romance, Undoubtedly: Billiards, Targets, Ridicules

Coverdale's affinity indexes a more general fixation, as bagatelles and billiards swept through the mid-nineteenth-century United States.[31] In fact, supporting Phelan's anecdotal description of the increasing number of tables mentioned earlier, a healthy proportion of patents for innovation in game design in the period between 1836 and 1875 were incremental improvements in the design of billiard and bagatelle tables—not to mention croquet (another intensely popular and operationally analogous game).[32] New designs focused on rearranging the elements of the game to make it more "fair"—largely through increased mechanization and miniaturization. Emphasizing targeting and social interaction, these games directed player attention to how the table arrangement might change, therefore changing the targets, after other players introduced their own outcomes. As a result, winning the game was a function of cumulative configuration, being able to adjust one's interventions such that they might create a personally fulfilling harmony of individual target-achievement and opponent outcomes, of directed strategy and on-the-fly reassessment. With typical billiard hall sessions measured by time at the table rather than by number of games played, winning was not necessarily an end point but rather a moment to pause, reset, and begin anew. Failure, similarly, was part of an agential continuum, the price paid for the opportunity to learn, decide, target, and arrange for oneself.[33]

Games highlight this theme generally, as they attune us to the power and capacity of *failure* within procedural environments. To clarify, I do not want to equate success directly with the conditions of "winning" in a game; in the same vein, by failure I do not necessarily mean "losing" with all of the psychological and social baggage the term brings with it. Although this perspective is important, it often dominates discussions of the social role that games play. Consequently, it may be productive to talk in a supplemental way about success and failure, as I have above, within an agential continuum. Success is the deployment of a strategy that increases the value of the game as a local engagement between the actors involved; successful gameplay tactically reconfigures the text/paratext relationship across which the game takes place. To illustrate this, the manipulation of the in-game algorithms might be narrated as a second-person commentary relating the players to each other as a social unit that is delimited by the game rules but also in excess of the rules: for example, "You *now* have more/fewer points *than you did*," "You *currently* play in a certain way that is *conveying* a certain kind of character," or "You won the last game/made me laugh earlier/are a frustrating opponent." Timing and situation have as much if not more relevance to a total gameplay situation than any purely operational result. Success, even in games that have a discrete "winner," is the tactful navigation of a social system that includes the players (as social entities) as much as the rule algorithms. Beating a child at chess and beating a grandmaster do not the same sort of success make (even if you beat them using the same moves).[34]

Failure, on the other hand, stems from the local inadequacy of a given strategy, but it is also an opportunity to adjust strategy, to see what worked and what did not. In this way all games are modeling devices on a number of levels. They reduce the scope of agency to a particular subset of actions and exaggerate the social importance of these actions. Playing a game of billiards is temporarily to entertain the fantasy that the only thing that matters *in the world* is the way you play your own ball at certain angles to knock the object balls into the pockets. Are you rich? It doesn't matter. Does the earth revolve around the sun? It doesn't matter. Is your leg broken? If you can still use the cue, it *doesn't matter*.[35] The world of billiards is a world of hands, arms, sounds, angles, felt, and a thin slice of space-time. The object formed in the playing of the game proceeds as if nothing but the angle of one's elbow and the firm crack of contact between the leather cue tip and the solid ivory ball mattered in terms of adjudicating the world. On a simplistic dismissal, this is what makes games escapist, but in fact this is also what makes games *productive*. Because of this reduction, games provide a platform for the exploration of mastery within a newly limited range of behaviors, much like Coverdale's Blithedale or Hawthorne's use of the historical Brook Farm. The characterizations developed within these artificial arrangements—ways of thinking, looking, or feeling—are transposed out of that environment, although not always in a one-to-one ratio with their utility within the game.

In addition to foregrounding these themes, the introduction of billiards as a historically specific game referenced in *Blithedale* further orients our attention to tropes of directed focus and targeting, to the cued "contact" of "spheres" at the heart of social arrangement and rearrangement in the novel.[36] If the "fixed idea" to which our narrator makes reference can form a shell of possibility around the narrative, anticipating the "dim shadow" of things to come through the medium of Coverdale, then we might understand this idea as the cue ball of the text, a neutral term limiting the possible targets through its position on the table. Coverdale himself might then be considered as the cue stick (a metonymy for the operator), moving this ball from point to point with linear force, directing our attention from one view to another, taking a wide view and limiting it in specific intentionally meaningful ways. The nature or significance of these intentions is left for us to interpret in the torque between different "targets" or from the accumulated tendencies of this targeting.

From limited yet variegated views we form a sense of the narrative through the comparison of individual textual objects at different levels of scope. At times Hollingsworth is narrated as one of a cluster of personalities all having bearing upon the total story ("Hollingsworth, Zenobia, Priscilla! These three had absorbed my life into themselves") and at other times he is more directly "under our microscope . . . insulat[ed] from many of his true relations," a target for individual interpretation that, as a result, bleeds into our sense of the other characters and their motivations.[37] Through all of this, Coverdale, as the first-person narrator, conducts our attention, not informing but *cueing* us to possible interpretive leaps that might be made in the juxtaposition of various narrative registers. Similarly, billiards itself was thought to act as a *cue* to ways of behaving that were taking place off the table. Much of the power the game held on the popular imagination had to do with its capacity to foreground this transactional space between the social world and the game provisionally placed at its center.

The emphasis here was not so much on mastery as on the exploration of what worked and what did not work, or what specific varieties of agency might look like. On the one hand, billiards was thought to model basic physical and geometric interactions via a reduction enabled by the rules and materials of the game. Phelan writes, "The game . . . may naturally assist the scientific man in the elucidation of his abstruse studies, and furnish him with some useful hints respecting the laws of motion, central gravity, etc."[38] On the other hand, the player uses these materials to model a given approach, thematizing his or her own agency in a social space, perhaps gaining insight, as Phelan suggests, into "the philosophical resignation to fate, the indifference of success, and all the multiplied and manifold passions of the human mind."[39] In *Billiards without a Master*, he makes physical control and decision-making style almost as central to his depiction of the game as the geometry of particular shots, writing, "To the physiognomist and the silent observer of human nature, there is no game that more thoroughly discloses the various dispositions of men than Billiards."[40] "Disposition" is read through a succession of individual movements accumulated over the course of a game, how one holds the cue, what one targets, and how one strings together these targets to accumulate more points than one's opponent. A later, 1859 edition of Phelan's book demonstrates this focus in the form of an anonymous bit of verse, claiming that "distinguishing traits are most forcibly shown / In a game, which of late, has most popular grown; / A very correct psychological steelyards / For character weighing—of course, we mean billiards."[41] Committed to proving that one's "Attitude Is Everything" (the title of the lyric), the author uses depictions of various billiards operators in action to make assessments about the general character of these players, using the game as a "steelyards" (a weighted scale on the principle of those used in medical offices today). With the game materiality providing a discrete and consistent environment, the human element is isolated as a core variable of the model in play, and therefore afforded a nearly quantitative interpretative value.

Developing the relationship between this and *Blithedale*, it may be useful first to think briefly about how *modeling* works, beginning with billiards and then folding this discussion into an analysis of Hawthorne's editorial and authorial style in the early 1850s. As articulated earlier, billiards operates via a reduction of the world to certain discrete elements: planar relationships, spherical masses subject to physics, muscle contraction, precision of movement, and the capacity to imagine a range of future outcomes based on a local targeting operation. The nature of this reduction is such that a new "whole" is created from a variety of previously available parts—where there was just a stick, a table, and some balls, now there is a social happening, a competition, an arena of motion and emotion. Emphasizing this (arguably phenomenological) wholeness, Phelan writes: "If any professional *litterateur*—or professional player, for the matter of that—should take exception to any of the matters which he has here laid down . . . he can only say that he will be happy to meet them in his own, or any other billiard saloon where the tables are correct, and decide the question in dispute by a direct appeal to the balls. . . . They might teach him 'the whole duty of man,' upon paper; but, on the tables, he could teach them the whole duty of a billiard-player."[42] There is an unexpected *equality* in these "whole dut[ies]," as presented here, that is brought into sharper focus by Phelan's feeling that becoming a good billiards player may have bearing on one's moral and social temperament. (He argues that wives would do well to allow billiard tables at home—foregoing the fears of its connection to gambling and moral vice—because it will encourage mental, social, and physical activity in the household that will radiate into a good middle-class home life.) As with Milton Bradley's *Checkered Game of Life*, it was thought that a focus on navigation and tactical reconfigurations would allow people not only to make peace with the importance of this kind of formalized decision making in everyday life but also to use these environments to workshop desired outcomes or behaviors in the broader world.[43] The "whole duty of man" could be given nuance or reterritorialized by the "whole duty of a billiard-player," with the fiction of ludic wholeness *de-realizing* the mundane wholeness of everyday character or disposition (to return to Marin's term). By this reading, billiards wrests sticks, tables, and human bodies out of their common usage in order to stage different *modes* of character and social interaction, augmenting the traditional significance attached to these objects in their more mundane contexts.

This, at its core, is a utopic operation native to games, although seldom discussed as such; the utopia displays a model of the current reality wherein alternatives might be imagined—if not necessarily fully expressed in the utopic text itself. In this way, a stylized and selective model *of* reality becomes a threshold model *for* achieving a different reality, Coverdale's "avenue between two existences."[44] The distinction between types of models, *of* and *for*, is discussed succinctly by Willard McCarty in his essay "Knowing . . . : Modeling in Literary Studies": "A model *of* something is an exploratory device, a more or less 'poor substitute' for the real thing. . . . In contrast a model *for* something is a design, exemplary ideal, archetype or other guiding preconception. Thus we construct a model *of* an airplane in order to see how it works; we design a model *for* an airplane to guide its construction."[45] A model *of* imagines a solitary object as a self-enclosed whole, while a model *for* invests a schematic with a specific intentionality. I would suggest that utopic modeling troubles this distinction, and that games offer insight into how that troubling occurs (perhaps not surprisingly, considering that the utopian text is the most obviously game-like of the literary genres). A model *of* an environment might be thought of as the cue ball that extends a radius of bounded possibility around it: it narrows the scope of the world to a distinct register of possibilities. The model *for* directs a certain momentum into the model *of,* directs it as a cue stick via one specific, narrower internal register of scope—what I've been calling targeting. A solid crack of the stick and the scene changes: the relationship of object balls changes, as well as the perspective of the cue ball. While the cue ball provides a limited perspective on a given range of object balls, the cue stick puts this wider scope into contact with the player's investments and vision, with his or her own narrower range of scope. This is represented in Phelan's manual through schematic views of particular shots. Through the contact of these two scopic registers we learn something about the player; an interpretation emerges as a function of targeting, which is always a measure of lining up two or more registers of scope. Since the dominant theme in billiards is this type of targeting operation, the game highlights the productive elements of scopic contact in the insistent interplay between models *of* (the relational layout of the balls) and models *for* (the linear decision making of the player). Because of this, Phelan's contention that the game's benefits might extend beyond the felt surface of the table feels more natural than it might otherwise (given the decidedly abstract nature of gameplay).

To wit, Phelan realizes that billiards itself (or its invention) is not necessarily social change: it is simply a reduction of the world to a simple set of terms, objects, and rules (a model *of*). Yet, on the other hand, he asserts that playing billiards can be a platform for certain types of changes: in play this model *of* a particular world becomes a model *for* a particular kind of mind, a particular kind of social interaction, and consequently a new kind of "world." Via the above, one of the victories of billiards, as a model, is a nonrepresentational change of affective association (what Phelan calls "disposition" or "attitude") that might, in turn, change behaviors and representational outcomes.

Hawthorne observes this as well, writing at one point in his notebooks (referring to an adolescent girl at Brook Farm who would later become his template
for Priscilla in *Blithedale*), "It would be difficult to conceive, beforehand, how
much can be added to the enjoyment of a household by mere sunniness of
temper and smartness of disposition."[46] Note that this change (an addition of
"enjoyment") comes about not via some kind of escape from the currently
existing system but rather by *using* the existing system in a special way—
inventing new objects and new models from within—by using the ambiguity
of the existing system (the multiplicity of its perspectives or scopic registers)
in sympathetic ways: "sunn[y] or "smart" perspectives in Hawthorne's observation here.

From a reduction of the world to the specific locality of the game table,
the game of billiards in general—and Phelan's view in particular—emphasizes
the narrowing of a potentially chaotic and enticing field of possible targets to
a given methodical perspective on a sequence of strategic strikes, and within
this to the singular act of a measured and precise contact between the player's
ball and the object ball. The precision of this interaction then expands to become a figure for a more general precision within the billiard hall, producing
players who understand the value of "combining the '*suaviter in modo* [gentle-
ness in manner] with the *fortiter in re* [fortitude in execution],' partaking
largely of the former."[47] The formal micro-materiality of interaction in a player's turn sheds light, in Phelan's view, on the larger formal protocols (social
materialities) of public interaction in a quasi-serial fashion—with each register of complexity introducing excesses not present at the smaller level and
therefore creating productive critical friction.[48]

This corresponds to the agential aesthetics of scope in the nineteenth-
century United States, which has been a recurrent theme throughout this
book. In Barnum's American Museum, the arrangements of text and paratext
that operate within a single exhibit are expanded to allow complex interrelated arrangements among the artifacts within the museum. On one level, the
exhibit-creator takes the role of a configuring curator tactfully trying to prod
the viewer's imagination; on another, the audience arranges its view of artifacts as it meanders through the museum space, self-curating the experience.
With the brick man advertisement, Barnum uses a further level of expansion,
bringing the metaprotocols of the "thoughtful looker-on" into the streets of
New York City. By doing so, he makes the case that the pedestrians surrounding the museum are already a part of a kind of museum-going game. In each
case here, the legible action is a function of targeted differentials of scope, a

focus on the changed arrangement of existing elements: the exhibit-creator controls the tenor and variety of outside themes that are brought into play with an exhibit, suggesting meaning in the interface of these two registers; the thoughtful looker-on habituates socialities by reducing the expanse of the museum to a controlled collection of personally significant exhibitions along a targeted theme of interest, thereby expressing a general public character; and the brick man promotion exerts influence over an audience by expanding the scope of museum contemplation into the surrounding streets. In all cases, the structuring of an environment, a paratext to an assumed text, constitutes the major act of invention at play.

A variation on this same aesthetic is why the general drive toward reform in the United States relied on what Steven Mintz calls an "Enlightenment faith in the shaping influence of environment."[49] American reformers (of which game designers can be considered a class) believed that selective navigation through the world created an experiential scene that would reciprocally produce a certain type of citizen—in this way, environment was the *ground* to the avatar *figure*. While imagining things from the perspective of an embedded avatar requires an emphasis on the procedural stylistics of decision and navigation, making the same point from the perspective of environment (the substance of the avatar's embedding) requires an emphasis on the aesthetics of scope, on how a series of choices reduces or expands the world in which the avatar acts, and how those changes reflect upon the agent's public character.

This environmental view of invention illustrates the way that a kind of *editorial* approach to the modularity of arranged objects was becoming the ground for various social agencies. Indeed, Hawthorne—himself an editor of relatively technical writing in his early career at the *American Magazine of Useful and Entertaining Knowledge*—seems to take this approach to his duties as an author, both in the creative use of journal materials cited above and in the sequencing of his narratives. Discussing the textual production of *A Wonder Book*, a collection of classic children's tales published in the same year as *The Blithedale Romance*, textual critic Fredson Bowers notes that Hawthorne wrote the tales of *A Wonder Book* separately and "allowed a blank leaf to stand at the end" in order to "keep each story as a unit, and thus movable in order."[50] Bowers continues, "Each story is separately numbered, and there is no continuous numbering anywhere in the manuscript. Each story, moreover, begins on the recto of a leaf, even if the preceding verso was blank. Together, these facts suggest that Hawthorne wished to keep the final order of the stories fluid until the last moment."[51] Though the publishing process required him to make final decisions regarding the placement of these discrete text objects, Hawthorne formulates standalone pieces that can be arranged later to achieve a desired compositional effect; he then tellingly nests these pieces in a framing metanarrative that places each story in the voice of an authorial cue, an older friend and storyteller to the children of Tanglewood named Eustace. These interstitial segments, with Eustace setting up the stories and fielding questions from children, place the tales of *A Wonder Book* in a wider environmental scene: the foggy vapors surrounding Monument Mountain, the babbling waters of Shadow Brook, and the changing seasons of the Berkshires provide a kind of "outside show" that localizes the classical myths of the collection. This localization foregrounds the formal choices made in the arrangement of *A Wonder Book*'s stories, as a kind of targeting operation, by imagining that "we" are *watching* this formation happen naturally (in both the environmental and the emergent sense). Phelan points out, "Good players often succeed admirably, and make very long runs, by what in Billiard parlance is called *nursing the balls* [that is, carefully arranging them through savvy play]."[52] Similarly, readers observe Eustace as he develops a story order appropriate to the changing scene, nursing (in the sense of providing directed education to) the children of Tanglewood in the process of this arrangement. Watching the way that Eustace "nurses," readers learn something about who he is and how they might make themselves through a similar decision-making process that insistently frames one limited figure (or story) in terms of another.

Eustace himself draws attention to his role as a targeted inventor, lamenting an old guard less sympathetic to the transparent reconfigurations that constitute the new grounds of authorship: "No man of fifty, who has read the classical myths in his youth, can possibly understand my merit as a re-inventor and improver of them."[53] Eustace reinvents these tales by locally arranging them in such a way as to emphasize a more "gothic" style; he expands the scope of the tales to include emotional valences not emphasized in the more austere classical narratives. By doing this, he suggests that such a rescoping is an inherently productive activity (an "improve[ment]" of the story); yet he also sees authorship (again, as a type of agency) not as whole cloth creation but rather as a navigation of existing terms. Accordingly, his role in *A Wonder Book* is to emphasize the critical work that happens in the movement between two registers of scope: the discrete story object and the meta "telling" story, the figure and the interpretative process that is expressed through a kind of targeting or localization.

Hawthorne then takes this a step further by injecting himself into the text as an even more expansive narrative frame. Beginning with a preface that ties his authorial voice to that of the narrator in the interstitial text, he draws attention to the fact that Eustace's story is, in fact, being related by another, different first-person storyteller, employing the narrative tactic of *metalepsis*.[54] Before the opening of Eustace's tale of the "Miraculous Pitcher," Hawthorne writes: "As for the story, I was there to hear it, hidden behind a bush, and shall tell it over to you in the pages that come next."[55] Later, in the closing of *A Wonder Book*, the precocious Primrose asks Eustace about a peculiar author who lives near their Tanglewood home:

> "Have we not an author for our next neighbor?" asked Primrose.
> "That silent man, who lives in the old red house . . . I think I have
> heard of his having written a poem, or a romance, or an arithmetic,
> or a school-history, or some other kind of book." "Hush, Primrose,
> hush!" exclaimed Eustace, in a thrilling whisper, and putting his
> finger on his lip. "Not a word about that man, even on a hill-top! If
> our babble were to reach his ears, and happen not to please him, he
> has but to fling a quire or two of paper into the stove; and you,
> Primrose, and I . . . would all turn to smoke, and go whisking up
> the funnel! . . . Something whispers to me that he has a terrible
> power over ourselves, extending to nothing short of annihilation."[56]

In addition to playfully foregrounding the multiple story frames at play (and thus the thematic of scope), Primrose seems here to link romance to arithmetic. Why? One relevant parallel between these genres of writing (and perhaps the other two mentioned, although more obliquely) is the way that they make the combination of figures central to the text. If arithmetic situates number objects under the sway of operators in order to produce new objects (expanding their effective scope), then we might argue that the romance, at least as employed by Hawthorne, is a similar combination of known quantities under the sway of an operator (a narrator or avatar like Eustace, or as we shall see shortly, Coverdale) with the purpose of producing creative new outcomes.[57]

Here I simply want to emphasize that the combined effect of these various framing devices is to direct attention to the nested nature of the various formal structures at play: the mythic classical tales deal with allegorical themes that are then recoded as naturalistic moral and oral themes (via Eustace) and further recoded as ludic mental and written themes, as styles of thinking or habitual dispositions. We might imagine each scopic register a progressively larger cloth laid over a small pool of dyed water; the shape of the blot in the smallest cloth is absorbed by the next, yet the context changes as the spot gets proportionally smaller and the absorption more minute. Similarly, each layer (or scopic register) has its own native significances that bleed into the layers above it, much as Phelan's well-formed billiards player enables a seepage of significance between the smallest layer (the single turn) and the larger layers of play (the social activity of the hall or parlor). By drawing readers into and out of different scoped frames, Hawthorne asks them to inflect each frame with a trace of the previous frame, which has the effect of targeting a given narrative within the scope of another. He underscores this activity further by bringing the narration into a direct, and somewhat unsettling, contact with the reader that breaks with the indirect third-person style dominating the text. This motion creates a critically suggestive seepage between layers that echoes the effect of Coverdale's secondhand narration in *Blithedale*—a similarity perhaps not unexpected given that *Blithedale* was written in the immediate aftermath of *A Wonder Book*. One might even see the narrative style of this earlier work as a kind of simplified workshop for the mechanisms Hawthorne employs in the later text—not to mention those used by William Simonds a year later in the Aimwell Stories discussed in Chapter 2.

The Blithedale Romance's most ostentatious display of scoping mechanisms appears in the series of narrative frames that surround Zenobia's tale of the Veiled Lady (a character that we later learn is one and the same as the mysterious Priscilla). Here we are almost lost in the series of increasingly secondhand narrations. While Hawthorne has already prefaced the entire novel in order to establish distance between his own recollections of Brook Farm and the recollections of *Blithedale*'s primary first-person narrator, now Coverdale prefaces Zenobia's tale with a similar disclaimer before presenting her words in first-person as well: "I know not whether the following version of her story will retain any portion of its pristine character. But, as Zenobia told it, wildly and rapidly, hesitating at no extravagance . . . we caught the freshest aroma of the thoughts . . . and thus heard, the legend seemed quite a remarkable affair."[58] The "pristine character" of the story matters less here than the "aroma of the thoughts," which convey the "remarkable" ("notable," but also perhaps "re-marked" or remade) affair to the reader at one remove. Again this draws attention to the prospect of a relationship between the different narratives at play, with one narrative acting as an ambiguous figure that draws attention to potential interpretative possibilities in the other. After a line break, we read the heading "THE SILVERY VEIL" and immediately jump into this new frame of narration:

You have heard, my dear friends, of the Veiled Lady, who grew suddenly so very famous, a few months ago. . . . Now, listen to my simple little tale; and you shall hear the very latest incident in the
known life . . . of this shadowy phenomenon. A party of young gentlemen, you are to understand, were enjoying themselves, one after-
noon, as young gentlemen are sometimes fond of doing, over a
bottle or two of champagne; and—among other ladies less
mysterious—the subject of the Veiled Lady, as was very natural,
happened to come up before them for discussion. She rose, as it
were, with the sparkling effervescence of their wine, and appeared in
a more airy and fantastic light, on account of the medium through
which they saw her. They repeated to each other, between jest and
earnest, all the wild stories that were in vogue; nor, I presume, did
they hesitate to add any small circumstance that the inventive whim
of the moment might suggest, to heighten the marvellousness of
their theme.[59]

Bordering on diegetic ridiculousness, the men begin to tell each other the
stories that *they* know of the Veiled Lady—stories that are narrated by Zenobia, as remediated by Coverdale, a character of Hawthorne's novelistic "theatre."[60] These stories radiate like the effervescent bubbles of the champagne
they drink, up through each layer, and at each layer imply something about
the narrator who directs our attention to them: Zenobia's interest in the Veiled
Lady speaks to her frustrated relationship with Priscilla, while the interest
Coverdale has in Zenobia's story indicates his continued interest in somehow
linking the story of the Veiled Lady's bondage to Zenobia's character and sexual history.

Hawthorne presents each of these as inroads to the readers' interpretations of the novel's characters. At the same time, he foregrounds the fundamental operations of scope that enable interpretative agency despite the
limitations that bound each consecutive layer in turn. The story of the "Silvery Veil," though framed within a deeply nested world, envelopes Priscilla in
Zenobia's final dramatic gesture: "Zenobia, all this while, had been holding
the piece of gauze, and so managed it as greatly to increase the dramatic effect
of the legend, at those points where the magic veil was to be described. Arriv-
ing at the catastrophe, and uttering the fatal words, she flung the gauze over
Priscilla's head. . . . Her nerves being none of the strongest, Priscilla hardly
recovered her equanimity during the rest of the evening. This, to be sure, was

a great pity; but, nevertheless, we thought it a very bright idea of Zenobia's, to bring her legend to so effective a conclusion."[61] Zenobia's action, callous in the total framework of *Blithedale*, brings together two locally independent registers of scope: that of "Theodore" tracking down the Veiled Lady and demanding to see her face, and that of the events that have come to pass until this point with Priscilla. By doing so, Zenobia explicitly puts these two registers into contact, directing attention to emergent themes of possession, aggressive discovery, and a cultural rejection of female ambiguity. Isolating Priscilla as the target of the story, its arrangements are propelled into our reading of her—the literary power of the veil here layered upon her body as a translucent presence shading one's view of the young girl. Covered or bound by the myth that "The Silvery Veil" presents, Priscilla's figural mystery is at least partially stolen away as she is linked with the sordid past of the Veiled Lady's performances, a conceptualization that Zenobia seems to hope will drive Priscilla out of the community and away from Hollingsworth. As Coverdale notes in the preceding chapter, people care not for Priscilla's figural "realities . . . but for the fancy work with which [they] have idly decked her out."[62]

From the comfort of his leafy "hermitage," Coverdale offers similar sweeping conceptualizations of the Blithedale community in a manner that again evokes the metanarrative device of targeting. Yearning for time alone to contemplate his various writing projects, he discovers a knot of trees woven together by a single resilient "wild grapevine." Within this "inextricable knot of polygamy" he finds a "hollow chamber, of rare seclusion . . . formed by the decay of some of the pine-branches, which the vine had lovingly strangled with its embrace, burying them from the light of day in an aerial sepulcher of its own leaves."[63] Of course, this hermitage, a kind of woven purse of foliage, evokes the social situation of Blithedale, with Zenobia, Hollingsworth, Coverdale, and Westervelt all bound together by affiliation with the "wild" Priscilla, herself a purse maker.[64] Yet it is from within this "natural turret" that Coverdale "open[s] loop-holes" and, "peep[ing], in turn, out of several of its small windows," gains perspective on the community and its players.[65] This space becomes a natural symbol of the scopic layers that enable these interpretations, as Coverdale aims his view from person to person, bringing them into contact with his literally more expansive view of the situation and passing judgment on them as a result.[66] Zeroing in on Hollingsworth, he interprets the philanthropist's opinion of humankind as "but another yoke of oxen"; why, Coverdale wonders, should he and his companions "waste our strength in dragging home the ponderous load of his philanthropic absurdities? At my height above the earth, the whole matter looks ridiculous!"[67] He then sets his sights on the community at large, commenting on "the folly of attempting to benefit the world" before noting that "our especial scheme of reform, which, from my observatory, I could take in with the bodily eye, looked so ridiculous that it was impossible not to laugh aloud."[68] The "scheme" that from within held so much potential at the outset of Coverdale's narrative has here been defined, conceptualized as it were, as "folly," on the same level as Hollingsworth's "absurdities." From Coverdale's scopic vantage, everything attains the taint of the laughable or "ridiculous."

This term, "ridiculous," recurs throughout the text, such that it deserves its own singular attention. When Coverdale attributes to Zenobia "a destiny already accomplished" (that is, a lack of virginity), he attempts to diminish this interpretation of her character as "a ridiculous piece of romance."[69] Later Zenobia observes, "What I find most singular in Priscilla . . . is her wildness. . . . It is quite ridiculous."[70] Attributing a pervasive cynicism to Professor Westervelt, Coverdale claims that his "tone represented that of worldly society at large, where a cold scepticism smothers what it can of our spiritual aspirations, and makes the rest ridiculous."[71]

Ridiculousness, in addition to the simple delineation of something as laughable, seems in the world of Blithedale to index a singular conceptualization or interpretative targeting of the object in question. Zenobia, defending Hollingsworth from Coverdale's accusation that he is driven by only one idea, admits, "Blind enthusiasm, absorption in one idea, I grant, is generally ridiculous," yet she contends that "a very high and powerful character [may] make it otherwise."[72] This may be because, typically, the "one idea" becomes an encompassing reading for the character in question, rendering him or her a permanent target; but in the case of a sufficiently vast character ("high" or "powerful"), the self manages to remain unencompassed by the idea in question. While Coverdale understands that Zenobia's lavish fashions and luxurious residence make her "gorgeous" and inscrutable, he adds that such things "would have been ridiculous in the poor, thin, weakly characters of other women," giving the lie to a deep insecurity beneath the outer vestiges.[73] That which adds to Zenobia's mystery or figurality (because of her character's "gorgeousness") would become a defining conceptual veil for other women. It would make them "ridiculous" or containable within the scopic register of empty worldly luxury, targeted as vain and commodified by their proximity to the wide world of monetary objects. That which has no ambiguity becomes, for Hawthorne, laughable in its almost mechanical scopic knowability or predictability (a predictability that might be linked to the "puzzling" of characters discussed in Chapter 2 with regard to Melville's *Confidence-Man*). Recanting her earlier view of Hollingsworth, Zenobia eventually cedes his "ridiculous" absorption within one idea, inveighing, "Are you a man? No; but a monster! A cold, heartless, self-beginning and self-ending piece of mechanism. . . . You have embodied yourself in a project."[74]

This directed enveloping of character also happens in more local moments of active focus under the cognate terminology of *ridicule*. Coverdale alternately wants to avoid being "the butt of [Zenobia's] endless ridicule," resents Westervelt's "ridicule of a friend," and comments on the way the world "disbelieve[s] and ridicule[s Hollingsworth], while hardly any do him justice, or acknowledge him for the wonderful man he is."[75] At the same time, seeing Coverdale smirk at her declaration that she plans to lobby for "women's wider liberty," Zenobia asks, "What matter of ridicule do you find in this, Miles Coverdale?"[76] Whereas the "ridiculous" object has become solely defined by one scopic association, "ridicule" here implies a circumstantial evaluation of a person in a certain unambiguous range, a local targeting operation or small act of modeling among an implied ambiguous multitude. Coverdale himself clarifies this when discussing his time at Blithedale with old friends in the city: "Meeting former acquaintances, who showed themselves inclined to ridicule my heroic devotion to the cause of human welfare, I spoke of the recent phase of my life as indeed fair matter for a jest. But, I also gave them to understand that it was, at most, only an experiment . . . [one which] had afforded me some grotesque specimens of artificial simplicity, and could not, therefore, so far as I was concerned, be reckoned a failure."[77] Drawing a range of affordances from his time at Blithedale, despite in one view being an object of ridicule, Coverdale holds on to the ambiguity of the experience as neither success nor failure. To be an object of ridicule was to become stripped of ambiguity for a moment on some level, to be, as Coverdale puts it in an early passage, "insulate[d] from many of [our] true relations"; but becoming this kind of targeted object in brief moments could also be, as he notes, productive as long as one did not remain long enough to become a ridiculous "failure."[78] The capacity for ridicule merely relates to the temporary contact of a person with a larger range of scope that, for a moment, appears to dictate behavior and therefore engross him or her. At this point of contact, the larger scopic register *targets*, or appears to give a singular motivation to, the smaller, therefore making it an object of ridicule—here the world at large makes the activities of Blithedale look contrived, contained, mechanical, and therefore silly. This is nearly always the case in the world: there is always some imaginable view that, when put into contact with our current actions, might make them seem unnecessary, mechanically single-minded, or dull-headed.[79] *Blithedale* makes a distinction, however, between being *ridiculed* and being *ridiculous*, with the latter being an almost institutionally permanent position, ideologically putting a character into contact with a single scopic register that envelopes him or her, much like Coverdale's grapevine hermitage or one of Priscilla's purses.

This is significant, as "ridicule" was also a punning term for a woman's knitted purse, a fashion very much of the moment in which Hawthorne was writing.[80] Named after the netting technique used to weave them, "reticules" originated at the end of the eighteenth century in response to changing fashions in women's dresses, as newly streamlined styles could no longer accommodate pockets. The term "reticule," derived from the same root as "reticulated" (netted), could also refer to the gridded scope one used to aim a rifle or a telescope. Because of the spoken similarity of the words, it is unclear whether the initial conflation of the terms "reticule" and "ridicule" was intentional, but it stuck nevertheless. We might remember this as we recall that when we are first introduced to Priscilla, Coverdale observes: "She now produced, out of a work-bag that she had with her, some little wooden instruments, (what they are called, I never knew,) and proceeded to knit, or net, an article which ultimately took the shape of a silk purse."[81] Priscilla, come to find out, is a talented producer of ridicules/reticules. Indeed, Coverdale is uncharacteristically observant when he wonders if these purses "were not a symbol of Priscilla's own mystery."[82] Linking together all of the novel's leads in varying ways, Priscilla not only makes purses of silk but also weaves through the text to make a kind of purse of all its characters.

At the center of this purse, as one might expect, is an awful lot of money. The fortune of "Old Moodie" has been under the care of Zenobia—provisionally, we learn—and stands to fall instead to his favored daughter, Priscilla, if Moodie should find out that she has been mistreated in any way. It is this sum of money that draws Hollingsworth to Zenobia, as he plans to use it as capital to build the philanthropic institution at the center of his monomania. Understanding that she might otherwise lose her love, Zenobia plots to return her sister to the employ of Westervelt, a plan that Hollingsworth apparently supports. But when this action leads Moodie, in turn, to revoke Zenobia's inheritance, giving all to Priscilla, Hollingsworth abandons Zenobia, swooping in to "save" Priscilla and take advantage of her love for the purpose of his philanthropy. Like the mysterious mesmeric substance that the audience at Westervelt's show believes has the power to turn the human mind into a kind of controllable mechanism—"soft wax in [the spiritualist's] hands"—so does Moodie's purse threaten to make each of the core players at Blithedale *ridiculous*, defined by their possession (or lack) of it and by what they are willing to do to get it. Coverdale narrates the power of this money again in the rhetoric of spiritualism rather than economy: "It is unutterable, the horror and disgust with which I listened, and saw that, if these things were to be believed, the individual soul was virtually annihilated, and all that is sweet and pure in our present life debased, and that the idea of man's eternal responsibility was made ridiculous."[83]

Like Coverdale's forest hermitage, the vantage of which allows him to target all of Blithedale as ridiculous, the perspective of the purse also carries the deep social danger of providing a scopic register that engulfs (that is, reti-cules or nets) and consequently defines all of the behaviors and relationships that have driven the action of the romance. It threatens to make all action unambiguously cynical and directed by raw avarice, circumscribing "all that is sweet and pure in our present life," as money becomes the singular interpreter of all social value and success, the final cue of an abstract and operative social body. From a number of ambiguous interpretative targets, *one* emerges both thematically and stylistically to steal away the readerly agency that has shaped our dispositional relationship with the text—a relationship that until the final chapters is built upon the variety of interpretations left open to analysis. In its last pages, the novel appears to succumb to this ridiculous master interpreta-tion via Coverdale as he reveals that the object of his affection throughout, the "one secret, hidden beneath many a revelation," was Priscilla, a metonymy for the purse (and near homonym, "Purse-ella") that demands we interpret all through its reticule: "I—I myself—was in love—with—Priscilla!"[84]

As readers we rage, yet it is worth noting that we are dispositionally driven to rage at this moment in the text, in a sense trained by our experience of the romance to feel this way: our dopily absent narrator, our avatar through-out this otherwise ambivalent text, has made a singular choice without us. He has rendered the ambiguity of the narrative into a singular love story, a Hollingsworth of a romance.[85] How dare he? We pore back over the text with a renewed energy to make it about something, anything, other than Cover-dale's weakly revealed love, finding new points of "ridicule" in the service of staving off this interpretative "ridiculousness." And in this motion we reveal the strategic critical power of Hawthorne's story space.[86]

To have one choice, to diminish the range of targeting in favor of a single target, thus diminishing the insistence of ambiguity to a single outcome is, given the ambiguity of our perspective throughout the novel, ridiculous. Zenobia, often the character equivalent of ephemerality and variability in the text (with her name itself evoking the Greek *xenos*, stranger), expresses the dominant theme of the novel in execution, "Why should we be content with our homely life of a few months past, to the exclusion of all other modes? It was good; but there are other lives as good, or better."[87] Spurred by Zenobia's suicide, a death that signals the coming closure offered in Coverdale's "confession," we are thrust from this admission back into the book—looking for other targets, pouring over the schema in search of other concepts, "other lives as good or better." If the catastrophe predicted by Coverdale's dream early in the text is indeed Zenobia's death, and this death is the direct outcome of an interpretative "pursing" or final conceptualization, then the "fixed idea" referenced in the dream passage might be construed as the event horizon of death as concept, with a fulfilled agential life being constituted by the conversation that radiates around this fixed point, a point meaningless in itself. Hawthorne evokes this image in the iterated scenes at Eliot's pulpit, where, after giving a dramatic speech about his singular idea, Hollingsworth would "fling himself at full length on the ground, face downward," in a performance of death while Zenobia and Coverdale would "[talk] around him on such topics as were suggested by the discourse."[88]

This would appear to be the work of *The Blithedale Romance*. It leverages a specific operative idea of romance as conspicuous layering to figure various shades of Hawthorne's moment in order to create interactively felt "topics" for discussion: the reduction of family to the purse (economic abstraction), the enclosure of female agency (gender domination), the danger of living by a single idea of any kind (institutionalism), and the troubled hopefulness of the social operator (limited imagination and configurative agency). Each of these is shown to have complex indirect relationships with each of the others as they are mapped onto the central characters, Priscilla, Zenobia, Hollingsworth, and Coverdale/Westervelt, respectively. Yet at the same time Hawthorne's style gestures at the very mechanisms of gesturing—the kind of continually retargeted billiards agency that we have been pursuing throughout—by revealing the "purse" as simply another interpretative frame, the reticulated veil surrounding an immanently "fixed idea." "Romance," and billiards as quasi-romance in Michael Phelan's way of styling it, figures what would now be identified as a "theoretical" disposition toward social media: a layering of frames whose work is performed in the torque of those frames, as well as the residues that they leave on each other. The point is to make local commitments, to understand that any object (or commitment or perspective) is potentially an object of situational ridicule; ridicule is indeed an always-present byproduct of making such an investment. The truly *ridiculous* thing is not to continue retargeting and reinventing, as it renders one mechanical, predictable, and therefore nearer to personal and civic "catastrophe."

The world of *Blithedale*, as in the world of "unseriousness" associated with nineteenth-century gameplay more broadly, is a world in which one must make one's peace with ridicule but need not be ridiculous. The effort to use media to maintain social fluidities in the face of more and more deeply circumscribing arrangements of scope and scale was addressed through attempts at prompting different interactive styles, different genres as different relations to media. Tracking this reveals the impact that certain underlying genre practices could have—as habitual modes of engagement, not just *tropes* through which things could be categorized. Whether it was literature that pivoted emphasis to iteratively targeted reading styles or gaming practices that highlighted iteratively targeted playing styles, cultural producers on both fronts faced the challenges accompanying a media environment that was not simply *reflecting* social meaning but *making* certain forms of social meaning possible or impossible. To note that at least some book reading might have unfolded in a manner better framed as billiards playing—and that authors like Hawthorne may have been attempting to stage such a different mode of reading—is to note an alternative social realm surrounding books that supplements the model of informational "circulation." Circulatory on one level, yes, but also transformational and defined by associative seepage between and among media, pages, spaces, and people. In the next chapter, this porous model of relation between media interaction and social space is exemplified by the first original runaway hit game in the United States, an unassuming enough "family" game called *Dr. Busby*. Here the boundaries between media forms and social practice were at their most permeable, as a game about community relations transformed into both a *book* and a *game about books* that helped entangle books and their authors with feelings of communal belonging.

CHAPTER 5

The Net Work of Not Work

The process of making character is something like making a cable. First, there are the little fine fibres of hemp; a great mass of these, twisted together, become yarn; several yarns make a strand; three strands make a rope; and three ropes make a small cable. A fibre of hemp is a very small and weak affair; but twist enough of them together, and they will hold the largest ship in the gale. So the little trifling acts and habits of the child seem very insignificant; but, by-and-by, when they are spun into character, they will become as strong as cables.

—William Simonds, *Whistler* (1856)

We would invite attention to the advertisement for a Tea Party at Hamilton Hall, this evening. It is to be under the management of an association of young Ladies, and we cannot hesitate to assure all who may be disposed to attend that they will find ample arrangements for passing an exceedingly pleasant evening. The Salem Ladies always do such things well.

—*Salem Register*, 26 December 1844

Mention is made of her here for the same reason that the buccaneers will likewise receive record; because, like them, by long cruising among the isles, tortoise-hunting upon their shores, and generally exploring them; for these and other reasons, the Essex is peculiarly associated with the Encantadas.

—Herman Melville, "The Encantadas, or Enchanted Isles" (1854)

There must have been a bit of a crisis on Essex Street. Sometime in mid- to late 1844—while the nation was in the midst of the contentious political cycle that would elect James K. Polk, while the U.S.S. *United States* was making the final maneuvers of its trip back to New England with a twenty-five-year-old Herman Melville in tow, while Sophia and Nathaniel Hawthorne were settling into their second year of marriage at the Old Manse, and while P. T. Barnum was in the early days of his European tour with Tom Thumb—the bookselling interest of William and Stephen Bradshaw Ives was eagerly anticipating a sure-fire best seller for the year-end gift-giving season. In the previous year, the Ives brothers had stumbled into a surprise hit that had dramatically changed their path as publishers—not a book at all, not the sort of thing they would usually do, but, against all common sense, a *pictorial card game* that outsold their modest initial print run of five hundred copies four times over in its first three months.[1] This card game, invented by a thirty-four-year-old Salem woman affectionately (if somewhat patronizingly to modern ears) remembered as "Miss Annie Abbot," was called *The Improved and Illustrated Game of Dr. Busby* (1843), and though neither Abbot nor the Ives brothers could know it, it would remain a part of the American gaming vernacular for the next century.[2] Their version alone—and there would be many imitators by the latter quarter of the nineteenth century—sold more than one hundred fifty thousand copies during the same period when the brothers' sometimes associate, sometimes competitor John Punchard Jewett was stunning the country by selling roughly three hundred thousand copies of Harriet Beecher Stowe's *Uncle Tom's Cabin*.[3]

If a game could sell this well, the Ives brothers must have reasoned in early 1844, why not a book drawn directly from its now well-known characters? "Messrs Ives, having a set of wood engravings of the personages in 'Dr. Busby,' employed the author of the game to write a story thereto," they write in the preface of Abbot's novelization. "It was presumed that no one was so well able to satisfy the curiosity of the juvenile public about Dr. B. and his neighbors."[4] Anne Wales Abbot, as she would do for the rest of a prolific career in game making, authorship, and editorial work, delivered. The book, expanding on the world of families and objects in *Dr. Busby*, spooled out into a world of narrative associations called *Dr. Busby and His Neighbors* (1844). But it wasn't exactly what William and Stephen had expected. When Abbot's handwritten pages arrived at their Essex Street office, they were a source of considerable tribulation: "The manuscript was sent off in haste, without any caption to the chapters, in consequence of which neglect, the blank spaces between were disregarded, and the proofs not passing under the eye of the author, who was rambling about the country, the mistake passes uncorrected."[5] Perhaps with more time, the publishers and author could have scrambled to make such corrections. It's fairly certain that Abbot did not intend her book to lack chapters or standard paragraph breaks. She was a fastidious writer on the whole, undoubtedly concerned with putting her best foot forward. But Stephen and William couldn't, or wouldn't, wait.

Disjointed, meandering, and downright *meta* in its opening pages, Abbot's novel eventually coalesces around a standard morality tale of a bad boy gone good, the sort of story that would set the stage for William Simonds's "Aimwell Books"—also endeavors in genre mixing, metanarration, and gameplay—in the decade to come. Reviewers in Salem and Worcester were charitable, looking past the jarring style, to note Abbot's "keen perception of character."[6] Yet, the anxieties that faced the Ives brothers in late 1844—as they committed the manuscript to print in the absence of their "rambling" author—are laid bare in a bracing preface:

> Whoever may chance to take up this book, ought to have fair warning of certain shocks he will meet with, from an abrupt transition of subject. Should he get out of patience and toss the book aside as a clumsy production, we cannot blame him. It is unjustifiable and disrespectful for an author thus to take an unsuspicious reader off his feet, and set him down in a new place, where he stares about him, wondering where, in the name of common sense, he may be. Should he read this preface, we trust our contrite apology will induce him to pass over these surprises, and other errors, in a forgiving spirit. . . . No scribbler impressed with a proper idea of the responsibility of authorship, considers his work done when he has covered the prescribed number of sheets.[7]

Though a "forgiving spirit" may be a precondition for enjoying Abbot's book, it is not entirely clear that the "certain shocks" the preface attributes to the work aren't, in some manner, the best way to represent Abbot's hit game in novelistic form, evoking the persistent though patiently normalized transitions and removals that were native to its playing. This was a book—like a movie about *Angry Birds* or a television show about the travails of Donkey Kong and his son—that did not need to exist. But like the game upon which it was based, the novel *Dr. Busby and His Neighbors* seems predicated on sharing, collecting, and developing story spaces simply "because you asked" and because the pictorial content invites it. Echoed by a broad swath of games and mixed media "panoramas" that were made in the waning days of Milton Bradley's direct stewardship of his company, the transmedia world of Abbot's *Dr. Busby* was an operational invitation to ramble, to waste time, and to revel in the communally "productive" qualities of not working. It seemed perfectly suited to the kind of pleasant ambling socialization that Bradley had observed while selling paper to the "mill girls" of Lowell. Indeed, *Dr. Busby* likely played a role in Bradley's childhood interest in games. In 1886 he fondly recalls, "This game will be remembered by many of the parents of the present day as among the earliest ever learned and possibly played at first on the sly, fearful of a reprimand should the report reach headquarters that they were 'playing cards.'"[8] Playing "on the sly" suggests a layering of worlds, overlapping modes of everyday theatricality with indirect dispositional effects akin to those discussed in the previous chapter, but in a less targeted, more multivocal way. This diffusive layering led to social performances one might justifiably dub "clumsy production[s]"—but something was produced all the same.

In what follows, I unpack the "clumsy" qualities of Abbot's early and all-but-forgotten work with Dr. Busby and his associates—the dislocations and perspectival breakages, the hard-and-fast closures based on time and not on plot fulfillment, the story-less and story-full ekphrastic magnetism of pictures—in order to understand the kinds of sidelong networks that were being produced not just within gameplay but also as potentials around gameplay. Patrick Jagoda, drawing on Susan Stewart, has recently argued that "networks reconstellate our ways of communicating, imagining, relating, and becoming—the forms of perpetual and everyday change that Stewart describes as 'the *poesis*, or creativity, of ordinary things.'"[9] Clearly, the reverse is also true: things like games that encourage certain structured ways of "communicating, imagining, relating, and becoming" also reconstellate our notion of what networks are. To adjust this notion of meaningful interconnection is, as a result, to adjust what counts as socialization, and what certain types of association *do* and *produce*. It is, in other words, to change the *net work* of a particular arrangement of people, things, and actions. And perhaps the analytical staging of gameplay practice as a method of sociological capture, a "network" yielded by various interlacings of characterological "hemp" and operational "knots" (or nots), isn't so far from what game makers of the period saw as a key potential of ludic media experimentation. We might recall that even the 1872 U.S. Patent Office classification puts games (uncannily) in the same category as "Traps and Nets."[10]

Slantwise Moves ends with a look back, to *Dr. Busby* and its immediate descendant *Authors* (1861), two games that themselves set the stage for Milton Bradley's reification of the game industry. In fact, alongside *The Checkered Game of Life* and croquet, Bradley's other patented best seller was a popular evolution of *Authors* called *Authors Improved*—which boasted a tractable lineage from the unruly rehearsals of material and method in the antebellum era to the comparatively more stable and canonical mediascape of the Gilded Age. In the first two-thirds of the nineteenth century, the divisions between media forms were messy enough that books and games often shared meaningful resonances that I have touched on in previous chapters. This messiness and reciprocity is given further contour below, as I examine the transmedia emphases of Abbot's early work and its indirect culmination in a game of literary canonicity. As we've seen, the vitality and cultural power of games and puzzles—as light and adaptable material media forms—lay in their amorphousness, their protean mutability, and in the pleasurable challenges they posed to the ideas of form that often dictated (though did not entirely define) literary taste. Yet the last quarter of the nineteenth century saw a massive influx of games that increasingly ruled out this sense of medial reciprocity, in favor of recognizable genre divisions and a subordinate relationship of the ludic to the literary. This feel of a nearly ontological divide was solid enough that points of contact had to be aggressively and artistically thematized in early twentieth-century literary experiments like those of the Oulipo—as if gameplay practices were a kind of outsider art in relation to the culture of books.

As a threshold figure, Bradley's *The Game of Bamboozle, Or the Enchanted Isle* (1872) serves as the landing point of our medial meditations, offering a moment to look in two directions at once. It allows us to sketch the trajectory of the industry in the closing moments of a baroque emergence, the end of a thirty-year era of strikingly experimental momentum, before tidy generic expectations cemented ideas of what games were, what childhood was, and what distinguished games from other paper media like literary books. I began this book with the provocation that games are experiments in genre. The book concludes in a moment when that experimentation itself was giving way to market pressures that imposed certain definitional assumptions that I have resisted—fixations on numerical competition and accounting, on recognizable ready-made mechanisms and types, and on novel content rather than novel operation. If *The Checkered Game of Life* intervened as both a *model for* and *model of* a certain type of aspirational and inspirational agency—implicitly

precoded as "manhood," defined by judgment and frenetic choice making—
and if this intervention was in part a way of demonstrating the straightforward pedagogical utility of games in an environment that tended to imagine
them as sinful at worst or "childish" and "feminine" at best, then Bradley's
1872 *Bamboozle* plays, by contrast, like a complicated critique of the game industry, an embrace of earlier "unproductive" or "noninstructive" game values
like those of *Dr. Busby*.

To effectively trace where commercial home entertainment media was
going in the early 1870s, it's not enough to see the market forces of this period
in isolation. We must also have a sense of memory for where it had been, for
what Bradley may have thought the industry stood to lose as it found a permanent place at the table. The historical "why" of this chapter is somewhat
simple. I close chronologically by fleshing out the games on either end of
those that have formed our primary objects of scrutiny: the beginning of mass
market games with *Dr. Busby* in the 1840s and the emergence of the rationalized industry represented by the McLoughlin Brothers, Parker Brothers, and
the post–Bradley Milton Bradley Company in the 1880s and 1890s. But the
critical why of this chapter is a bit more complicated, reaching at the why of
gaming more broadly—at the value of pastimes in the literal sense of things
that "pass the time" and create attachments but that are assertively *not work*.
In Anne Abbot's case this was a function of socionarrative exchange—the potentials for differing stories offered by pictorial movement and the promise of
shared time, stolen time, time without purpose—demand, flux, and memory
were the name of the game. Sharing this sensibility, *Bamboozle* returns to the
idea of *not* deciding in procedurally encoded ways, lingering in pictorial sea
chambers with mermaid figures, whales, and serpents. Both Abbot and Bradley invest in an aesthetic of linger that is neither unproductive nor the frenzied
"productivity" of *The Checkered Game of Life*'s self-generation engine. Instead,
these games emphasize a certain laxity of movement, producing operational
story spaces that enable time without purpose to find its reservoirs.

Even Their Silence Had a Language: Social
Nots and Ambiguous Entanglements

When Anne Abbot first brought the prototype of *Dr. Busby* to Stephen Ives,
he was uninterested. Charles E. Trow, a Massachusetts congressman whose
memoir regarding Ives's "Old Corner Bookstore" forms one of the only extant

narratives, recalls, "He gave her no encouragement, so she went to Boston and saw some of the publishers there,—possibly Crocker & Brewster, William D. Ticknor, Gould & Lincoln, and others,—but met with no success."[11] Milton Bradley adds, "Although the price asked was very low, there was no recognized demand for such merchandise and the manuscript was declined."[12] Facing a chorus of indifference, Abbot was unflappable. She returned to Salem and finally persuaded Ives to purchase the game "at a nominal price" for a small run beginning distribution during the somewhat nonstrategic season of late winter—after the holidays, but before the rainy days and sunny leisure of spring and summer.[13] The game was to be called *The Improved and Illustrated Game of Dr. Busby*, the "improvements" likely referring to its marbled pasteboard container and overall standardization from the prototype Abbot had been shopping around. But these improvements came with logistical problems: "[As] printing had to be done in Boston, there was considerable delay before the Salem end came to time, and many a day good-natured expressman Adrian Low had to wait patiently at the store for the plethoric packages which were sent to Boston, New York and Philadelphia."[14] Offering slivered filaments of insight into the particular sensation created by the game, Ives made sales volume an explicit part of his company's marketing strategy, as numbers were rigorously tracked in consecutive ads: in June 1843, "this most beautiful and popular game, has been published short of three months, and nearly two thousand copies have been sold"; by fall 1844, "upwards of fifteen thousand have been sold in the last eighteen months"; while the Christmas-adjacent ads in the *Salem Register* saw another bump to "upwards of sixteen thousand" by year's end.[15] This may not have been the skyrocketing success of Bradley's *Checkered Game of Life*, but it was impressive nevertheless for a piece of media that was concurrently revealing and inventing its own market. By way of comparison, *The Mansion of Happiness* (1843), a game the Ives brothers rapidly localized from its English source material (seemingly to expand their repertoire and increase awareness of their newfound specialization), had sold "between four and five thousand" copies after its first year.[16]

Dr. Busby's peculiar success unfolded within a network of driven, professionally minded women along the urbanizing northeastern region of Massachusetts. Alongside newspaper ads for the game and reviews for Abbot's book, these women were promoting meet-ups among neighbors that were often explicitly political (in favor, for example, of temperance or abolition). But they were sometimes less direct, conceivably using games as cover for a more nebulous and evolving set of collective interests and intimacies: "[You will find] ample arrangements for passing an exceedingly pleasant evening," as one ad put it. "The Salem Ladies always do such things well."[17] Responding to these networks of shared investment, Ives also copyrighted and began publishing *Characteristics of Distinguished Persons, male and female* (1843), a historical memory game invented by Roxbury's Louisa C. Tuthill (listed only as "A Lady" on the box).[18] The popularity of both games opened the door for others, like Eliza W. Ward, a Salem teacher who devised the "game of letters" that would come to be known variously as *Logomachy* or *Anagrams*.[19] And the Ives catalog in general was given many positive reviews by a writer they glowingly referred to as "the talented editress" of the *Boston Evening Transcript*—Cornelia Wells Walter, the first female editor of a major U.S. newspaper.[20] If nothing else, *Dr. Busby* was an indication of an especially vital community of women creating innovative and marketable media, despite the fact that visibility and success often depended on male endorsement.[21] This creative energy was catalyzed by a comparatively democratized prototyping process for game design, facilitated by low-cost materials that could be readily found in domestic spaces. *Dr. Busby* was the signal of both social and material innovations—a strategic seizing of the state of the available—and the neighborhood of people and things from which it emerged was echoed by the associational continuum of the game itself.

Yet for all the things *Dr. Busby* represented, it was also plain to see what it was *not*: it was not a pack of standard playing cards (Figure 13). This was a significant part of its genius. With only twenty cards, labeled neither by numbers nor by text, the game was arranged by colors along the border edges that corresponded to different pictorially represented families. This meant that the typical numerical combinations that characterized games like brag, whist, or cribbage could not be approximated with the deck (for example, straights and additive target numbers). Instead, the colorful and gesturally interesting cards required players to forge an intimate familiarity with different "family" members and objects associated with each family's group: in the blue set, a giant eye ("ONE EYE") accompanies a piano-playing "WIFE," a rough-housing "SON" in the midst of a fight with another boy, and a white-gloved, ink-shaded "SERVANT" of "MR. NINNY-COME-TWITCH," the head of the family. The coyly postured "DOLL the dairy-maid" leads the red-edged cards, clustered with "her FATHER, BROTHER, SERVANT, and PAN of MILK." In the yellow group, "SPADE the Gardener" occupies a kind of visual joke, with the "spade" of traditional cards converted into a literal garden implement that sits alongside the gardener's "WIFE, SON, [and] SERVANT." Finally, the titular Dr. Busby appears on the brown-edged

Figure 13. *The Improved and Illustrated Game of Dr. Busby*. Salem: W. & S. B. Ives, 1843. Courtesy of American Antiquarian Society.

cards, standing in front of a medicinal storefront with a family that includes "his WIFE, SON, SERVANT, and Doll the dairy-maid's black-eyed LOVER."[22]

Though the game could be played—and was likely developed with—a subset of standard playing cards (10 through king, with the aces added), the operation could not be easily reversed, as the above list makes clear. Numbers and sequential hierarchies among cards are obliterated in favor of lateral imagistic association—a design element appreciated by early reviewers, who consistently applauded the cards' "spirited and beautiful" artwork.[23] Pushing the player into a richly populated story space, the visual and relational disruptions of the cards also served to make *Dr. Busby* a more challenging game of memory and classification than it might have been otherwise. Since you must remember *all of the cards*, methodically calling them from the hands of your opponents to win, an initial memorization of pictures and names is central to basic gameplay: "Any one of the players may begin the game by calling upon his right-hand neighbor for any card which he has not in his own hand. If his neighbor has the card he calls for, he must give it up to him. He may then call for another, and go on till he calls for one which his neighbor has not in his hand. . . . When a player has called every card from the hand of his right-hand neighbor, thus putting him out of the game, he may continue to call from the next on the right hand. At the close of the Game, the victor will have all the four families united in his hand."[24] Even beyond the mysteries of the initial deal, the deck is stacked against players: if they forget what a card looks like, who currently has it, or what it's called, they are likely to fail. Any successful turn that doesn't result in total victory—which is to say *most* turns— prompts a migration of cards, a flux of "neighbors" (the characters represented) among "neighbors" (the term conspicuously used for players) that must be attentively tracked and enunciated. The instructions warn, "The game is made longer and more complicated by every failure of memory." But these "failures" were rendered nearly certain, especially in early play sessions, as each family had a slightly different configuration of associated people and things. As a result, players searching for a mnemonic aid could not assume a categorical commonality in each five-card grouping. For instance, though most families were defined by their father's names—Busby, Ninny-come-twich, and Spade—Doll the milkmaid's family is headed by Doll. One must remember that her father, who is nameless except by relation, must be called for separately. As an added twist, Doll's family, rather than having a "son" like the rest, instead has a brother, again defined by his relation to Doll. All of the families have "servants" (two white men, one white woman, and a black man—more on the racial dynamics of the game in a moment), but only some groupings have objects associated with them. So, while Doll's family is rounded out by a pan of milk (sipped at by a tiny cat) and the gardener's family by a spade (sitting silently against a garden wall), Dr. Busby's family is instead completed by a man defined in relation to a *different* family, that is, Doll's lover.

This is simply to say that the names and relations could be easy to forget. This challenge is made materially evident by the fact that some players took the time to short-circuit the difficulty by transcribing the quick descriptions from the back of the box onto the cards themselves.[25] Later editions of the game by different publishers would add the names to the cards, but the lack of text in the first Ives edition seems to align with a preoccupation in Abbot's design philosophy with memory and association via pictorial evidence. It's also possible that the lack of text was an inadvertent omission, since Abbot's immediate follow-up, *Master Rodbury* (1844), would add typeface text to the base of the images, clarifying the relation of character and name in a vastly more complex game. Whether intentional or not, the challenges of pure pictorialism and verbal recall had a decided impact on people's pleasure in the amusement: two Boston-area newspapers lingered on the "healthy" and "capital exercise" the game offered "for the memory," while the *New York Commercial Advertiser* admired the fact that the cards were "a little gallery of pictures, very neatly executed, and affording amusement *per se*, without reference to the game of which it is the instrument."[26] The lack of text invited a broader latitude of potential use—the cards could serve as tiny paper dolls, for instance—while also conditioning players to be both synesthetically and gesturally "attentive" during gameplay.[27]

To obtain Doll's father, for example, you need first to remember that he is *not* "Mr. Doll" (depending on the strictness of the game), but you might also recollect that, in Doll's family, the patriarch is in a seated position with a pipe, by contrast with every other male character (the others, without exception, are in standing positions). If you had trouble placing the members of the family at first, the particulars of his bodily posture might lead you there, sticking in your mind because of this singular distinction of "attitude" (to think back to Michael Phelan's term for the coincidence of bodily arrangement and temperamental disposition). Similarly, when one "pictures" the Ninny-come-twitch family, it could be easy to confuse the father and the servant, as they are dressed nearly alike, the only differences being the darker complexion of the servant and the fact that the father has a dog next to him. In Abbot's *Dr. Busby*, race and gender become subtle shorthands for social placement, but they do not decide the issue in and of themselves. Rather they are registered as one of a number of relational details that plot a given character within the scope of a given family in the community of "neighbors." Moreover, though all families have servants—planting the local relations of the game in a specifically classed white northeastern milieu—and though the border color would cue you into the cards that you needed, it could be difficult to know, when glancing at your hand, whether Spade's servant was the man with the fruit in front of his face or the man hoeing the garden. Time would create habits of mind and familiarity among players, and it would seem that this familiarity was as deeply caught up in the *connections* that located a person as it was in the *distinctions* that could tell you who they were not.

Dr. Busby was, on one level, a functional model of social memory and categorization. Note the basic movements inherent to the game: see certain people, see where they go, call them over, know who they are, know whom they belong with, and remember them through their associated objects and gestures. "Acquaintance" could be seen as a pivot term here between rote memorization and a more personal form of "getting to know," which was seized on by at least one reviewer: "Dr. Busby and his eccentric family, cannot fail of affording a fund of amusement for all that become acquainted with them."[28] In parallel to this, the game was also a demonstration of the ways that waiting, recitation, and leisurely intimacy could productively entangle people, pictures, and utterances—converting amusement into a machine and platform for sighting and citing details in low-stakes social exchanges. With a number of recognizable community tokens in play, certain types of discussion might be subject to implicit coding, just as was undoubtedly the case with the conversation cards mentioned at the opening of this book.[29] A double discourse creates both openings and alibis: calling for the "lover" could prompt either conversation or raised eyebrows; calling for the "doctor" could be an invitation to discuss another player's health; calling for the "spade" could perhaps be a slightly naughty reference to the card games that this, *assuredly*, was not. Put differently, you might have a conversation while playing cribbage, but it was a conversation that you would have to take full responsibility for. The content of Abbot's game, by contrast, provides social cover. In the language of the previous chapter, *Dr. Busby* offers cues that both pictorially and algorithmically scope a territory for external targets. It was appropriate in this context that the single body part isolated by the game would be Mr. Ninnycome-twich's giant staring eye ("ONE-EYE"). Players stare at the cards and at each other, and the cards stare back. Though the graphic elements were not entirely necessary to the operative gameplay, there is not an extant version of *Dr. Busby* that doesn't have pictures. The "little gallery" of cards encouraged a kind of storyboarding in the off-moments of gameplay that Abbot and Ives saw opportunity in as the Christmas season approached in 1844. This time, and for all of her productions in the aftermath of *Dr. Busby's* success, Abbot herself would secure the copyright.

The notion of a shared world, populated by the varied actors at play in the game of *Dr. Busby*, was at the heart of Abbot's attempt to render these social movements as story sequences in the book *Dr. Busby and His Neighbors*. Expanding the significance of gameplay through a reciprocally inflected "outside show" (to employ Barnum's term), Abbot's novel revels in the notion that the players and the characters on the cards could slip into and out of different narrative associations with each other—players imagining themselves as characters, and the characters, strangely, imagining themselves as both game pieces and parts of the same community as the players. Doll and her Lover discuss this extranarrative slippage early in the book:

> "Did you hear that some wag has put out a game, called Dr. Busby, with pictures, real likenesses of you and myself and Harry besides, and your father, pipe and all, &c."
>
> "An impudent, good for nothing sight!" exclaimed Doll, half laughing, half pouting. "I hope I have my silk gown on, and my white bonnet."
>
> "Not you! There you are carrying the milk-pail, with bare arms, not half so round and white as yours are; you are looking roguishly over your shoulder, just as—"
>
> "As I look when I have said something on purpose to tease you."
>
> "Well, I tell you he has made your hair all flying in tangles!"[30]

Making a date to play "Fox and Geese" later in the night, Doll and her Lover—appropriately enough given their boundary-breaking relationship across the game's operative family structure—disrupt the boundary between the functional "neighbor callings" of gameplay and the friendly and imaginative house calls that were the site of its playing. The novel emphasizes an exchange between the associations of gameplay and the associations of the illustrated world suggested by the deck, arranging features (both people and things) from *Dr. Busby* and Abbot's immediate follow-up, *Master Rodbury*, upon a cooperative stage.[31] Characters like Spade the gardener and Ninny-come-twich's son, Quarrelsome Bob, are introduced with an assumed familiarity: his "pugnacious propensities, as well as his odd and somewhat uncouth name" are something with which "the reader is not unacquainted."[32] And Abbot winks at her audience's pictorial knowledge by claiming that the young Dr. Busby's son "will sit for hours like an image."[33]

Layering expansive characterological paratexts, oblique reference to mechanics, and gestures toward materials, Abbot performs the game of *Dr. Busby* as a rich territory for story making that could go beyond what was possible in a game with traditional cards—rendering "family gathering" as both an operative mechanism and a literary opportunity. The players sitting "around a table" (as suggested by the instructions of the game) are echoed in the novel by clever moments that use this familiar arrangement to stage other forms of narrative drama. At one point an informal bit of social mediation that is centered on Doll's brother, Harry, configures the principals as they might be in a standard game: "Around a table at one end sat the general committee, with a great arm-chair for the chair-man and pen and ink for the clerk. On one side all those who felt aggrieved by Harry's conduct . . . had ranged themselves in solemn rows across the room, while Spade, the gardener, and his son . . . drew up in an equally imposing battalion, opposite to them. . . . Leaning on the chimney piece, stood Mr. Ninicumtwich. . . . When Harry came in, and bowed round to this formidable array of friends and foes, he was so confused that he could hardly distinguish an individual."[34] With characters facing each other—drawn up, aligned in rows, and leaned against furniture—readers could recognize themselves in the narrative scene differently than through a more straightforward psychological identification. Harry's worry about being able to "distinguish an individual," for instance, reads differently in a transmedia context operatively concerned with parsing out and locating individual cards. Conditioned by performative memories that were spatial, active, graphic, and interpersonal, the associational scope of a reader's imaginary world was coupled to familiarities that outstripped standard bibliographic genre expectations of plot or character. Because of this, as in the scene above, the multiplying clusters of characters in various scenes could participate in a more immediately gestural evocation of the room layout involved in standard gameplay, which required clusters of interaction rather than two-person intrigues: without at least four players, *Dr. Busby* would hardly function, since the locations of all cards would be too easily tracked from the onset, with little to no mystery in the deal. Thus a moderately large room of players move a large community of characters from place to place. In this sense it feels appropriate that, as we might recall from the apologetic preface, the book also deigns to "take an unsuspicious reader off his feet, and set him down in a new place, where he stares about him, wondering where, in the name of common sense, he may be."[35] In this universe, readers and cards weren't so different after all.[36]

Though the term "interplay" is typically used to define the relationships among players, rules, and materials, here it might do well to invoke a secondary notion: "interplay" as *what happens between plays* (just as an "interstate" is a pathway between states). While an unduly narrow critical scope might see these interplays as dislocations from the official algorithmic or spatial boundaries of gameplay, they were also the places where games did considerable work to stage new affinities and new acquaintances by weaving together what Abbot calls "fibres of association and affection."[37] Indeed, if character was represented as a compound but regularized length of rope—the twisted "yarns" referenced in the opening of this chapter—then forms of interpersonal connection, immersion, and fixation often developed this figural space into a language of "knots" (recall Hawthorne's "Knot of Dreamers" in *Blithedale*). And though Abbot represents gameplay only indirectly in her novel, William Simonds, writing shortly after, in an installment of his Aimwell series, gives us some of idea of the messy entanglements that could arise:

> A variety of games and amusements were resorted to, and were entered into with much spirit. Sometimes all the company were engaged in one play. At other times, they would scatter into a number of little groups, each diverting itself in its own way. Two or three of the more sedate ones might be seen in a corner of the room absorbed in the examination of some curious object or illustrated book. In another corner, perhaps, a mischievous boy is about to play off a joke upon an unsuspecting little fellow, who is quietly watching the progress of a game in which he has become interested. Another is relating a laughable story, or propounding a puzzling charade, to a *knot* of listeners; and another, still, is very complacently "paying a forfeit" which she has just incurred.[38]

Producing affective "knots" even among more adult players, *Dr. Busby* was an opportunity to create specific intimate arrangements as powerful visual entanglements of stories, moves, and bodily proximities.[39] This was encouraged by the fact that it had no central board, which meant it could be played while on the move, or by a group standing off in the corner at a party (Figure 14). Moreover, the game lacked a regularized timing between or within turns. A single round of *Dr. Busby* could be incredibly elastic, as it had no discrete temporal endpoint, with players continuing to call for neighbors until they won the game or miscalled a card. With this loose turn mechanism, you might even walk away for a bit with cards in your pocket, returning to the game in a locale different from that in which it was begun.[40]

The medial sensibility of "waiting with" in games of this sort compels players to find associative targets beyond whatever has defined "action" or "active play" up to that point in the activity—it strategically breaks the tool of rational game time (fairness with regard to the number of turns and the corresponding time of each turn) to encourage stretchy interplays of memory and paratextual storytelling. The interplays of *Dr. Busby* involve patiently

Figure 14. From Caroline Smith, *Popular Pastimes for Field and Fireside, or Amusements for Young and Old*. Springfield: Milton Bradley & Co., 1867. Courtesy of American Antiquarian Society.

watching and remembering names and things (that is, the specific content of cards one will call for), as well as a flux of personal emplacements for those names and things (Who has that card right now? What should I call for from the person next to me at the next turn?). On the one hand, this continual shifting of ready-made actors into differing arrangements highlights a content-oriented theme of characterological and social mobility with regard to the fictional characters on the cards. On the other hand, this movement of cards also conditions close *listening to* and *awareness of* the nonfictional persons filling the room. Abbot figures this in a number of ways in her novelization, as in moments when gesture is as important as dialogue: "Doll exchanged many a droll smile with Harry. . . . But even their silence had a language."[41] This kind of coded communication extended to a general sense of domestic drama, in that the exchanges of gameplay were sometimes frowned upon by more conservative actors circulating at the periphery. Here, it's important to remember Bradley's notion, referred to earlier, that this game was often played "on the sly, fearful of a reprimand."[42] To play on the sly was to be constantly aware of the interplay we are pursuing, with play itself situated by fears that the cards would be captured by someone other than the players. This fear would have existed in an ironic and layered relationship to the "good feeling[s]" one Charleston reviewer acknowledged that the game produced "through a whole company."[43] If some members of that "company" were critical or suspicious of game playing, then these good feelings would be under persistent threat of attack (however low the stakes might be). Ironically, as time went on, the game itself would be employed in an unspoken effort to reinforce white middle-class feelings about community insiders and outsiders.

Sensible Associations

In the years that followed, *Dr. Busby* became a pervasive standard produced by any number of different companies. Moving away from the communal localizations of Abbot's Massachusetts, the game's training function was obliquely fused with more indexical memories that could be quickly linked to ways of speaking about and picturing racial and social stereotypes—a dark side of play that grew especially vicious by the last quarter of the nineteenth century. Tracking almost along the same chronological vectors that saw *Uncle Tom's Cabin* shift from an abolitionist icon of racial sympathy to later re-stagings that reinforced explicitly racist imagery, subsequent renditions of *Dr. Busby* cribbed the mechanism and pictorialism of the game but abandoned Abbot's original arrangement of characters to deploy a set of animalistic and racist tropes: a newly added "Cod" family of fishmongers as grotesquely bug-eyed fish; a "Butcher" family similarly rendered as cows; and the African American family of "Dr. Busby's Coachman," now defined by the frustratingly familiar racial caricatures of watermelons and bright red lips. In these iterations, the central Busby family is singularly tasked with representing the entirety of a "normal" white middle class, while farmers, servants, and other blue-collar laborers recede into a bestial visual domain of difference.[44] Gone are signs of class critique like rich Ninny-come-twich's inappropriately pugilistic son, object associations like the pan of milk or spade, or crossover characters linking families like "Doll's Black-eyed Lover." The memory functions of the revised, reprinted, and reimagined game oriented neighborhood interactions via intensely projected differences centered on the faces and bodies of persons, both encouraging certain habits of associative recall and ensuring that those memories were held in starkly delimited lines, sutured to feelings of "comical" excess and physical disgust. Each family now represented a different biosocial world—not actors in a shared space that might share the pages of a narrative, however disjointed. By contrast, for Abbot in 1843, the distinctions of race or face were employed to a more muted effect, one in a series of differences, rather than the central organizing code of the Busby universe.

Through the success of Abbot's game, the stage had been set for a range of other similar amusements, from direct rip-offs with names like *Dr. Fuzby* and *Old Dr. Busby*, to adaptations like *Uncle Tom's Cabin* and *The Lamplighter* that used the family-matching mechanism as a way to suggest the ruptures and reconciliations of the novels from which their characters were drawn (Figure 15). Given its strong associations with paratextual storytelling—despite this aspect not being narrated explicitly by its instructions—it's not exactly shocking that Abbot's game found itself wrapped up in literary affairs. *Dr. Busby* revealed the potential for games to be associational story-making mechanisms on top of anything else that they might train or reflect—a potential further underlined by Abbot's novelization. That these "literary" alliances were, in fact, *recognized* as belonging within the scope of American literary culture may help to explain the appearance of a genetically related game that directly represented prominent icons from this culture. While in subsequent cases the associational narratives of *Dr. Busby* were harnessed to forms of racial "storytelling" and sighting, the most successful follow-up to Abbot's game used the situationally interlocking mechanisms of card movement and associative

Figure 15. *Game of Uncle Tom and Little Eva*. Providence: V. S. W. Parkhurst, ca. 1852–1861. Courtesy of American Antiquarian Society.

narration to both produce and cite a cultured authorial canon. In *The Game of Authors* (1861), these indexical elements of group association fused author's names to a selective list of their respective works. The "family heads" conceit of *Dr. Busby* was revised and expanded to reflect respected authors, with "families" constituted by a range of popular publications (Figure 16). As *Authors* was the best-selling conceptually literary game of its time, it is useful to linger for a moment on it as a critical link between the antebellum period of commercial American game design (and literary culture) and the postbellum industry defined by competition between Milton Bradley and the McLoughlin Brothers (discussed further below).

Authors bore many genetic debts to *Dr. Busby*, both operationally and in terms of the labor networks that led to its production. Sometime in early 1861,

Figure 16. *The Game of Authors*. Salem: G. M. Whipple & A. A. Smith, 1861.
Courtesy of American Antiquarian Society.

"a young man" representing "a coterie of bright young ladies" in Salem brought A. Augustus Smith the idea (or prototype) for an educational amusement that matched authors to their works.[45] Smith had been a junior partner at the Ives company in the heyday of *Dr. Busby*, but by the 1860s this company was no longer interested in game innovation, primarily producing pieces from Stephen and William's back catalog. I suspect that Smith's move down the street, from the Ives's "Old Corner Bookstore" to Henry and George Whipple's game and book shop at 190 Essex Street, was at least partially predicated on the desire to produce and market this *new* game that had recently come to his attention. As one of the first products of the newly formed Whipple & Smith, the bet paid off. *Authors* was even more popular than *Dr. Busby*, attaining, Bradley later notes, "a permanence and an aggregate sale, probably never equaled by any other modern social game."[46] In the years that followed, versions of *Authors* became ubiquitous, some adding pictures, some prefiguring the "expansion packs" of our own gaming age by lingering on subsets of authors, such as the "Queens of Literature," and some including signatures to expand the paratextual authority attributed to the cards.[47]

This was a game that could be readily condoned, even among scrupulous adults, as something not quite as frivolous as other forms of card playing—a way to produce a sort of middle-class conversational cultivation, since "the constant repetition of the names of authors and the association with the names of their works, serves to fix them all in their proper relations in the minds of the players."[48] Indeed, in her own fictional reflection on the social entanglements of gaming in the first part of *Little Women* (1868), Louisa May Alcott places the "sensible game of Authors" among croquet and other story games that Jo March uses to "refresh [the] minds" of her sisters and friends.[49] It was, undoubtedly, a win-win for the industry: widely considered a "sensible game" for its educational content, *Authors*, much like other card games before it, also allowed producers to repurpose widely available materials like cardstock without any other special requirements. Yet even beyond this, the ostensive goal of the game was precisely to remind people of the books and authors that were out there—works being sold nearby, either in the same shop or a few doors down. Just as *Dr. Busby and His Neighbors* used a book to reinforce the media presence of one game (*Dr. Busby*) while introducing another (*Master Rodbury*), by the early 1860s *Authors* could use the market reach of games as a way to enhance the effective reach of books.

This was precisely the moment when Milton Bradley, surfacing from beneath a glut of beardless Lincoln portraits, had seized his own "capital chance" by diving into the production of *The Checkered Game of Life*. With the help of Samuel Bowles and his printing facilities, Bradley soon expanded his catalog by adding a number of thoughtful improvements to existing games that would allow him both to patent and to establish a name for himself as an industry innovator. *Peter Coddle* was given a makeover and rewritten as *Sam Slick* with a set of entirely new cards, and croquet was given standardized rules and a redesigned set of target bridges. *Authors*—achieving considerable notoriety after Whipple & Smith's release—was a safe bet for Bradley's particular brand of operational and material reengineering. As a part of the "New England Series" of games produced by Milton Bradley & Co. during the Civil War, *Authors* could be easily slotted into Bradley's quasi-pedagogical project because of its prestige content and memory-training functions.[50]

Signaling a sidelong relation the original Abbot and Ives *Dr. Busby* through the advertising value of "improvement," *The Game of Authors Improved* was aggressively marketed with reference to shifts in mechanic, material, and cultural novelty. Bradley added numbers and special modifier cards into the mix, quickly patenting this particular change to monopolize the "interest" these rule innovations added to the game. Always looking for ways to capitalize on the material differences between traditional printing and lithography, he advertised his cards as both more fair and more aesthetic as a result of the "perfectly flat surface of stone" used in a manufacturing process that "avoid[ed] the impression on the back, which is objectionable and unavoidable in the ordinary process of type-printing."[51] Finally, he saw to it that there were annual adjustments to the list of authors, increasing the scope of the game's canon-producing potential as well as motivating new purchases: "This annual revision is a feature peculiar to this game, and must recommend it to the public in preference to those stereotyped editions of ten years' standing, and which consequently can be gotten up for one-half what it costs to make the *Improved* edition. Ask for Authors IMPROVED and take no other, as the price is the same for the stereotyped editions."[52] Yet though these changes enabled *Authors Improved* to circulate an evolving series of associated personages and stories, the performative play that had defined at least some part of *Dr. Busby*'s initial success was largely absent. Filled with literary content rather than literary methods, the game was primarily citational rather than creative on the player's end.

The more imaginatively entangled worlds of narrative association and performance in miniature were left, in Bradley's early catalog, primarily to toys rather than games. Pictorialism and storytelling were modes of amusement linked to historical and cultural education in sliding panoramas like *The Myriopticon* and *The Historioscope*, and in more freeform venues like *Kris Kringle's Christmas Tableaux*, where little wands introduce tiny pigs, trains, and carpet-bagging travelers onto a shared stage (Figure 17). In a game like *The Checkered Game of Life*, these looser story-creation mechanisms fade into the background in favor of individually oriented choice making and choice watching. These were the urgent moment-to-moment decisions that iteratively produced what Bradley had called the "exercise of judgment" in an implicit rejection of the more passive mode of game-watching native to a game like *The Mansion of Happiness*. It wasn't until after the Civil War had ended that Bradley would return to the type of easy interplay—snares of storytelling and game movement—that had been critical to the phenomenon of *Dr. Busby*.

Life and *Authors Improved* each sought to seize the cultural authority of education. By contrast, a game called *Bamboozle, Or the Enchanted Isle* sought to reclaim elements that might be ruled out in the effort to imbue gameplay with pedagogy. By the late 1860s and early 1870s, while pursuing pet projects

Figure 17. *The Myriopticon: A Historical Panorama of the Rebellion*. Springfield: Milton Bradley & Co., ca. 1865. Courtesy of American Antiquarian Society.

in color theory, Bradley had begun to see a value in pure amusement and pictorial reverie over and above the pedagogical apparatus attached to a game. "We learned years ago by experience, that which many others seem not yet to have understood," he observes in a telling bit of ad copy, "if too much instruction is loaded on to a Game it will sink, and hence the object aimed at, be lost."[53] With its weird unspoken allusions to Melville's oeuvre—sperm whales, steamboats, vortices, and fishing wrecks evoking the awful deaths of Hunilla's husband and brother in "The Encantadas"—along with its fantastical references to fairy tales and sentimental novels, *Bamboozle* floats through the clinkers of nineteenth-century amusement ephemera to reveal a renewed interest in gameplay as a special entanglement of both operationally enabled movement and spellbinding failures of movement.

Not in the Least Instructive: Drowning in Color

The Game of Bamboozle, Or the Enchanted Isle occupies an odd place in the
Milton Bradley Company's early trade catalogs (Figure 18). The game went
into production in 1872, while Bradley himself was still a regular presence on
the factory grounds, and went through new editions well into the twentieth

Figure 18. *The Game of Bamboozle, Or the Enchanted Isle*. Springfield: Milton Bradley
& Co., 1872. Courtesy of American Antiquarian Society.

century—noted as one of the company's most popular games before abruptly disappearing after 1926.[54] In its inaugural listing, it is given a privileged status on the same page as Bradley's flagship *Checkered Game of Life* and alternatively marketed as "more for the money than any other game ever published," "adapted to youth and adults," and based "on an original principle never before applied to a similar game."[55] These were remarkable claims from a game designer not prone to hyperbole, but the peculiar descriptions didn't cease there. Later catalogs affirm with dry candor that the game is "not in the least instructive" and that it has "no instructional value whatsoever"—nothing if not curious, given that Bradley was a persistent reformer at heart.[56] After all, this was the entrepreneur who spent a good portion of his profits manufacturing and advocating alongside Elizabeth Peabody in support of the U.S. kindergarten movement; who in early advertisements organized games into instructional categories like "Art and Design," "Mechanism," "American History," and "Temperance and Morality"; and who originated some of the basic color theory that standardized paint and crayon colors in elementary schools.[57] To say that *Bamboozle* had no instructional value was to make this game different from almost everything in the company's early catalog. It sounds nearly like a kind of wry in-joke—something designed to cue the suspicion of consumers and historians alike. To the latter, Bradley's conspicuous copy prompts pointed questions about timing: what happened in the early 1870s to make this seasoned game designer decide that a renewed marketing focus on getting "more for the money" and "entirely new principles" was necessary? In a word, McLoughlin happened.

Although Bradley's production base was in Springfield, Massachusetts, a good portion of the company's sales were made in booksellers' and stationers' shops in New York City, where he had a reputation for quality and thoughtful design. Bradley knew how to market his use of new technologies to appeal to the sensibilities of his costumers, as we saw earlier with his promotion of the "perfectly flat" impressions that set his version of *Authors* apart from those of other manufacturers. Color was undoubtedly a part of this as well, as he used hand painting, stenciling, and two-color lithography to direct the eye and establish a distinct style for his games. But by 1870 the New York–based McLoughlin Brothers firm—producing its own card games and children's books since at least the late 1850s—had begun to expand its production facilities, opening one of the largest print factories in the United States and substantially increasing its capacity to create full-color images.[58] Part of this expansion included a flurry of new games, repurposing the work of its teams of book and valentine artists, printers, and chromistes to enchant the market that Milton Bradley had developed for striking new board games.[59] Gone was the flat and often sloppy stencil coloring work of the copper-plate era or the simple, clean color geometry of Bradley's *Checkered Game of Life*, to be replaced with a range of rich and deep colors, realistic shading, and scenic variety (to a degree nearly obscene, given the amount of labor involved). Mega-collections like *Aunt Louisa's Home Games for Little Boys* (1870) were essentially layered grids of numbers over beautifully rendered storybook scenes, creating an impossibly economical compilation of six games for the price of one (especially given the detail and aesthetic quality) (Figure 19).

In terms of their mechanics, these games were hardly new; most were

Figure 19. "Game of Bear Hunt." From *Aunt Louisa's Home Games for Little Boys*.
New York: McLoughlin Brothers, ca. 1870.
Courtesy of American Antiquarian Society.

some version of dice matching or simple racetrack games. But their vibrant playing fields diverted the eyes and immersed children by creating their own contexts of color—interesting or novel rule design be damned. The ur-media for McLoughlin Brothers was the picture book, not the algorithm, and many games in the immediate aftermath of its expansion drew on existing properties to port narrative sensibilities into standard operative formats. In twenty-first-century archives, these boards are often suspiciously well preserved, hinting that players may not have returned to these diversions as frequently as they did to games like *The Checkered Game of Life* and *Dr. Busby*. But that didn't hurt initial sales. John and Edmund McLoughlin capitalized on both the strengths of the new technology and an especially talented stable of artists that included Thomas Nast, Ida Waugh, and Palmer Cox (Figure 20). The magnetizing effect of the chromolithograph in a storefront or under a Christmas tree was real, especially among adults who had grown up in a more single-tone and hand-colored era: the simple light blues, rose reds, and crayon greens of *Dr. Busby*'s world. In high contrast, the McLoughlins offered reasonably priced prints that looked *expensive*.

Figure 20. McLoughlin Sample Show Room. Undated.
Courtesy of American Antiquarian Society.

Bradley was quick to respond. After buying land in 1870, he opened his own new factory, with the space and labor force necessary to fully enter the chromolithographic arms race.[60] You can almost hear his competitive (and perhaps a bit frustrated) tone in a preface to an 1870 Christmas ad: "Few teachers can originate a good Game. The authorship of Games is an art to be acquired only by natural talent with much practice. It requires but little ability and a good Cyclopedia, to get up a Game played like Authors, only having a different name and nomenclature, or to make a set of cards for playing whist or euchre, by discarding hearts and spades, and substituting some other emblems. . . . Our list is not made up of such duplications of old methods under new names."[61] While the full-spectrum depth of *Bamboozle's* chromolithographed board signaled the boom competition for immersive color game experiences, it may also have demonstrated Bradley's attempt to make the compelling appeal of images instructive in its own right. Akin to Melville's metanarrative reflections in *The Confidence-Man* and resistance to narrative progression in "The Encantadas," *Bamboozle* might be seen as a metagame: a snarky reaction to McLoughlin Brothers' beautiful but operationally vacuous game design. At the same time, unwilling to produce a game that was merely pictures on a racetrack, Bradley's particular slant on the Enchanted Isle feels like an experiment in the effective social work that such boring game design could, in fact, accomplish if turned in on itself. It was a return to the dynamics of social "interplay" that had likely played a role in *Dr. Busby's* unexpected popularity.

At eighteen by eighteen inches, *Bamboozle* was one of the biggest game boards Bradley had ever printed. He filled the space with a range of curious and confusing designs, numbers, visual layers, and forking linear paths—as though he were combining all six of the *Aunt Louisa* games mentioned earlier. There's a sea scene with a mermaid evoking Benjamin Sand's fantastical metamorphic picture books, scenes of hardscrabble life and domestic tranquility likely drawing on the popular currency of narratives like Maria Susanna Cummins's *The Lamplighter*, a German-fairytale-like forest scene in a nod to McLoughlin's storybooks of a similar genre, not to mention a wild gesticulating man at the bottom gate, who may or may not be Bamboozle himself (it is never explained). The board is a suggestive pictorial story space—divided into a number of different sectors that nevertheless bleed over into each other. In a rare move for games of the period, it is printed on the diagonal, encouraging a persistent movement of the eyes and head as one tracked along the whirlpool that defined the outer field of play. At nearly two feet wide, it was an image that would surely absorb a small child or group of children. The whirlpool design itself gestures at this interplay of insides and outsides, an iterative zeroing-in and zooming-out that evokes the romantic operations of scopic play discussed in the previous chapter, even as the content suggested similar continuities with the sensibility of Romanticism. But this was a game, not just a picture toy—and its mechanics revealed its true eccentricity.

More than anything else, *Bamboozle* was a fantastical series of operative thresholds players were required to pass over and through, looping from one path to another, backpedaling, interleaving, circling, and tying themselves in knots in order to reach the end goal of Mr. Goodfellow's Castle. Despite its genetic similarity to the typical spiraling race game of the era, the sheer number of paths and misdirections of *Bamboozle* moves it into different territory, as it is a game that encourages you to get lost on its board. Contrary to the design simplicity of *The Checkered Game of Life*—where proper gameplay is easily learned by looking at the record dials (which tell you what rolls do and how many points you need to win) and the board (which directs with helpful manicules)—*Bamboozle* seems intent on confusing, ensnaring, and enchanting with a set of images and nonobvious gameplay elements. If you were a child, you were probably going to need to get your parents involved in explaining the rules.

Examining these rules more closely, one is immediately arrested by a dense cluster of text: a tiny font fills the borders and proliferates with "if" scenarios. These were not the meticulously standardized instructions that were the pride of the Bradley company name in its patented version of croquet; instead, these rules offer far too little and far too much all at once. Too little, in that there is no sense of a story offered for the titular character (a villain). His counterpart, the inviting Mr. Goodfellow who beckons you toward his mansion at the top of the playfield, is equally undeveloped. The mermaid in an upper corner receives similar treatment. In fact, backstory in its entirety is contained within a single prefatory line: "This game illustrates the trials experienced in getting from the old, tumble-down town of Hardscrabble to Goodfellow's palace on the Enchanted Isle." Adding to this relative lack of orientation, a player expecting a linear and methodical approach to the rules is met only with a knotted series of explanations and backtrackings—a textual counterpart to the tangles of the playfield. "Suppose four persons are playing," begins a representatively exhaustive section of the rules,

and one has spun one and entered his man on station 1. Another has spun two and entered at 2, another at 3, and the fourth at 6.

The first player spins [the] dial and moves his man from station
1—on the track leading directly to Bamboozle's gate—as many
points as the numbers spun. In succeeding spins he goes in at Bamboozle's gate, and turning to the right goes over 17, 18, and 19 on to
the lightning rod, and thence to the palace. But if he stops at 17, he
must by the next spin go to the left, as shown by the arrow, and
enter at the left door and through the castle out on to the ladder,
and reach Goodfellow's that way if possible. If he stops at 18, he
must enter the castle at the right door and then out on to the ladder
as before. If 19 is hit, he must by succeeding spins go down to the
lower round of the ladder and climb that, but there is no detention
at the bottom of the ladder.[62]

This is not to say that the sequence described is impenetrable. Obviously any
race game can lead to a series of scenarios based on the roll of the die or the
spin of the teetotem. But a convoluted narration of the play makes things
sound more confusing than is strictly necessary. The rules for *The Checkered
Game of Life* did not explain every possible move one could make at every part
of the board, and yet *Bamboozle* consistently treats the diligent reader to
mind-bending conditionals and reversals: "If you land at 14, and get on to 21,
you take the indirect track to the left; but if you do not hit 21, you keep the
direct track to the palace, unless you hit 22, in which case you must switch off
on to the indirect track to the left."[63] An algorithmic "if" prefaces a near majority of the sentences in these rules, constantly placing focus on different
options, but not in a way that allows for the exercise of judgment (as in *Life*).
Rather, these options are seemingly in the service of a multiplication of outcomes designed to dizzy the young reader—or even the mature one. The grace
of "if . . . then" more often than not becomes the tangled profusion of "if . . .
and . . . then . . . but . . . unless." These obfuscating removes culminate with
the wise reassurance, "If it be remembered that all red spots with white figures
are points of detention where the player must lose as many turns as the numbers indicate, that the white stations are landings, and that the arrows are always to be followed, there will remain but few other points to be remembered,
and they are as follows. . . ." This prefaces four other special rules, one explanation of a rare strategy, and a final declaration: "A player may be bamboozled
several times and then win the game."[64] Indeed, to make use of these rules
requires a high level of patience and a continual reconsultation of the board.
There is a throttling back-and-forth between the text and the numerical

indices of the game track that stalls gameplay and, tellingly in any play-through, prompts conversation. The textual lines cross with the visual, as one tries to keep a ludicrous number of if-thens "in mind" while doubling back between the two sources of operational authority: the board and the instructions. This action of doubling back serves to extend the gameplay and build some degree of "waiting while we figure this out" into the operative dynamics of the game in its playing. "Interplay" rises to the foreground as weird rules overlap with arresting images to provoke discussion, storytelling, and paratactic associations.

Overlapping with this is perhaps one of the more fascinating and innovative game dynamics, the previously mentioned "points of detention." Each of these requires a player to wait for as many turns as are listed in the red circle, in some cases as many as five or six turns. This could be quite a long time if one recalls that up to *six people* might be playing the game at once. The images that accompany many of these spots are interesting in themselves, suggesting that one is "detained" by being caught up in looking at something: an image of a princess, a lighthouse, and a will-o'-the-wisp. In other words, one is detained by the very things that might arrest one's attention about the game board outside of the game proper, that is, when encountering this playfield as a piece of art in the domestic space. This breaking of the "fourth wall" is something that one can imagine would happen frequently as a result of getting snared in a "detention," caught in one of the game's many knots. As players waited for their turn to recommence they would have to become engaged in the patient watching of another person's path, meditative moments, storytelling, and other amiable activities outside the constant thrust of a race game. In *The Checkered Game of Life* only "Prison" forces you to wait, and even then the waiting is only for one turn. This folded in with a certain middle-class spirit of constant movement and upward mobility that regarded stasis as akin to an evil: "There is no such thing as a stationary point in human endeavor," writes a young clerk named Edward Tailer in an 1850 diary entry, "he who is not worse today than he was yesterday is better. And he who is not better is worse."[65] If lives like Tailer's were those Bradley had effectively represented on the playfield of his first successful game, *Bamboozle* seeks something less driving, more aimless, but perhaps just as productive, if in different ways.

Incorporating these structured moments of waiting was arguably Bradley's way of forcing players to fixate on the other thresholds involved in the domestic playing space, again as they had in a game like *Dr. Busby*, and to develop relationships with the other players through these fixations. In this way, waiting and detention—"knot work" holding a person fast in the "gales" of human interaction—are powerful and active inactions that direct attention to a social moment, to the other people and other objects in the room. Much like the chromolithographic process that enabled the production of this game—which composed a multicolor image through a sequenced multitude of overlayed hue inkings—a regular return to the ludic story world of *Bamboozle* trains players to appreciate a snarl of interrelated layers, perspectives, and possible points of creative fusion between these layers. As a game about "knot playing" (through its various entangled pathways) that created moments of "not playing" in between active moments of gameplay, *Bamboozle* highlights the affiliative and social networks that might be produced within a game but outside its formalized borders.

In this way, *Bamboozle* is undoubtedly of a piece with Bradley's other home amusements of the era in its highlighting of layers and *immersion*—not just because winning the game requires players to spiral into the whirlpool that surrounds the board but also in the sense of immersive sociality, inquiry, and storytelling. Perhaps because of his personal experience with invention as a patent draftsman, and perhaps because of his own breadth of knowledge with regard to the history of game design, Bradley, like Abbot and Barnum before him, understood the way that situating documentation and illustration could change the meaning of an object. He had begun to experiment with this in the late 1860s and 1870s, but primarily in the domain of toys rather than through games. In the stencil-colored *Kris Kringle's Christmas Tableaux*, for instance, he encouraged children to develop a layered view of background, multiple foregrounds, stage proscenium, and external story (not to mention the potential for homemade pieces, suggested by the simplicity of the design). He even plays with the simple hierarchy of these layers: the Main Street warehouse where the game was produced shows up as a part of the miniature scene, the toy engulfing the world of the player in a manner analogous to Abbot's ludic engulfment of the narrative world in *Dr. Busby and His Neighbors*. In Bradley's more directly historiographic *Myriopticon* and *Historioscope*, a panorama of views—of scenes and watchers, and watchers of watchers who are themselves waiting and being watched by the parlor circle—are accompanied by a script, but also a set of paratextual materials that were intended to help children market and create buzz around the unveiling of the panorama. All of this creates the sense of an event that is both self-contained and radiating out into its surrounding world, much like Barnum's American Museum culminated in a rooftop city view that framed the outside as a kind of inside.

Bamboozle attempted to code this scopic and pictorial interplay into its operative world, using failures of action to place the emphasis on proximity and association. Because the medium refused to do anything but build that world and *ensure* players inhabited it for a time, players and readers were cued to do the work of producing a social meaning for their activity, to tell their own story within certain "assigned limits" (to return to the language of Abbot's preface). Yet while the game itself persisted, the "new methods" touted by the trade catalog copy didn't necessarily stick. As the nineteenth century wore on, and Bradley ceded control of his company to others, major commercial board games largely stripped out operative innovations in favor of the simpler nonstop forward-backward mechanics of *The Game of Goose* or *The Mansion of Happiness*: the nonoperative pictorialism of McLoughlin Brothers had, in some ways, won the day. You might get lost in the board on your own time, but there was nothing about the rules of the game that codified these enchantments. Links to the literary persisted, but mainly as a mask placed over endless repetitions of the same game—often games of upward mobility (replacing Christian grace), as in the case of several games by Parker Brothers that were based on Horatio Alger novels. The directed indirection of *Bamboozle* gave way to a minimal narrative of persistence and success, not a story to invent, but a plot to reinforce. The power of object associations—of suggestive collectives of things, images, and people—to reorient life was, in some ways, no longer a mysterious force to be mobilized in a number of different ways (a ludic take on the hazy indirections of romanticism), but a familiar and accepted "reality." Games like *Dr. Busby* and *Peter Coddle's Trip to New York* had done a certain work to create comforts with the anxieties that accompanied the expanding urban world of people and things, and by the end of the century this comfort had been achieved.

Conclusion: Peter Coddle Blanks Out

As the nineteenth century wended toward the twentieth, so a familiar story goes, American literature changed. A pervasive romanticism—at least partially defined by its misty and marvelous take on historical potentials, its moody effusions of emotion, and its suggestions of interplay between the real and the fictive—gave way to pointed sociological genres like realism and naturalism, genres less overtly concerned with figural or formal provocation. The domain of directed indirection, tracking with the modernist sensibilities of the early twentieth century, would become more readily allied with a playful poetic experimentalism that was the purview of artists, tastemakers, and scholars but not necessarily the reading public as a whole. Settling into a different cultural landscape, games went their own way, drifting from operative invention even as a slew of colorful new skins were applied to classic game genres. *The Checkered Game of Life* continued with the same form into the twentieth century, only to be revised in 1960 as the pink-and-blue-car, rainbow-dial race game most know today. *Bamboozle* remained on the books for fifty years, shifting materials slightly but still as opaque in 1922 as it was in 1872. Tangrams and billiards saw some cosmetic improvements but were not fundamentally altered (barring the wholesale evolution of pinball from earlier parlorizations of bagatelle). *Dr. Busby* and *Authors* saw some additions and revisions but, in the case of *Busby*, continued using fairly standardized box art representing the sociable doctor in front of his medicine shop. Yet *Peter Coddle*, before being operatively reborn as *Mad Libs* in the 1950s, underwent a curious transformation.[66]

Following the box art as the game traveled both manufacturers and time, the adolescent Coddle envisioned on Simonds's original Gould & Lincoln edition had, by the 1880s, become a middle-aged greenhorn—increasingly identified by a tawny growing beard and distinctive green umbrella. There were exceptions, but in the later 1880s and 1890s Coddle began to approach Rip Van Winkle territory, depicted as a white-bearded old man with a genial but sometimes wild look in his eye. Then, in the 1930s, a series of Milton Bradley editions begin to dim the lights on the figure. In one, a dark, featureless shadow outline is surrounded by the signs and bustle of the city; in another, a similar phantom form appears only in profile to look over the polygonal protrusions of the skyline. By 1936 there is no Coddle at all, just a colorful horizon populated by skyscrapers (Figure 21).[67] Peter Coddle games themselves vanish from the market shortly after.

This was not a character under any single artist's control. Like child-friendly pop icons from the twentieth century such as Snoopy and Mickey Mouse, Coddle was, of course, free to remain forever ageless. These versions were coming from different designers, undoubtedly watching each other in a crowded field but not exactly meeting to discuss character development. So how can we account for the gradual aging and evaporation of the character? One can only speculate, but it is at least plausible that the very idea of urban material anxiety was aging in a way reflected by Coddle's representation. In the 1850s and 1860s, the new world of things and their capacity to change a

Figure 21. *Game of Peter Coddle's Trip to New York.* Springfield: Milton Bradley Company, 1936. Courtesy of The Strong, Rochester, New York.

person through specific arrangements and in particular proximities could be felt as a problem for the young adult. *Peter Coddle* was a game in which such anxieties were made humorous, tractable, and socially creative as a group of players used these things (both on the cards and the cards themselves) to construct a collective narrative. By the 1890s, it was only the doddering old man who could be imagined as shocked and forever changed by the things that accompanied the new industrial economy. In the end, as the twentieth century entered its second quarter, this was not a story of a person at all but simply a reflection of the city itself, with its endlessly exchangeable varieties of new and old things (people, perhaps, included). The anxieties that had registered a field of invention, a site of potential transformation, however dangerous, had simmered down as engagement with new commercial media was domesticated. A set of comfortable genre protocols emerged, modes of recognition that could be projected onto what had previously been seen as a "heterogeneous heap."

The transition from *Peter Coddle* to *Mad Libs* might be seen as a meaningful shift from "things" to more functional demands: in the latter, the blanks are not filled by things *given to you*, cards that come from the outside to change the story, but are instead supplied as a variety of linguistic units summoned from one's own verbal stockpile to fit a given grammatical place. The things (not to mention adjectives and verbs) were *inside you* now, words and concepts to be produced on demand. In a way, the United States had become a population of naturalized "Peter Coddles," comfortably situated in a world of object associations so pervasive as to feel like the world itself ("society" perhaps) rather than some vital animating substance or dangerous invader. This is not to say that these knotted ligatures—of things, materials, ideas, forms, and people—ceased to exert influence along the vectors of indirection and vicarious effect we have followed. It is simply to suggest that such effects may have ceased to *feel* as such, lost in a preoccupation with content-centered approaches to meaning, taken for granted as the "is" of objects or the "is not" of mere association.

The historical media criticism unpacked in this book has a variety of ends, loose and otherwise, even as we wind toward an ending. Yet they are all caught up in the attempt to grasp a sense of the potentials that exist in re-narrating these complex associative entanglements. Reintroducing games into the field of print and literary culture has been a way to continue the cultivation of a more accurate and inclusive (if messy) picture of the nineteenth-century media ecology. To open new views on the reception and production practices of the moment has been a way to dilate the interpretative field in such a manner as to at least sketch the experiential contingencies of genre experimentation more broadly. That is, it has allowed us to ask differently oriented questions about why specific experiments were taken on, or about what types of practiced interaction allowed players to both recognize and take pleasure in particular forms of media. These recognitions and reinforcements have been understood as at once tactile and tactful, touchy and talky, in nontrivially related ways. Whether book, game, or otherwise, a media form comes to us as a "thing" even as it comes to us as an object or set of ideas. It is something we can "use" in creative ways or something we can simply "get used to." As Robin Bernstein and others have insisted, things "invite us to dance," and that dance has effects that are hopelessly attached to feelings of social belonging, habits of social arrangement, and the perceived boundaries of social invention—what we might call in a more effusive mode the ends of "imagination."

At the close of this inquiry, I am also aware of a methodological conditioning that has been at work on me throughout. Again, it is not so much new as it is powerfully reinforced by the methods required of the game analyst and by what I've called "close playing": a necessary fixation on the multiple layers of interaction that create both meaning and effect in a piece of media (where meaning, indeed, might just be one of many potential effects). These layers are often afforded different relative statuses in literary criticism—differential relationships I have attempted, with whatever limited success I've had, to flatten. To interpret a game responsibly, it has been necessary to trace the interwoven associations between "paratextual" elements like marketing and pictures as indirectly but meaningfully connected to the intimate connections, charged interactions, and communal attachments being formed among the players of a game in the local privacy of their own playing environment. At the same time, even as the rules of a game—its "genre"—structure an operative model of interaction and association within these given constraints, the content of the game plants itself firmly in memory of those constraints, those paratexts, and those people.

The challenge throughout has been to think in a similar way about the work of literary texts, to use specific nineteenth-century games as a way to reorient readings of nineteenth-century books in a manner sensitive to often metalinguistic notions of form and interaction. An alternative perspective on historical "reading" practice is the consequence here—a perspective that remains open to different kinds of potential that may have been seen in the production and consumption of books, however canonical they may be and however settled their social significance may seem now. The door is cracked for finding meaning in fragmentary readings, operative readings, and slant readings tracking with the "material" vectors of understanding that existed alongside the semantic vectors of a text. It is hard to imagine reading practice in this environment as *ever* only a start-to-finish linear production, a straightforward circulation of ideas through the arteries of culture. Instead, social effects emerged through a series of dislocations, reversals, frame breakages, material dalliances, and simple proximities that were part and parcel of *what it meant to produce* within specific cultural and technological constraints. The sense of unity would come only later.

As our own contemporary media become even less transparent with regard to their material and operative underpinning—presenting us with endlessly manipulable "content" framed by proprietary interfaces designed (optimally) to disappear from view—this attention to alternative notions of what mediums do, and what their effects are, is even more important to reinforce. Moreover, it is essential that we achieve this reinforcement in ways that do not lose the dimensions of inquiry that have traditionally been the purview of literary study: figurality, metaphor, and associative logic. Associations can be technical, material, and procedural as often as they can be linguistic. If, for instance, boredom and frustration are feelings we are inclined to see as linked to *broken* media—whether it be an undergraduate lamenting a long-form description of a garden in a nineteenth-century book or a professor lamenting a long stare at his or her own smartphone while an app that *had been working just fine* pauses to update—the example of games forces us to imagine such moments as features rather than bugs, as a part of what our media are doing to or for us, and not external to questions of meaning. We bamboozle ourselves when we imagine that such "knot work," tying us down or tripping us up, is "not work"—that it doesn't condition us in specific ways that are part of our social fabric, our networks of everyday life.[68] Games have provided a historically embedded way to reinforce the thematics of timing, engagement, and material encounter throughout this book. Explicitly developed as dispositional *tools* in the nineteenth century (and always beholden to the marketing angle of being "instructive" as well as "amusing"), they have offered insight into the ways that literary media were also conceived of as something *used* and not simply *absorbed*.

Earlier, I employed Milton Bradley's *Checkered Game of Life* to illustrate the shift from passive Lockean absorption to an ideology of use in procedural terms, exemplifying this split in the operational difference between Bradley's freeform grid and previous single-track board games. Situated and sold in the same urban milieu (though Bradley's game was undeniably more pervasive), Walt Whitman's *Leaves of Grass* depicted agency via a literary representation of the same avatar position present in *Life*, a structured "you" that was simultaneously a performed "I." Like the public signs and handbills that both structured and empowered the independent movement of urban strangers in nineteenth-century New York, both *Life* and "Song of Myself" proved themselves to be invested in, as David Henkin writes, "facilitating forms of access and interaction that did not require personal acquaintance . . . or recognizable individual authority."[69] Within this model, authority was socially dispersed and the individual was reconceived as the social nexus conveyed by the interaction of the I-position and the you-position of Whitman's poem—embodied by the avatar marker of Bradley's game. From where we stand now, this "interactivity" might be seen as an aesthetic of scopic contacts, with the "I" represented as the iterative, accumulated experience of one social actor (his or her social character) that must always be in contact with the wider scope of affordances and limitations conveyed by cultural materials (in order for that character to be comprehensible). The interactive avatar figure was an attempt to imagine how something like individual agency might exist in a world that continually pushed back at any attempt to make its objects anything less than social—filled with and surrounded by agencies outstripping the singular actor. Bradley and Whitman provide models for how irreducibly social objects were nonetheless captured in descriptions of private and individual proportions; for both, the emphasis was iterative, algorithmic, and targeted.

Both "Song of Myself" and *The Checkered Game of Life* anticipate Friedrich Nietzsche's later observation, "If one has character one also has one's typical experience, which recurs repeatedly."[70] Yet Melville, as we saw, troubled the issue. *The Confidence-Man* asks how *change* might occur in a world where "character" rules, where agential legibility is defined by a "typical experience, which recurs repeatedly." Melville's engagement with this problem left us with a troubled utopic figure, that of the Confidence-Man who acts as a surrogate for the lost agency of state machine subjects, the operator filling in the blanks of his or her interior Peter Coddle game. Melville's Confidence-Man gestures at a solution by showing that, despite its seemingly *interior* machinations, character was driven (and thus ideas of change were driven) by the contact of the state machine subject with registers of scope outside itself. Here an operator targets his marks both in the sense of making them a prey *and* in the sense of bringing their "interior" layer of scope into contact with his own. The problem is that the *Fidèle* passengers do not see themselves as targets—but, of course, readers know that they are. And that rehearsed awareness of the frame may have been the point. Even as it cannot overcome its own narrative problematic (the book simply ends with the Confidence-Man ambiguously walking into the night), Melville's novel represents and encourages playerliness within an emerging world that needed to find comfort in the mechanisms of "ridicule" in order to avoid stagnation and begin staging change. Here, the Confidence-Man might be seen as sketching a picture—with his "little arguments"—alongside a tangram, contouring and reconfiguring a meaning that was delightfully volatile, situational, and "tactful." Indeed, P. T. Barnum found his own comfortable profits on this particular media stage by allowing his audiences the opportunity to test out new social characters and protocols through persistent rearrangements of focus in the American Museum.

And Michael Phelan also showed this configurative opportunity to be central to his theory of billiards, as even the abstract physical operations of targeting are seen as occasions for vicariously adjusting one's "dispositions" and therefore changing one's (domestic or social or personal) world. Drawing this reading into *The Blithedale Romance*, I argued that Hawthorne aggressively performed the "targeted" approach to change through narrative style, but also through the symbol of "ridicule," both a purse (a container) and a "loophole" in Coverdale's organic netting through which he targets (a reticule). True, it may be too much to suggest that Hawthorne explicitly modeled his novel on billiards (despite his references to Coverdale's interest in the game). However, reading *Blithedale* in conversation with the cued targeting mechanics that defined this culturally pervasive amusement allowed us to see elements of literary engagement in Hawthorne's text that echoed the engagements pursued in the "proper" playing of billiards narrated in Phelan's manuals, not to mention those more spatial interactions native to Barnum's work.

Existing in a shared historical space of production, reception, and transmission, the games discussed in this book show an interface between literary representations and these more bodily, social, and operational concerns in the nineteenth century. In a wider discussion of twentieth-century new media technology, Lev Manovich writes: "The advantage of placing new media within a larger historical perspective is that we begin to see the long trajectories that lead to new media in its present state, and we can extrapolate these trajectories into the future."[71] Similarly, seeing "old media" within a shared continuum of production and appropriation not only enriches our capacity to produce significant comparative insights but also gives us additional perspective on structures of thought and medial instantiation in the twenty-first century. As all media are becoming increasingly driven by the goals of interactivity and social markup—by proceduralization and attention to operational aesthetics that go far beyond the truth-or-falsehood schematizations that Neil Harris saw at work in Barnum's exhibits—we might find such a viewpoint instructive. Old cues might find new targets, holding the potential for directing us to "other lives as good, or better."[72] Telling these new stories requires a sense of the social infrastructures that began to emerge from the rippled circles of *Bamboozle* or *Dr. Busby*, not the comfortable and expected straight lines of *The Mansion of Happiness*. For better or worse, we must maintain a perspective on the move, receptive to the various slants in motion, and disposed to play both with and around them. We must be willing to get stuck on things, on people, and on unfinished ideas—and to value the work that is being done while we are.

NOTES

INTRODUCTION

1. *Bradley's Holiday Annual of Home Amusements and Social Sports, 1872–3* (Springfield: Milton Bradley & Co., 1872).

2. Though neither is a scholar of games as such, Clifford Geertz and Michel de Certeau offer particularly resonant reflections on the imaginative work performed by situations of gameplay in the construction, not simply the reinforcement, of the aggregate associations we come to call "society" or in a more active, procedural rhetoric, "social dynamics." In "Deep Play," Geertz notes that a game is often "not a depiction of how things literally are among men, but . . . of how, *from a particular angle*, they imaginatively are," and continues by arguing that these "art forms generate and regenerate the very subjectivity they pretend only to display (25 and 28, emphasis added). In *The Practice of Everyday Life*, Certeau lingers similarly on the constructive action modeling enabled by games in their various retellings: "To be memorized as well as memorable, [accounts of games] are *repertories of schemas of action* between partners. . . . These mementos teach the tactics possible within a given (social) system . . . the models of good or bad ruses that can be used every day" (23). In this book, I am interested in what we can learn from these "repertories" as indicators of broader media engagement, as well as how formal experimentation within the production of games itself might shed light on the "schemas of action" that were being conditioned by the materials and practices of media circulation in the U.S. nineteenth century. See Clifford Geertz, "Deep Play: Notes on the Balinese Cockfight," *Daedalus* 101.1 (Winter 1972): 1–37, and Michel de Certeau, *The Practice of Everyday Life* (Berkeley: University of California Press, 1984).

3. This could be termed "operational fidelity" to emphasize the way that games replicate and resituate a limited range of behavior *as if* it were the only cluster of behaviors that mattered for a given time. Game theorist Jesper Juul explains that "the rules of a game add *meaning* and *enable actions* by setting up *differences* between potential moves and events" (19, emphasis original). Because games are iterative, these differences or expectations of meaning can become habits of mind, structuring a way of looking at the world—which is precisely why games have been taken seriously as a site of cultural pedagogy at least since the nineteenth century. From the other direction, this practice of "simplifying and crudely schematizing," as Gregory Jackson notes in "A Game Theory of Evangelical Fiction," "reveal[s] the underlying structure" of certain practices that bind social groupings. By invoking the term "fidelity" I want to reflect the fact that though these *models* of practice are undoubtedly there to be revealed, they never pretend to capture anything like a total picture of social action; they are most useful in their "crude" and unabashed facet-iness. See Jesper Juul, *Half-Real: Video Games between Real Rules and Fictional*

Worlds (Cambridge, Mass.: MIT Press, 2005); Gregory S. Jackson. "A Game Theory of Evangel-ical Fiction." *Critical Inquiry* 39.3 (Spring 2013): 451–485.

4. Many attempts to define games double back to provocative and foundational pieces by Roger Callois and Bernard Suits, folding in more recent work by Katie Salen and Eric Zimmer-man (see below). Nevertheless, critics offer their own takes even as they summarize and compile. In *Gaming*, Alexander Galloway begins: "A game is an activity defined by rules in which players try to reach some sort of goal" (1). Mary Flanagan's definition in *Critical Play* is less end directed: "Games can be thought of more productively as situations with guidelines and procedures" (7). And before moving into an excellent digest of twentieth-century definitional scholarship, Jesper Juul offers a "classic game model" derived from a variety of sources, in which a game is "1. a rule-based formal system; 2. with variable and quantifiable outcomes; 3. where different outcomes are assigned different values; 4. where the player exerts effort in order to influence the outcome; 5. the player feels emotionally attached to the outcome; 6. and the consequences of the activity are optional and negotiable" (6–7). I am influenced by and indebted to each of these general ac-counts, though, as I discuss, my aims in this book are more particular. See Roger Callois, *Man, Play, and Games* (New York: Schocken Books, 1961); Mary Flanagan, *Critical Play: Radical Game Design* (Cambridge, Mass.: MIT Press, 2009); Alexander R. Galloway, *Gaming: Essays on Algo-rithmic Culture* (Minneapolis: University of Minnesota Press, 2006); Juul, *Half-Real*, esp. 29–54; Katie Salen and Eric Zimmerman, *Rules of Play: Game Design Fundamentals* (Cambridge, Mass.: MIT Press, 2004); and Bernard Suits, *The Grasshopper: Games, Life and Utopia* (Toronto: Uni-versity of Toronto Press, 1978).

5. Milton Bradley, "The Uses and Abuses of Games," *Good Housekeeping* 2.8 (20 February 1886): 225–226.

6. *Classified index of subjects of invention adopted in the U. S. Patent office.* "Class 46." 1 March 1872. United States Patent Office, 67.

7. Bradley, "Uses," 225.

8. Ibid., 226.

9. Here I'm drawing on Lisa Gitelman's excellent rethinking of genre in *Paper Knowledge*: "Genre is a mode of recognition instantiated in discourse. Written genres, for instance, depend on a possibly infinite number of things that large groups of people can recognize, will recognize, or have recognized that writings can be for. . . . Genres—such as the joke, the novel, the docu-ment, and the sitcom—get picked out contrastively amid a jumble of discourse and often across multiple media because of the ways they have been internalized by constituents of a shared cul-ture. Individual genres aren't artifacts, then; they are ongoing and changeable practices of expres-sion and reception that are recognizable in myriad and variable constituent instances at once and also across time" (2). Genre here functions less as a set of narrative tropes and more as set of protocols that condition the way you use something (for example, the rules of a game or the instructions for an administrative form). Though there are similarities, you typically read a mys-tery novel differently than a romance, a poem differently than a novel. "Don't just give me any book, I like science fiction" is a way of registering the things one wants to *do* with a book, where "reading" is often a black box for a massive variety of visual, mental, and physical actions—explicit and implicit rules of engagement. The "genre" invention component of a new game is often registered, as I see it, by the anxiety and frustration that can accompany learning a new game: "I don't know what to do! I don't know if I want to do it! This is *stupid*." When the mech-anism proves familiar, when the game really isn't that new—"Ahh, this is like *Monopoly*!"—we tend to settle more quickly into the comfortable gestalt of action that accompanies notions of genre and affinity. See also Johanna Drucker, "Entity to Event: From Literal, Mechanistic

Materiality to Probabilistic Materiality," *Parallax* 15.4 (2009): 7–17; Lisa Gitelman, *Paper Knowledge: Toward a Media History of Documents* (Durham: Duke University Press, 2014); Virginia Jackson, *Dickinson's Misery: A Theory of Lyric Reading* (Princeton: Princeton University Press, 2005); Bonnie Mak, *How the Page Matters* (Toronto: University of Toronto Press, 2011).

10. Sacvan Bercovitch, "Games of Chess: A Model of Literary and Cultural Studies," in Robert Newman, ed., *Centuries Ends, Narrative Means* (Stanford: Stanford University Press, 1996), 17.

11. Striving for a term that can account for the difference between traditional narrative and "cybertext" or algorithmic narratives like a Choose-Your-Own-Adventure book, Aarseth constructs this term from the combination of "ergon" (work) and "hodos" (path), suggesting the nontrivial effort a user exerts in order to produce an expressive "path" through the performance space of the object (1). This term, he argues, "centers attention on the consumer, or user . . . as a more integrated figure than even reader-response theorists would claim. The performance of the reader takes place all in his head, while the user of a cybertext also performs in an extranoematic sense." See Espen Aarseth, *Cybertext: Perspectives on Ergodic Literature* (Baltimore: Johns Hopkins University Press, 1997).

12. This terminology is indebted to José Muñoz's useful gloss on Giorgio Agamben, "Unlike a possibility, a thing that simply might happen, a potentiality is a certain mode of nonbeing that is eminent, a thing that is present but not actually existing in the present tense" (9). See José Muñoz, *Cruising Utopia: The Then and There of Queer Futurity* (New York: NYU Press, 2009).

13. The terminology of "vehicle" and "tenor" is borrowed from I. A. Richards, *The Philosophy of Rhetoric* (Oxford: Oxford University Press, 1936). And though the philosophy of metaphor is a program of study in itself with important touchstones from Max Black, Stanley Cavell, Donald Davidson, José Ortega y Gasset, and many others, I am especially partial to Ted Cohen's series of essays in *Thinking of Others: On the Talent for Metaphor* (Princeton: Princeton University Press, 2008). On material objects as occupying an important metaphorical space for reconsidering cultural histories, see also Katherine C. Grier, "Material Culture as Rhetoric: 'Animal Artifacts' as a Case Study," in *American Material Culture: The Shape of the Field*, ed. Ann Smart Martin and J. Ritchie Garrison (Winterthur: Winterthur Museum, 1997), 65–104.

14. Geertz, "Deep Play," 26.

15. *Virginia Gazette*, "Sketchy's Newly Invented Conversation Cards," Williamsburg, 11 November, 1775, 1.

16. *The Diary; Or, Loudon's Register*, New York, 31 July 1793, 4.

17. David M. Henkin paints especially vivid pictures of urban extraliterary print as a platform of communicative transaction in *City Reading*, noting that in the mid-nineteenth-century United States the "proliferation of 'little bits of paper' in the expanding city signaled a world far removed from the exchanges of spoken words among the personally acquainted" (19). See Henkin, *City Reading: Written Words and Public Spaces in Antebellum New York* (New York: Columbia University Press, 1998), and "City Streets and the Urban World of Print," in *A History of the Book in America: The Industrial Book, 1840–1880*, vol. 3. (Chapel Hill: University of North Carolina Press, 2005).

18. *Komikal Konversation Kards* (Boston: Adams & Co., 1866), n.p.

19. As Elizabeth Maddock Dillon has recently pointed out, "the print public sphere is decisively limited by literacy in such a way that often renders this limitation largely outside the field of political and cultural vision and analysis. Individuals who do not read and write in English in the eighteenth-century Anglo-Atlantic world tend to disappear from view in accounts of the print public sphere; more significantly, the a-literate are erased from the scene of cultural

analysis as if access to literacy were a preexisting, structural constraint rather than a contingent, political division among diverse peoples" (14). It is a guiding hope of my project that attention to the alternative social "literacies" of gameplay will aid in developing sidelong accounts of cultural engagement—productively supplementing critical analyses that rely on accounts of association produced and reinforced by traditional print literacy. See Dillon, *New World Drama: The Performative Commons in the Atlantic World, 1649–1849* (Durham: Duke University Press, 2014).

20. *Conversation Cards* (New Bedford: Benjamin Lindsey, 1811).

21. Lauren Berlant and Sianne Ngai provide an excellent introduction to the subtleties of the comedic in their recent collaborative work, "Comedy Has Issues," where they also land in the territory of genre inquiry: "[We approach] the question of genre not just as an aesthetic topic but also as a scene of affective mediation and expectation" (*Critical Inquiry* 43.2 [Winter 2017]: 239).

22. George Noyes registers as much in his 1856 piece, "Good Conversation and Prose Writing": "The manner, the expression, the tone, the gesture, the lively anecdote, the brilliant wit, the sharp repartee, the well-conducted argument, the workings of different minds, the animation depicted on the countenances of the speakers, the natural eloquence flowing from the heart, excite a deeper interest, and make more lasting impressions of pleasure on the mind than the perusing of a book in solitude, however elegant or agreeable be the style, and however exciting or instructive be the theme" (quoted in Augst 99). For further discussion of the role of feeling and "animation" in nineteenth-century conversation and political discourse, see Thomas Augst, *The Clerk's Tale: Young Men and Moral Life in Nineteenth-Century America* (Chicago: University of Chicago Press, 2003), esp. 62–113.

23. My use of the term "operation" and its cognates develops from Ian Bogost's definition: "In systems analysis, an operation is a basic process that takes one or more inputs and performs a transformation on it. . . . Mathematical operations offer fundamental examples. . . . Other kinds of operations include decisions, transitions, and state changes. I use the term operation very generally. . . . Brewing tea is an operation. Steering a car to avoid a pedestrian is an operation. Falling in love is an operation" (*Unit Operations: An Approach to Videogame Criticism* [Cambridge, Mass.: MIT Press, 2006], 7). Though susceptible to overgeneralization, Bogost's core point is useful: an operational perspective sees actions broken into discrete stepwise procedures that narrate the interrelationships necessary to produce given results within a given system. My use has been further inflected by the discourse of "mechanism" that pervaded the nineteenth-century American mind. See Neil Harris on the "operational aesthetic" of the nineteenth-century United States in *Humbug: The Art of P. T. Barnum* (Boston: Little, Brown and Company, 1973), 61–89.

24. Stephen Ramsay discusses a similar move in Eve Kosofsky Sedgwick's *Between Men* through Sedgwick's use of the triangle as a "graphic schema" by which to identify and discuss male homosocial exchange. Throughout the work, Ramsay argues, the triangle acts as "a pattern transducer—a machine for mapping one symbol set onto another. . . . To suggest that such triangles may lie elsewhere, and to use the triangle as a means for clarifying and elucidating the hidden, nondominant motives of a text is to deform with a purpose" (55). Indebted to such schematic efforts to "deform with a purpose," the opening move of most chapters in the present book is to sound out the meaningful operational schema of particular games as a way to remap the literary texts in play. See Ramsey, *Reading Machines: Toward an Algorithmic Criticism* (Urbana: University of Illinois Press, 2011), and Sedgwick, *Between Men: English Literature and Male Homosocial Desire* (New York: Columbia University Press, 1985).

25. Robin Bernstein, *Racial Innocence: Performing American Childhood from Slavery to Civil Rights* (New York: NYU Press, 2011), 80.

26. Ibid., 79.

27. My view of "liminality" draws on cultural anthropologist Victor Turner, who argues that social practices like games are "are liminal, in the sense that they are suspensions of daily reality, occupying privileged spaces where people are allowed to think about how they think, about the terms in which they conduct their thinking, or to feel about how they feel in daily life" (Turner 22). This metareflection is made possible not because a game detaches one from the "real world" but *precisely because it doesn't*—because the performance of detachment is always incomplete, fragile, and fragmentary. Contrary to Johan Huizinga's influential and pervasively Romantic notion of gamespaces as surrounded by a "magic circle," Karen Sánchez-Eppler reminds us that "self-articulated play is never fully a 'stepping out of "real" life,' but rather that the nature and possibilities of play are always socially constructed and constrained" (180). Steven E. Jones introduces a materialist angle equally compatible with my view: "We might do better to imagine the space set aside in a game in more material, less magical terms, perhaps an actual chalk circle" (15). As much as possible, I attempt to adopt a sensibility more indebted to the sonic and tactile associations of chalk than to the dramatic illusions of impossible depth that characterize magic. See Victor Turner, "Liminality and the Performative Genres," in *Rite, Drama, Festival, Spectacle: Rehearsals toward a Theory of Cultural Performance* (Philadelphia: Institute for the Study of Human Issues, 1984); Johan Huizinga, *Homo Ludens: A Study of the Play Element in Culture* (London: Beacon Press, 1955); Karen Sánchez-Eppler, *Dependent States: The Child's Part in Nineteenth-Century American Culture* (Chicago: University of Chicago Press, 2005); and Steven E. Jones, *The Meaning of Video Games: Gaming and Textual Strategies* (New York: Routledge, 2008).

28. Quoted from back matter in George Arnold, *The Sociable; or, One Thousand and One Home Amusements* (New York: Dick & Fitzgerald, 1858), iii.

29. William B. Dick, *American Hoyle; or, Gentleman's Handbook of Games* (New York: Dick & Fitzgerald, 1864), 398.

30. "Games for the Soldiers or Family Circle," *Scientific American* 11.24 (10 December 1864): 382.

31. *Springfield Republican* (15 December 1866).

32. Race is considerably more difficult to speculate on, at least within the sphere of mass circulation that delimits this project. My focus on new games that sold and circulated throughout the mid-nineteenth-century United States allows me to sketch a mobile picture of what can easily be assumed to be the associative practices of the white majority (with particular slants on the production end into a male notion of what *was* and *could be* in the social world). Alongside this world of comparative privilege, I pause at strategic moments to speculate on how similar or contrastive practices might further loosen our view of gameplay's potential to adjust social feeling. Though they purchased these games in great volume, literate middle-class whites of the era were unlikely enough to *document* their practices of play—perhaps because of how unimportant it seemed in the grand scheme or because they feared projecting unsavory or unproductive character to associates (for example, soldiers ditched dice on the battlefield the same way a person might clear a salacious web browser history today). How much more social pressure to occlude certain "minor," "silly," or "ephemeral" practices of play—even when one had the leisure to consider them—must there have been for more marginalized actors, those without such social cover? I have hope that by tracing the more easily documented contours of the archives I will create opportunities to aggregate further traces of minority reception.

33. Sex and allied sexual practices are one way to trace and produce these slantwise moves—something the designers of *Twister* were undoubtedly all too aware of—but there are other modes of physical and associational play that occupy the labile territory often mapped by sex in critical discourse. If sex can allow us to reinvent ourselves through intimate and at times risky figures of play that exceed the normative forms projected by gender, then it is perhaps worth remembering that sex isn't the only game in town. Michel Foucault, "Friendship as a Way of Life," in *The Essential Works of Foucault, Volume 1: Ethics: Subjectivity and Truth*, ed. Paul Rabinow (New York: New Press, 1997), 138.

34. "L'homosexualité est une occasion historique de rouvrir des virtualités relationnelles et affectives, non pas tellement par les qualités intrinsèques de l'homosexuel, mais parce que la position de celui-ci 'en biais,' en quelque sorte, les lignes diagonales qu'il peut tracer dans le tissu social permettent de faire apparaître ces virtualités." Michel Foucault, "De l'amitié comme mode de vie," *Gai Pied* (1981), http://yagg.com/2015/01/26/michel-foucault-%E2%80%A8de-lamitie -comme-mode-de-vie-entretien-au-gai-pied-1981 (accessed May 2016).

35. W. J. T. Mitchell attributes a similar layered bouncing and redoubling "language game" to Foucault in *Picture Theory*, arguing that in Foucault's famous discussion of *Las Meninas* the point is to make these images "harder, not easier to talk about" (60). Mitchell, *Picture Theory: Essays on Verbal and Visual Representation* (Chicago: University of Chicago Press, 1995).

36. Here I think it's critical to flag archival limitations once again, this time on the production end of the spectrum. More than others, I double back to Milton Bradley, both because he leaves behind enough breadcrumbs to initiate the work of doing this history and because he is fascinatingly aware of his position as a media maker throughout his sustained career. Even beyond the fact that games have a sparse and irregular presence in the archives, nonwhite, nonmale designers of nineteenth-century games—with the exception of Anne Abbot, discussed below and in Chapter 5—have been hard to track. This is not, undoubtedly, because they didn't exist but because they were not afforded the cultural capital of putting their name at the head of a company or securing copyright (not to mention taking the substantial financial risk of patenting and producing mass-market game media). I offer sensitive readings of those who did persist so that we might begin the work of unearthing more, and so that curators and critics can see the value in continuing to fight an increasingly difficult battle over the preservation of so-called ephemera.

37. Emily Dickinson, "Tell all the truth" (1872, manuscript leaf). Amherst: https://acdc .amherst.edu/view/asc:12239 (accessed May 2016).

38. The goal here is to follow Lisa Gitelman's lead in "resist[ing] any but local and contrastive logics for media" (*Paper Knowledge*, 9). This view represents one of the most vital methodological insights of "media archaeology"—a critical movement catalyzed by critics like Gitelman, Lev Manovich, and Friedrich Kittler. In short, these critics insist that media and technology don't progress in a linear fashion (in a master narrative of techno-determinism). Instead, "new media" emerge in the transposition and transformation of existing models—emerging from conflicts and interactions and blind alleys that are as material as they are conceptual.

39. Bradley, "Uses," 225.

40. For more on the invention of "childhood," see Sánchez-Eppler, *Dependent States*; Sarah Chinn, *Inventing Modern Adolescence: The Children of Immigrants in Turn-of-the-Century America* (New Brunswick: Rutgers University Press, 2008); Patricia Crain, *Reading Children: Literacy, Property, and the Dilemmas of Childhood in Nineteenth-Century America* (Philadelphia: University of Pennsylvania Press, 2016).

41. Augst, *The Clerk's Tale*, 22.

42. A lifelong ally of Elizabeth Peabody, Bradley was an avid proponent of the kindergarten movement in the United States. In an 1894 memorial issue of the *Kindergarten Review*, Bradley writes with admiration about "the fidelity with which Miss Peabody always prosecuted the promulgation of Froebelian educational methods," continuing: "Miss Peabody was my faithful guide and critic in every move made in the preparation of the material, and in many subsequent talks she gave me great encouragement to persevere. . . . Well do I remember many sharp criticisms from her called forth by my ignorance of the true spirit of the new education in the preparation of what I considered improvements in material. But whenever Yankee ingenuity or business experience suggested something which she could honestly approve, no one could be more appreciative or more cordial in expressing her approbation, both publicly and privately." Bradley was first convinced of the value of the kindergarten after seeing Peabody give a magnetizing talk on the topic at a Springfield public school. See Milton Bradley, *Kindergarten Review* 4.2 (1894): 40.

43. The American field of "book history," growing out of influential pieces like Robert Darnton's "What Is the History of Books?" (1982) and D. F. McKenzie's *Bibliography and the Sociology of Texts* (1986), has provided some of the most compelling pictures of this promiscuous field of paper goods. The standard source for the mid-nineteenth-century United States is *A History of the Book in America: The Industrial Book, 1840–1880*, vol. 3, ed. Scott E. Casper et al. (Durham: University of North Carolina Press, 2007). See also Augst, *The Clerk's Tale*; Henkin, *City Reading*; Leon Jackson, *The Business of Letters: Authorial Economies in Antebellum America* (Stanford: Stanford University Press, 2008); Meredith McGill, *American Literature and the Culture of Reprinting, 1834–1853* (Philadelphia: University of Pennsylvania Press, 2003).

44. McGill, *American Literature*, 4.

45. See, for instance, F. & R. Lockwood, *The Traveler's Tour through the United States* (1822).

46. Bradley, "Uses," 225.

47. See George Coolidge et. al., *The Boston Almanac for the Year 1858* (Boston: Brown, Taggert, & Chase, 1858), as well as Laura Wasowicz's excellent database of imprint tracings, the "19th-Century American Children's Book Trade Directory," at the American Antiquarian Society: http://www.americanantiquarian.org/btdirectory.htm (accessed May 2016).

48. *Salem Register* (23 December 1852): 3; *Daily Atlas* (20 December 1853): 4; *Salem Register* (11 December 1854): 2.

49. *Salem Register* (26 December 1844): 3. For a more in-depth look at Jewett, see Michael Winship, "John Punchard Jewett, Publisher of *Uncle Tom's Cabin*: A Biographical Note with a Preliminary List of His Imprints," in *Roger Eliot Stoddard at Sixty-Five: A Celebration* (New York: Thornwillow Press, 2000), 85–111.

50. *The Boston Almanac for the Year of 1858*, 155.

51. Anne W. Abbot, "Hawthorne's *Scarlet Letter*," in *North American Review* 71.148 (July 1850): 135–149.

52. Not incidentally, the first commercial versions of this game were printed by G. M. Whipple and A. A. Smith, booksellers for Hawthorne's publisher, Ticknor and Fields.

53. Ann Fabian, *Card Sharps and Bucket Shops: Gambling in Nineteenth-Century America* (New York: Routledge, 1997), 2.

54. Michael Oriard, *Sporting with the Gods: The Rhetoric of Play and Game in American Culture* (Cambridge: Cambridge University Press, 1991), ix.

55. Discussed further in Chapter 1, this distinction between "formal" and "forensic" materiality is drawn from Matthew Kirschenbaum, *Mechanisms: New Media and the Forensic Imagination* (Cambridge, Mass.: MIT Press, 2008).

56. Lisa Gitelman, *Scripts, Grooves, and Writing Machines: Representing Technology in the Edison Era* (Stanford: Stanford University Press, 1999), 3.

57. Herman Melville, *The Confidence-Man: His Masquerade*, ed. Hershel Parker and Mark Niemeyer (New York: W. W. Norton, 2006), 36, 53, 195.

58. Walter Benn Michaels, *The Gold Standard and the Logic of Naturalism: American Literature at the Turn of the Century* (Berkeley: University of California Press, 1987), 18.

59. Sacvan Bercovitch, *The Rites of Assent: Transformations in the Symbolic Construction of America* (New York: Routledge, 1993): 373.

60. Scott A. Sandage, *Born Losers: A History of Failure in America* (Cambridge, Mass.: Harvard University Press, 2005), 72.

61. Christopher Castiglia, *Interior States: Institutional Consciousness and the Inner Life of Democracy in the Antebellum United States* (Durham: Duke University Press, 2008), 300, emphasis added.

62. Bercovitch, *Rites of Assent*, 369.

63. Priscilla Wald and Gerry Canavan, "Preface to *Speculative Fictions*," *American Literature* 83.2 (June 2011): 246.

CHAPTER 1

1. James J. Shea and Charles Mercer, *It's All in the Game* (New York: G. P. Putnam and Sons, 1960), 55. Though Shea's bias as then-president of the Milton Bradley Company is evident, this remains one of the only extant accounts of Bradley's life.

2. Patented in spring of 1866, Bradley's *Checkered Game of Life* bears only passing resemblance to the 1960s revision with which most today are familiar.

3. Milton Bradley, Social Game, U.S. Patent 53,561, 3 April 1866.

4. Karen Halttunen, *Confidence Men and Painted Women: A Study of Middle-Class Culture in America, 1830–1870* (New Haven: Yale University Press, 1984), 40.

5. Shea and Mercer, *It's All in the Game*, 51, 57.

6. In this chapter, and throughout the book, I use the typical shorthand "*Boy's Own* books" to refer to the genre of mass-market titles that can be traced back to Clarke's anthology (a significant majority of which employ some variation on that nomenclature). When referring to a specific volume, I provide the full title.

7. William Clarke, *The Boy's Own Book* (Louisville: Morton and Griswold, 1854), 6.

8. Trumps, *American Hoyle*, 4.

9. Dick and Fitzgerald, *The American Boy's Book*, 5.

10. Clarke, *Boy's Own*, 6.

11. In the preface to *American Hoyle*, William Dick (writing as "Trumps") observes: "Hitherto our market has been supplied exclusively with reprints . . . which do not at the present time meet the requirements of the American public. . . . . We need scarcely say, that many of our most popular Games are peculiarly American, while those of foreign origin have become so changed by American modification, as to make the European rules and descriptions quite as likely to mislead as to instruct" (3).

12. Supporting the notion of play as a testing space for social experimentation, Brian Sutton-Smith argues that its function "is to reinforce the organism's variability in the face of rigidifications of successful adaptation. . . . This variability covers the full range of behavior from the actual to the possible" (231). For more on the theory of play as a laboratory for adaption and

variability in behavior, see Sutton-Smith, *The Ambiguity of Play* (Cambridge, Mass.: Harvard University Press, 1997), esp. 225–231. On games or "liminoid" commodities as ways of enacting productive social subjunctivity, see Victor Turner's "Liminality and the Performative Genres," in *Rite, Drama, Festival, Spectacle: Rehearsals toward a Theory of Cultural Performance* (Philadelphia: Institute for the Study of Human Issues, 1984), esp. 20–27.

13. Milton Bradley, *Visit of Santa Claus to the Happy Children* (Springfield: Milton Bradley & Co., 1868), 7. This is not to take Bradley entirely at face value. Clearly some of the games in his catalog were old favorites (some discussed below). But there does appear to be an effort in the early days of the company to produce games that employed some degree of operative or material novelty—a strategic approach, given that *new* methods, rules, and mechanisms could receive the sole manufacturing protection of a patent.

14. Mark Stephen Meadows, *I, Avatar: The Culture and Consequence of Having a Second Life* (Berkeley: New Riders, 2008), 13. On the genesis of "avatar" as a term of art in video games, see Chip Morningstar and F. Randall Farmer, "The Lessons of Lucasfilm's Habitat," in *The New Media Reader*, ed. Noah Wardrip-Fruin and Nick Montfort (Cambridge, Mass.: MIT Press, 2003), 664–677. On "avatar" as a way of "performing objecthood," a practice I explore further in Chapter 3, see Uri McMillan, *Embodied Avatars: Genealogies of Black Feminist Art and Performance* (New York: NYU Press, 2015).

15. Here I mean to invoke the full punctuated disruptiveness that Bill Brown and Robin Bernstein (among others) have addressed in "things." Brown summarizes this by contrast with "objects" by noting, "We look through objects because there are codes by which our interpretative attention makes them meaningful, because there is a discourse of objectivity that allows us to use them as facts. A *thing*, in contrast, can hardly function as a window. We begin to confront the thingness of objects when they stop working. . . . The story of objects asserting themselves as things, then, is the story of a changed relation to the human subject and thus the story of how the thing really names less an object than a particular subject-object relation" (4). See Brown, "Thing Theory," in *Things*, ed. Bill Brown (Chicago: University of Chicago Press, 2004), 1–22; and Bernstein, *Racial Innocence*. On the "sociology of associations," see Bruno Latour, *Reassembling the Social: An Introduction to Actor-Network-Theory* (Oxford: Oxford University Press, 2005).

16. This terminology draws on Matthew Kirschenbaum's discussion of optical storage media in *Mechanisms*. It emerges as an attempt to distill a notion of materiality capacious enough to account for the fact that, in Johanna Drucker's words, "No amount of ideological or cultural valuation can transform the propensity of papyrus to deteriorate into gold's capacity to endure" (quoted in Kirschenbaum, 10 n. 16). Kirschenbaum coins "forensic materiality" to describe the distinctive limitations and affordances of a particular piece of physical media, resting "upon the principle of individualization (basic to modern forensic science and criminalistics), the idea that no two things in the physical world are ever exactly alike" (10). Formal materiality is, by contrast, constituted by a particular interface model or articulation schema applied to a set of data—what he calls "the multiple relational computational states on a data set or digital object" (12). I pivot this distinction outside of computational realms to address historical media more broadly, especially games, where these forms of materiality are often explicitly interwoven to produce the scene of play—a scene where the (forensic) physicality is always as much at issue as the (formal) rules.

17. Walt Whitman, *Leaves of Grass and Other Writings*, ed. Michael Moon (New York: W. W. Norton, 2002), 901.

18. Ed Folsom, "I am the poet: Whitman's Manuscript Drafts of 'Song of Myself' *Leaves of*

Grass, 1855," in *The Classroom Electric: Dickinson, Whitman and American Culture* (University of Iowa Libraries 2005): http://bailiwick.lib.uiowa.edu/whitman/ (accessed 9 August 2016).

19. Whitman, *Leaves of Grass*, 784.

20. Whitman, "1855 Preface," *Leaves of Grass*, 624

21. Horace Traubel, *With Walt Whitman in Camden*, vol. 2, 175 (Walt Whitman Archive): http://www.whitmanarchive.org/criticism/disciples/traubel/WWWiC/ (accessed 9 August 2016).

22. For more on Whitman's interlinking of physical and mental exercise, see the recently uncovered series by him on "manly health": Mose Velsor (Walt Whitman), "Manly Health and Training, With Off-Hand Hints Toward Their Conditions," ed. Zachary Turpin, *Walt Whitman Quarterly Review* 33 (2016): 184–310.

23. Whitman, "A Backward Glance," in *Leaves of Grass*, 484.

24. Whitman, *Leaves of Grass*, 785.

25. Shea and Mercer, *It's All in the Game*, 25–30.

26. Bradley, *A Successful Man*, 5.

27. Ibid.

28. Bradley, "Uses," 225.

29. Shea and Mercer, *It's All in the Game*, 19.

30. Ibid., 35.

31. Ibid., 39.

32. Ibid., 42.

33. Bradley, *A Successful Man*, 12.

34. The population of Springfield, Mass., at this time was 15,199; Bradley sold more than forty thousand copies of *Life* in 1860 alone. U.S. Bureau of the Census, "Table 9. Population of the 100 Largest Urban Places: 1860," 15 June 1998, www.census.gov/population/www/documentation/twps0027/tab09.txt.

35. Ibid., 66.

36. *Springfield Sunday Republican*, 21 February 1960.

37. Ibid., 69–70.

38. The animated effect was intensified by a number of scenes incorporating fire, including a long dramatic closing depicting the burning of Richmond.

39. The inclusion of games like *Twelve Men Morris* and *Fox and Geese* in these multipacks was certainly a way to cash in on the "old methods" I argued Bradley was critical of earlier in this chapter. Still, as I mention below, I think it makes a difference—however economically cynical our perspective might be—that Bradley is transparent and thoughtful about the historical connections to be made through play, whether familial (*My Grandfather's Games*) or national (*Games of 1776*). For Bradley, playing old games is not a way to connect with all eras (the utopic of timeless "childhood") but a way to connect with *specific* times in specific places.

40. Bruce Whitehill, *Games: American Boxed Games and Their Makers, 1822–1992: With Values* (Randor: Wallace-Homestead, 1992), 2.

41. Michael Oriard, *Sporting with the Gods*, 167. *The Game of Goose* was first published in England in 1597 and acted as a template for future games such as *The New Game of Human Life*, *The Mansion of Bliss*, and *The Mansion of Happiness*.

42. Though its U.S. manufacturing is novel, the game itself was not. By all appearances it was a direct reworking of Carrington Bowles's eighteenth-century British game, *A Journey through Europe*.

43. Whitehill, *Games*, 10.

44. As with most games in this era, die rolls were made with a teetotum—a six-sided top

marked with numerical values. Dice were a source of anxiety due to their association of with gambling: "The family taboo against dice was so strong that soldiers during the Civil War who carried them to gamble with would leave them behind when going into battle, so in case they were killed in combat, no dice would be sent back to the family as part of the soldier's personal effects. Because of this, Civil War battlefields are said to be an excellent place to unearth early bone dice" (Whitehill, *Games*, 11).

45. Emerson demonstrates his familiarity with the term in his well-known lecture "The New England Reformers": "Do you complain of our Marriage? Our marriage is no worse than our education.... Can we not play the game of life with these counters, as well as with those?" (Ralph Waldo Emerson, *The Essential Writings of Ralph Waldo Emerson*, ed. Brooks Atkinson [New York: Modern Library, 2000], 407). It is likely that Emerson's prescient reference to the "game of life" is either entirely metaphorical or a reference to the popular *New Game of Human Life*, an import from Europe that bore more resemblance to reform games like *The Mansion of Happiness* (discussed below) than to Bradley's game.

46. Ramsay, *Reading Machines*, 18.

47. Bradley, Social Game.

48. Ibid.

49. Ibid.

50. McKenzie Wark, *Gamer Theory* (Cambridge, Mass.: Harvard University Press, 2007), 31.

51. Not to be confused with the counted points that a player accumulates, a *decision point* is a juncture at which the game would not move forward without player involvement.

52. Bradley, Social Game.

53. Jill Lepore, *The Mansion of Happiness: A History of Life and Death* (New York: Alfred A. Knopf, 2012), xxvii.

54. Shea and Mercer, *It's All in the Game*, plate 11.

55. Similarly ambivalent and yet tellingly situated are squares like "Ruin" (near "Suicide," but also near "Bravery") and "Poverty" (where the only negative outcome is a valueless turn and the possibility of "Disgrace"; positive outcomes include "Honesty," "Ambition," and "School").

56. Whitehill, *Games*, 9, 11

57. Ibid., 9.

58. Halttunen, *Confidence Men*, 3–4.

59. John Locke, "An Essay Concerning Human Understanding," *Modern Philosophy: An Anthology of Primary Sources*, ed. Roger Ariew and Eric Watkins (Indianapolis: Hackett, 1998), 274.

60. Ibid.

61. Whitehill, *Games*, plate 9.

62. Ibid., 11.

63. Ibid., 11.

64. Bradley, Social Game.

65. Ibid.

66. Whitehill, *Games*, 11.

67. This is what makes it jarring when Mary Flanagan, otherwise excellent on the critical impact of games in the playing, discusses *Mansion* and states, "Success is attained through honesty and charity and players are wise to avoid idleness" (Flanagan 79). This takes the rhetorical moralism of the game's instructions at face value rather than working through the practical operations of gameplay. In actuality, success in *Mansion* is attained through continuing to spin the teetotum, spinning high values, and getting lucky about what you land on. There's no way to be

wise about avoiding "Idleness" (*Square* 17)—unless wisdom could be conveyed in the twist of a wooden top.

68. Janet Murray, *Hamlet on the Holodeck: The Future of Narrative in Cyberspace* (New York: Free Press, 1997), 128.

69. Bradley, Social Game.

70. Steven Mintz, *Moralists and Modernizers: America's Pre-Civil War Reformers* (Baltimore: Johns Hopkins University Press, 1995), 13.

71. Emerson, *Essential*, 83–84.

72. Bradley, Social Game. It should be noted again that the particular model of self that is offered by *Life* was of the sort that Bradley himself would have been most personally familiar with: white, Christian, adult, and male. "Fat Office" and "Congress" were not typical life options for women or the majority of nonwhite players. This raises interesting questions, however, when we take into consideration that Bradley absolutely presupposed that women—and non-working-age children for that matter—would be an audience for the game. As I mentioned earlier, one explanation could be a desire to create a deeper sense of performative understanding between family members and their respective patriarchs. At the same time, another layer of explanation might have been somewhat more pragmatic with regard to a game about agency: players of all types were expected to develop a practical understanding of agency by playing at those social actors with the maximal potential for expressing it. It's hard to imagine that the irony could have gone unrecognized.

73. He recounts some of the special difficulties of the early days in the business as follows: "The first pressman I had was one Riddle. This was his real name, but work became slack and Jack enlisted in the war. When he left he said he would come back with shoulder straps [i.e., honorable decorations], and so he did, but minus one arm. After he left I had some jobs to do and found one Jack Kelly, in Hartford, who could pull a press, when he wasn't drunk. One day I missed him, and after waiting for him to turn up, I found him sitting on a baggage truck at the depot, with just enough brain to say he had quit and wouldn't go back again. My greatest anxiety was to get off some prints of 'Christ Blessing the Little Children,' for Gurdon Bill, and as there was no other way . . . I went to work pulling the press myself. The result can well be imagined by any lithographer, but I ran the press till Mr. Bill began to suggest that the work was not as good as it had been formerly, which I was obliged to allow" (Bradley, *A Successful Man*, 13).

74. Shea and Mercer, *It's All in the Game*, 43.

75. Christopher Castiglia provides an excellent background on the aims and shortcomings of reform in the antebellum United States, noting, "Reform espoused self-management as achievable through habitual exercise and continual vigilance" (Castiglia, *Interior States*, 11).

76. Whitehill, *Games*, 9–11, emphasis added.

77. William Wordsworth, "Expostulation and Reply," in *The Age of Romanticism*, ed. Joseph Black et al. (Toronto: Broadview Press, 2006), 199.

78. William Cullen Bryant, "The Prairies," in *Nineteenth-Century American Poetry*, ed. William Spengemann (New York: Penguin Books, 1996), 20.

79. Ibid., 22.

80. Whitman, *Leaves of Grass*, 617, 664.

81. To be sure, in Whitman as in Bradley, accounting is not abandoned. Whitman calls to mind the passive accrual of counter-points in lines such as "I think I will do nothing for a long time but listen, / And accrue what I hear into myself . . . and let sounds contribute toward me" (*Leaves of Grass*, 683). Nevertheless, in what follows I argue that the priority of this accounting is displaced by the operational mechanics of his engulfing script. With Bradley we saw this

displacement visualized in the substitution of the freeform grid for the linear racetrack, moving the counting operations of the game into the hands of players and freeing up the game space for an algorithm of decision. In the final part of this chapter, I make the case that "Song of Myself" invokes the avatar figure of Bradley's game *textually* through the use of repetitive syntax and ambivalent pronouns. The effect is to foreground character as a kind of possibility-machine, the "current and index" (ibid., 680) through which accounting for the discrete units of American life becomes an opportunity for accountability and judgment.

82. By 1856, the image has come closer (read: bigger). A part of me jostles to address this as an indication that Whitman feels he has grown *closer* with a readership. The new edition preface—directly addressed to Emerson, rather than an abstract reader—signals that he now knows who he is looking at in that picture. But let's not get ahead of ourselves. I am aware that this is a flight of speculative fancy—however reasonably suggestive given the content of the book. Undoubtedly, the size of the image simply indicates a willingness on the part of Whitman and his publisher to invest in a larger engraving.

83. Ibid., 662.

84. Ibid., 663. Of course, the line that precedes this might be seen as a contradiction of this view, "You shall not look through my eyes either, nor take things from me." The apparent contradiction, aside from Whitman's own stated sympathy for contradiction, can be seen as a product of the high level of abstraction in his language, an abstraction rendered tractable by thinking of it against a board game metaphor. If you are out of the room when your turn comes up and, upon your returning, I declare, "I moved you," there is no confusion about what it is that I have moved. Similarly, Whitman's writing encourages the reader to take the position of the *poet* (a grammatical, decision-making position, like the marker in a game); it is not asking the reader to inhabit Whitman's physical body, "my eyes."

85. Ibid., 665.

86. For a notable discussion of Whitman's repetitive syntax yielding a sense of cognitive synchrony, see Wai Chee Dimock, "Whitman, Syntax, and Political Theory," in *Breaking Bounds: Whitman and American Cultural Studies.* ed. Betsy Erkkila and Jay Grossman (New York: Oxford University Press, 1996), discussed further below.

87. Whitman, *Leaves of Grass*, 692.

88. See Dillon, *New World Drama*, esp. 1–30.

89. Whitman, "1855 Preface," 622.

90. "The qualities which characterize 'Leaves of Grass' are not the qualities of a fine book or poem or any work of art but the qualities of a living and full-blooded man. . . . You do not read, it is someone that you see in action, in war, or on a ship, or climbing the mountains, or racing along and shouting aloud in pure exultation" (Whitman, *Leaves of Grass*, 785).

91. Ibid., 705.

92. Interestingly, the notion of movement and choice within the domain of "types" has additional resonance with Whitman's composition process during the setting of *Leaves*. Ed Folsom notes this in his analysis of early manuscript fragments: "Since so much changed between the making of these notes and the completion of the book (including the addition of the preface and the reordering of the poems), [Whitman's] manuscript reveals that [he] was actively making substantive last-minute changes—reorganizing, adding, and deleting, even while Andrew Rome was typesetting the poetry" (http://bailiwick.lib.uiowa.edu/whitman/). See also Matt Miller, *Collage of Myself: The Making of* Leaves of Grass (Lincoln: University of Nebraska Press, 2010).

93. Whitman, *Leaves of Grass*, 620.

94. Ibid., 646.

95. Dimock, "Whitman, Syntax, and Political Theory," 70.

96. Ibid., 71, emphasis added.

97. This loss of contingent agency "in effect" may explain the boredom adults find in playing race games like *Candyland* or card games like *War*: "I have no chance here, its all already determined by the order of the cards!"

98. Dimock, "Whitman, Syntax, and Political Theory," 78.

99. Ibid.

100. Whitman, *Leaves of Grass*, 684.

101. Ibid., 705.

102. Whitman, "1855 Preface," 621, ellipses original.

103. Ibid., 685.

104. Castiglia, *Interior States*, 13.

105. For interesting discussions of each of these important nineteenth-century ideologies see Castiglia, *Interior States*; Halttunen, *Confidence Men*; and Rosemary Garland Thomson, who argues, "Machine culture created new somatic geographies. . . . Rather than machines acting as prosthetics for the human body as they had in traditional cultures, the body under industrialization began to seem more like an extension of the machine" ("Introduction," in *Freakery: Cultural Spectacles and the Extraordinary Body*, ed. Thomson [New York: NYU Press, 1996], 11).

CHAPTER 2

1. Walter Aimwell, "Peter Coddle's Trip to New York," in *Jessie; or, Trying to Be Somebody* (Boston: Gould & Lincoln, 1858), 247.

2. Ibid., 257.

3. Ibid., 241.

4. The most detailed account of Simonds's life is a biography appended by his wife to his half-finished book, *Jerry*. Walter Aimwell, *Jerry; or, the Sailor Boy Ashore; to which Is Added a Memoir of the Author with a Likeness* (Boston: Gould & Lincoln, 1864), 151–153, 173. On journalistic accounting among young white men in this period of urban redefinition, see Augst, *The Clerk's Tale*.

5. Aimwell, *Jerry*, 96, 111–113.

6. Ibid., 173, 213.

7. Exploring the prevalence of documentary "fillability" in the context of blank books and journals, Lisa Gitelman notes: "Fillability in some cases suggests a moral economy (diaries and fern and moss albums, for example), and in many others it suggests the cash economy with which nineteenth-century Americans had grown familiar. Filling up evidently helped people locate goods, map transactions, and transfer value, while it also helped them to locate themselves or others within or against the sites, practices, and institutions that helped to structure daily life" (*Paper Knowledge*, 21–22).

8. Aimwell, *Jerry*, 214.

9. Some of this is, obviously, beholden to the didactic elements of the genre—a flat-footed instructionalism rather than a direct aesthetic challenge anticipating modernist experimentalism. Even so, attention to the specific generic differences of didactic and instructional pieces might have some bearing on our overall notion of what constituted typical literary reading and indeed nonliterary reading practices more broadly in this moment. Moreover, it's not certain that the authorial experiments of twentieth-century modernism can be seen as fundamentally

distinct from (and unindebted to) less valorized genres that were embedded in the very texture of these authors' early domestic lives.

10. Aimwell, *Jessie*, 43. Jessie seizes on the phrase as a way of reclaiming a schoolyard taunt: "Oh, it's that drunken Hapley's daughter, isn't it? I wonder who pays the bills. . . . If there's anything I despise, it's to see a poor girl all the time trying to be somebody." Jessie repurposes the "cruel remark" by putting it at the entryway of her determined exercise in self-accounting (ibid., 44).

11. Roughly a quarter of *Jessie*'s pages are devoted to games, whether describing them or narrating their playing (ibid., 172–185, 236–260).

12. Ibid., 295.

13. For more on amateur newspapers—which saw a surge in the 1840s and '50s—see the collection and short synopsis at the American Antiquarian Society: http://www.americanantiquarian.org/amateurnews.htm.

14. This draws on Bruno Latour for the insight that objects/things/mediators ensure the discretely limited sets of action that give abstractions like "ideology" their apparent analytic force and foundation. More often than not, one does not adopt a mental "framework" from out of the ether of ideas; instead, *things* enforce ideology through limitations and affordances that materialize as an intellectual second nature. The idea of a "framework," for Latour and in my own argument, is a *shorthand* and *manicule*, pointing to a cluster of human-media associations that condition forms of agency. See Latour, *Reassembling the Social*, esp. 173–190, 194, 203.

15. Melville, *The Confidence-Man*, 238.

16. See N. Katherine Hayles, *How We Became Posthuman: Virtual Bodies in Cybernetics, Literature, and Informatics* (Chicago: University of Chicago Press, 1999).

17. Juul, *Half-Real: Video Games between Real Rules and Fictional Worlds* (Cambridge, Mass.: MIT Press, 2005), 60, emphasis original.

18. Discussed below, both Wai Chee Dimock and William V. Spanos address this instrumentality in some depth, through the heuristics of "accountable selves" and "materialist optimism," respectively. See Dimock, *Empire for Liberty: Melville and the Poetics of Individualism* (Princeton: Princeton University Press, 1989), 180–196; and Spanos, *Herman Melville and the American Calling: The Fiction after Moby-Dick, 1851–1857* (New York: SUNY Press, 2008), 180–197. On *character*, see Karen Halttunen, *Confidence Men and Painted Women* and James B. Salazar, *Bodies of Reform: The Rhetoric of Character in Gilded Age America* (New York: NYU Press, 2010).

19. In the past twenty years, scholarship predominantly under the umbrella of New Media studies has made some headway into parsing the connections and distinctions between the literary and the algorithmic (for example, state machines); yet an overwhelming majority of these studies have fixated (understandably) on the twentieth century for their objects of analysis. See especially Aarseth, *Cybertext*; Bogost, *Unit Operations*; and Kirschenbaum, *Mechanisms*.

20. Respectively, John Bryant, "*The Confidence-Man*: Melville's Problem Novel," in *A Companion to Melville Studies*, ed. John Bryant (New York: Greenwood Press, 1986), 316; Spanos, *Melville and the American Calling*, 212; and Sianne Ngai, *Ugly Feelings* (Cambridge, Mass.: Harvard University Press, 2005), 50. And though she is not making a *computational* argument, Susan M. Ryan also gets at the functionalism of the novel through her examinations of the "etiquette of charity." Etymologically, "etiquette" refers to a flyleaf or label attached to an object detailing its contents and instructions for use—suggestively similar to the term "protocol" (OED). See Ryan, *The Grammar of Good Intentions: Race and the Antebellum Culture of Benevolence* (Ithaca: Cornell University Press, 2003), esp. 60–88.

21. For a useful digest of the novel's early critical reception—when it was largely dismissed as "baffling, unreadable, and incomprehensible"—see Bryant, "*The Confidence-Man*: Melville's Problem Novel," 331–334; see also Brian Higgins and Hershel Parker, *Herman Melville: The Contemporary Reviews* (Cambridge: Cambridge University Press, 1995). Updating this catalog of responses, Elizabeth Renker comments on the historical view of the novel's "unreadability" by arguing that it "*is* unreadable" because "in it [Melville] took on and explored the obstructing page that was at the core of his own writing anxiety; as he did so, he displaced his frustration with the page onto the reader" ("'A ———!': Unreadability in *The Confidence-Man*," in *The Cambridge Companion to Herman Melville*, ed. Robert S. Levine [Cambridge: Cambridge University Press, 1999], 116–117). And in a similar light, Rick Mitchell argues that Melville creates "an unstable text that continually frustrates the reader's attempts to gain (illusory) mastery . . . of the narrative" ("*The Confidence Man*: Performing the Magic of Modernity," *European Journal of American Culture* 23.1 [2004]: 62). Departing from the semiotic focus of these readings, this chapter approaches "unreadable" moments—such as the absent Mark Winsome exclamation that inspires Renker's title—as figurations of the operationalism that was emerging as a necessary part of everyday life in the nineteenth century United States. Where Renker and Mitchell see textual opacity and gestures toward deconstructive indeterminacy, my reading appends opportunistic structural engagements with figures of machinery and incremental reform.

22. Herman Melville, *The Confidence-Man: His Masquerade*, ed. Herschel Parker and Mark Niemeyer (New York: Norton, 2006), 62, emphasis added.

23. Melville, *The Confidence-Man*, 304–312.

24. As noted in contemporary reviews of the book, *The Confidence-Man* was sold at locales like H. P. Ives and A. A. Smith's shop in Salem and A. Williams and Co. in Boston—places also known for sales of games such as the immediate predecessor to *Peter Coddle* called *A Trip to Paris* (discussed below). *Salem Register*, 6 April 1857, 2.

25. Melville, *The Confidence-Man*, 77.

26. At the core of this reframing of nineteenth-century print culture is Meredith McGill's *American Literature and the Culture of Reprinting*. More recently, Ellen Gruber Garvey has expanded this sensibility to include amateur scrapbookers and less official sites of documentary aggregation, arguing that "people in positions of relative powerlessness used their scrapbooks to make a place for themselves and their communities by finding, sifting, analyzing, and recirculating writing that mattered to them. . . . Scrapbook makers' work mirrored the practices of newspaper editors, who continually clipped and recirculated material, so that a single article in a local paper potentially reached millions of readers throughout the country." See Garvey, *Writing with Scissors: American Scrapbooks from the Civil War to the Harlem Renaissance* (Oxford: Oxford University Press, 2012), 4.

27. See Lara Langer Cohen and Jordan Alexander Stein, eds., *Early African American Printing* (Philadelphia: University of Pennsylvania Press, 2012).

28. See Gitelman, *Paper Knowledge*, and John Guillory, "The Memo and Modernity," *Critical Inquiry* 31.1 (Autumn 2004): 108–132.

29. Though the precise cause of Simonds's death, beyond "lung hemorrhage," is unstated in the memoir compiled posthumously by his wife, it was likely tuberculosis contracted during his time as a printer that caught up with him, as complications from the disease were varied and long-term, even for those who survived early symptoms. A truly shocking number of people involved in the printing industry were afflicted with tuberculosis as a result of having to work in cramped and unsanitary conditions during the nineteenth-century printing boom. The chemicals used in printing were often breeding grounds for the bacteria that triggered and aggravated

lung infection, especially in poorly ventilated spaces. Records from the U.S. Bureau of Labor Statistics show that the average life expectancy for compositors in 1850 was only twenty-eight. See "Hygiene of the Printing Trades," in *The Bulletin of the U.S. Bureau of Labor Statistics* 209 (April 1917): 73.

30. William Simonds, "Hymn," in *Poems, Delivered, on Various Occasions, Before the Mechanic Apprentices' Library Association* (Boston: I. R. Butts, 1842).

31. *Boston Saturday Rambler*, 2 January 1847, 2.

32. Ibid. Ryan Cordell has recently shown that similar operations were at work in the recirculation and reconfiguration of Nathaniel Hawthorne's short story "The Celestial Railroad." See Cordell, " 'Taken Possession of': The Reprinting and Reauthorship of Hawthorne's 'Celestial Railroad' in the Antebellum Religious Press," *Digital Humanities Quarterly* 7.1 (2013): http://digitalhumanities.org/dhq/vol/7/1/000144/000144.html (accessed 9 February 2017).

33. Though boasting fifty thousand subscribers by the start of 1847, the *Boston Saturday Rambler* was consistently plagued by financial trouble that appears to have been the direct consequence of delinquent subscription payments (a common problem for newspapers of this moment). A darkly humorous subthread of editorials chastise readers for their failure to support the paper in none-too-subtle poems such as "Have I Paid the Printer?" An article on "Cheap Papers" echoes the sentiment: "All that we ask is . . . that they appreciate the advantages they enjoy, by promptly *paying* the trifling sum by which the printer furnishes them with their weekly sheet." *Boston Saturday Rambler*, 24 October 1846, 31 October 1846, and 2 January 1847. For more on the economics of the newspaper world, see Leon Jackson's excellent *The Business of Letters: Authorial Economies in Antebellum America* (Stanford: Stanford University Press, 2008), esp. 120–126.

34. *Boston Saturday Rambler* 7 November 1846.

35. Laura Wasowicz, "19th-Century American Children's Book Trade Directory," American Antiquarian Society: http://www.americanantiquarian.org/btdirectory.htm (accessed May 2016).

36. Herman Melville, *Typee: A Peep at Polynesian Life* (New York: Modern Library, 2001), 132, 145.

37. William Simonds, *The Boy's Own Guide to Good Principles, Habits and Manners* (Boston: Massachusetts Sabbath School Society, 1853), 13.

38. Mudge and Spooner disappear from the public record after this production—though Amsden and Company (later Adams and Company, a major catalog dry goods firm) continue to produce the game with the same text under the title "The Most Laughable Thing" for at least thirty years.

39. *A Trip to Paris* (Boston: Mudge and Spooner, 1857), 1. Mudge and Spooner draw their world of substantive things from popular culture, and perhaps even from interesting literary figures: an "Ourang Outang," "a sperm whale" and a "pop gun" all make potential appearances in *Trip*. A more exhaustive study of these transformation games than I have yet been able to undertake might find productive territory in a comparative chronological assessment of the "random" objects that were used. Each version—from Mudge and Spooner's *Trip* to Simonds's *Peter Coddle* to Milton Bradley's *Sam Slick* variations on the game—came with more than a hundred cards, and to my surprise, few cards ever repeat. One can imagine buying a new game *simply for the new cards* as they would have cross-operability (such as it was) with any other game of the sort, shifting it into a new register of object associations.

40. *Trip to Paris*, iv.

41. Ibid., 16.

42. By the 1890s, every major game manufacturer from Milton Bradley to Parker Brothers had seemingly created its own bootleg using Peter's name. Coddle traveled around the country, from Boston to Chicago, even making a brief stint on the battlefront of the Great War. See the International Games Database at the AGPC website: http://www.agpc.org/archives/gamecatalog.html (accessed 9 February 2017).

43. This allies Coddle's narrative with the developing genre of male career journaling, where the opening gesture is one of travel from home in search of the accountable experiences, things, and money that will define a free (masculine-inflected) "self." Enos White, for example, writes in 1821, "This Day I leave my Father after having got him to consent to my being Free. I leave in good spirits, although my prospects are very small, and the opinion of my friends is that I shall soon wish myself back again. I am now eighteen years and five months old with one decent suit of clothes and fifteen dollars in change to commence my career with" (quoted in Augst, *The Clerk's Tale*, 20).

44. Aimwell, *Jessie*, 242.

45. Ibid., 248–249.

46. Ibid., 257.

47. Ibid., 257–258.

48. It was only in playing the game strictly according to its rules with an entire class of sharp undergraduates at SUNY Oswego that I was able to see the way that timing and anticipation are critical elements of the game's overall pleasure matrix. I'm thankful to the students in both runs of my senior seminar Confidence/Games—especially Nadia Misir, Naomi Fogg, and Kayleigh Grimm—for their insights during these play-throughs.

49. Ibid.,

50. Twentieth-century computational scientists, like Claude Shannon, would use Boole's propositional logic as the basis of switchboards that would become the foundation of computing. See Andrew Emerson, "Obituary: Claude Shannon," *Guardian*, 7 March 2001, http://www.guardian.co.uk/science/2001/mar/08/obituaries.news (accessed 9 February 2017).

51. George Boole, *An Investigation of the Laws of Thought* (Amherst: Prometheus Books, 2003), 402, 407.

52. Ibid., 422.

53. John Corcoran, "Introduction," in Boole, *Laws of Thought*, xviii.

54. Melville, *The Confidence-Man*, 17.

55. This argument draws on the notion of "probabilistic materiality" developed (and performed) brilliantly in regard to form, format, and medium in Johanna Drucker's "Entity to Event: From Literal, Mechanistic Materiality to Probabilistic Materiality," *Parallax* 15.4 (2009): 7–17.

56. Of course, the name of the boat itself also evokes a certain changeless consistency despite the changing flow of the material world, punning on the French "fidélité" meaning "faith;" see the *Oxford English Dictionary* online, s.v. "fidélité" and "fidèle," http://www.oed.com.

57. Melville, *The Confidence-Man*, 15.

58. Melville invokes just such a metaphor of "function" and "argument" in his earlier novel *Pierre: or, The Ambiguities* (1852). Developing a scheme to rescue his supposed half-sister Isabel from poverty by pretending as though they are married, Pierre glosses over the role that his current fiancée, Lucy Tartan, will play in the (ultimately self-destroying) charade: "Lucy was so intimately interwoven, that it seemed impossible for him at all to cast his future without some way having that heart's love in view. But ignorant of its quantity as yet, or fearful of ascertaining it; like an algebraist, for the real Lucy he . . . had substituted but a sign—some empty *x*—and in

the ultimate solution of the problem, that empty *x* still figured, not the real Lucy" (Herman Melville, *Pierre: or, The Ambiguities*, ed. William Spengemann [New York: Penguin Books, 1996], 181). Appropriately enough, this moment occurs in "Book X" of *Pierre*. For more on Melville's education and particular interests in math, see Zachary Turpin, "Melville, Mathematics, and Platonic Idealism," *Leviathan* 17.2 (2015): 18–24, and Meredith Farmer, "Herman Melville and Joseph Henry at the Albany Academy; or Melville's Education in Mathematics and Science," *Leviathan* 18.2 (2016): 4–28.

59. Melville, *The Confidence-Man*, 9. It is worth noting, as does John Bryant, that the terms "stranger" or "other" are reserved nearly "exclusively for the confidence men both early in the novel and late"—being used more than a hundred times in this manner. Each of these "strangers" is indeed an "excellent rhetorician who molds himself and his arguments to fit the needs of a particular audience," though I would add a productive doubleness to the term "argument" as used here (Bryant, *Melville and Repose: The Rhetoric of Humor in the American Renaissance* [New York: Oxford University Press, 1993], 237–238).

60. Melville, *The Confidence-Man*, 10–11.

61. Ibid., 11–12.

62. Ibid., 12.

63. Gustaaf Van Cromphout argues that the deaf man is a symbol for the impossibility of knowing other minds, citing the "unenlightening" descriptors the passengers assign while watching him nap (Cromphout, " 'The Confidence-Man': Melville and the Problem of Others," *Studies in American Fiction*, 21.1 [1993]: 39). I would argue instead that the novel underlines the capacity of social interactions to determine personal legibility (one's own "mind" included). Melville foregrounds the constitutive sociality of anything that could be construed as what Cromphout calls a "true self" (39). In this way, I agree with Rachel Cole that the Confidence-Man "represents the possibility that personhood might be irreducibly social" (Cole, "At the Limits of Identity: Realism and American Personhood in Melville's *Confidence-Man*," *Novel* 39.3 [2006]: 386).

64. Melville, *The Confidence-Man*, 13.

65. Ibid., 13–14.

66. Aimwell, *Jessie*, 242.

67. See the *Oxford English Dictionary* online, s.v. "state," http://www.oed.com.

68. Eric Slauter, *The State as a Work of Art: The Cultural Origins of the Constitution* (Chicago: University of Chicago Press, 2009), 8–9.

69. James Chandler, *England in 1819: The Politics of Literary Culture and the Case of Romantic Historicism* (Chicago: University of Chicago Press, 1998), 121–122.

70. Ibid, 128.

71. See Gitelman, *Paper Knowledge*, 1–10.

72. See Benedict Anderson, *Imagined Communities: Reflections on the Origin and Spread of Nationalism* (New York: Verso, 2006).

73. Castiglia, *Interior States*, 7.

74. Ibid., 3–9.

75. Cultural anthropologist Victor Turner discusses this in terms of patterns of social intimacy that form around shared proximate experience—"communitas," in his terminology—that are memorialized and codified through social ritual: "Initially free and innovative relationships between individuals are converted into norm-governed relationships between social *personae*" (Turner, *From Ritual to Theater*, 47). In Turner's earlier work, such "personae" were explicitly discussed in terms relevant to twenty-first-century theories of posthumanism: "These individual

and group structures, carried in people's head and nervous systems, have a steering function, a 'cybernetic' function, in the endless succession of social events, imposing on them the degree of order they possess, and, indeed, dividing processual units into phases" (Turner, *Dramas, Fields, Metaphors*, 36). To both Turner's and Castiglia's formulations I think it is important to add that these "interiors" or "structures" are not dematerialized geometries of *mind* but practiced habits of bodily action, speaking, and writing. The sense of an "interior" is effectively produced through media engagements of the sort we saw at the beginning of this chapter with William Simonds—journaling, gameplay, and other forms of socialized documentary interaction that are then mis-recognized as individual and contained. See Turner, *From Ritual to Theatre: The Human Seriousness of Play* (New York: Performing Arts Journal Publications, 1982); *Dramas, Fields, and Metaphors: Symbolic Action in Human Society* (Ithaca: Cornell University Press, 1974); and "Lim-inality and the Performative Genres," in *Rite, Drama, Festival, Spectacle: Rehearsals toward a Theory of Cultural Performance* (Philadelphia: Institute for the Study of Human Issues, 1984).

76. Castiglia, *Interior States*, 10.

77. Bryant makes the point that the novel itself puts the reader in a similar position, writ-ing that, by the end, "Melville's argument seems to disintegrate for lack of a resolute voice, and readers must float between a 'maybe yes' and 'maybe no' " (*Melville and Repose*, 232).

78. Melville, *The Confidence-Man*, 26.

79. Ibid., 42.

80. Ibid., 240.

81. Ibid., 239.

82. Ibid., 135.

83. Dimock, *Empire for Liberty*, 195. For Dimock, the image of the "promising self" renders the individual a kind of victim by default, as they must perpetually account for how their accu-mulated actions measure up to this image (or frequently fail to): "A promising self is a commod-ity whose ownership must be continually renewed—whose ownership can be guaranteed only by endless acts of purchase. As a circuit of reflexive exchange, the promising self stands as a utopian marketplace. One that completes its production and consumption . . . all within the compass of a single individual" (196). Yet Dimock's focus on the "single individual" in this pas-sage deemphasizes the manner in which these transactions are always social (*The Confidence-Man* is a series of dialogues, not monologues). I would argue that one of Melville's accomplishments in the novel is precisely to trouble the apparent insularity Dimock registers by showing the ways in which the "circuit" is always already socially constructed in a network of figural *machines* and *arguments*.

84. Melville, *The Confidence-Man*, 17.

85. On this topic, I find Spanos's discussion of the Confidence-Man "de-centering" and then "re-centering" his marks useful (*Melville and the American Calling*, 180–181). The figure of "centering" is slightly misleading, however, as the Confidence-Man's interlocutors never truly find a "center" so much as they are given tactical "arguments" that allow them to produce legible statements of character—they find confidence in others reading them as they would like to be read. Legibility, in this qualified view, suggests the important social dimension of this process; their anxiety has to do with a desire to play a specific role within a social network rather than solely a desire to resolve their individual *being*.

86. Paul Brodtkorb argues similarly that "a precondition of knowing oneself would be a personal consistency, yet a man could be consistent only if . . . he had a static idea of Man good for all occasions to which he could refer as if it were his essence. Yet . . . the essence of human nature is probably inconsistency" (Brodtkorb, "The Confidence-Man: The Con-Man as Hero,"

Studies in the Novel 1.4 [1969]: 426). I take a more functional approach to the relationship between con man and mark, noting reciprocity between the *appearances* of consistency and inconsistency. Taken alone, the Confidence-Man may be a symbol of the latter, yet his interaction with the passengers of the *Fidèle* draws attention to the procession of ephemeral decisions (always potentially inconsistent) that constitute apparent stability.

87. Melville, *The Confidence-Man*, 42.

88. Ibid.

89. Ibid., 52.

90. Ibid.

91. Ibid., 52.

92. Ibid., 53.

93. Ibid.

94. Ibid., 53.

95. Ibid., 54.

96. Ibid., 33–36.

97. Ibid., 36. The original "confidence-man," the historical figure from whom the term is drawn, was a Manhattan operator who played upon the egos of urban newcomers. Lamenting the lack of "confidence" among city gentlemen in the modern era, Thomas McDonald would close his conversation with potential marks by asking them to demonstrate their confidence in the loyalty of old acquaintances by leaving him with their watch—promising to return it the following day before disappearing into the crowd with a chuckle. After months of theft, McDonald was arrested, and the story became a sensation in the popular press, prompting reflections on the optimism of the population and the growing necessity of skepticism in a changing world. See Johannes Dietrich Bergmann, "The Original Confidence-Man," excerpted in Herman Melville, *The Confidence-Man: His Masquerade*, ed. Herschel Parker and Mark Niemeyer (New York: Norton, 2006), 304–312.

98. Melville, *The Confidence-Man*, 54.

99. Ibid., 54, emphasis added.

100. Ibid., 55.

101. Ibid., 58.

102. To be discrete in this sense is to produce precisely one output state when given one input. This is why it is imperative that the Confidence-Man manage complete "confidence," "no ifs" (ibid., 81).

103. Ibid., 161.

104. Ibid., 135.

105. Ibid., 132.

106. Ibid., 133.

107. Ibid.

108. Ibid.

109. Ibid., 81.

110. Ibid., 142.

111. Michael Paul Rogin registers this modulation of character: "The cosmopolitan remains a single character, present throughout the novel's second half. But while the confidence man would be self-sufficient (if he had a self), the cosmopolitan demands relationship with other characters. . . . The confidence man defrauds his victims and leaves them; the cosmopolitan seeks ongoing connections. The confidence man is a success; the cosmopolitan is a failure" (Rogin, *Subversive Genealogy: The Politics and Art of Herman Melville* [New York: Knopf, 1983],

245, 247). Developing this, I would argue that, in fact, we have seen that the Confidence-Man is never truly "self-sufficient" and always signifies a form of contact, however damaging it might be. The "ongoing connections" sought in the second half of the novel are in fact the same connections figured in the first half, but from a reversed perspective—that of an agile cooperator. And while the lack of substantial monetary gain differentiates Frank Goodman from the previous incarnations of the Confidence-Man, I am hesitant to plot his action on the success/failure continuum that Rogin does. Games typically have locally determined winners and losers, but in a *social* continuum one is not a "failure" when one withholds from dominating a younger sibling in a game of pick-up basketball or backgammon. There can be joy and "success" in the playing, and in the losing. Melville explores this, skeptically of course, through the character of Goodman.

112. Bryant, *Melville and Repose*, 240, 250.

113. Melville, *The Confidence-Man*, 74.

114. Spanos, *Melville and the American Calling*, 181–182.

115. Louis Marin, *Utopics: The Semiological Play of Textual Spaces*, trans. Robert A. Vollrath (Amherst: Humanity Books, 1984), 14.

116. Merlin Bowen gets at this blind anticipation, noting, "*The Confidence-Man* is not a sermon . . . but a gesture" (Bowen, "Tactics of Indirection in Melville's *The Confidence-Man*," *Studies in the Novel*, 1.4 [1969], 418). Marin argues that utopic discourse always has this gestural quality as a consequence of its being a "schema in search of a concept" (*Utopics*, 163).

117. This connection is hinted at by Wyn Kelley, who notes, "[Melville's] concern with invention . . . seems emblematic of the larger project with which the American nation and its people were centrally engaged in the nineteenth century" (Kelley, *Herman Melville: An Introduction* [Oxford: Wiley-Blackwell, 2008], xv). Indeed, early on, the Confidence-Man takes an inventor's guise, claiming to have created the "Protean easy-chair" (Melville, *The Confidence-Man*, 47).

118. See the *Oxford English Dictionary* online, s.v. "invent," http://www.oed.com.

119. Herman Melville, "Letter to Nathaniel Hawthorne, May 1851," in *Moby-Dick*, ed. Herschel Parker and Mark Niemeyer (New York: Norton, 2006), 541.

120. Melville, *The Confidence-Man*, 237–238.

CHAPTER 3

1. Henry E. Dudeney, "Tales with Tangrams," *Strand Magazine* 36 (July–December 1908): 581. Dudeney, an important early twentieth-century puzzle maker in the United Kingdom and contributor to the *Strand Magazine* (famous for both its puzzle section and its serialization of Arthur Conan Doyle's Sherlock Holmes stories), writes that the game is "a recreation that appears to be at least four thousand years old, that has apparently never been dormant, and that has not been altered or 'improved upon' since the Chinaman Tan first cut out the seven pieces [that constitute the puzzle]" (Dudeney 581). Dudeney's mistaken (and widely circulated) account is directly drawn from that of Sam Loyd, discussed below. Even after it was debunked in 1911, this account continued to circulate for many years.

2. The name "tangram" originated in the United States, though its history is obscure. Jerry Slocum notes that the first book of these puzzles published in the U.S. was James Coxe's *Chinese Philosophical and Mathematical Trangram*, and that Coxe may have picked up the word "trangram" from a short-lived literary magazine called *The Trangram; or Fashionable Trifler*. This may

be, as games and puzzles in this period were often referred to as "trifles," as was the case in the popular billiard game of "bagatelle," which translates from the French as "little trifle." Later, educator and Harvard Divinity School graduate Thomas Hill was the first to coin the word "tangram" (without the "r") in his 1848 *Puzzles for the Young*. It seems likely that he removed the "r" from Coxe's earlier formulation to make the name more accurately reflect the game's Chinese lineage ("t'ang" being Cantonese for "Chinese"). See Jerry Slocum with Jack Botermans et al., *The Tangram Book: The Story of the Chinese Puzzle with over 2000 Puzzles to Solve* (New York: Sterling, 2004), 16–19, 23, 30.

3. Slocum, *The Tangram Book*, 38–39.

4. Ibid., 32, 70, 76. In addition to the Coxe edition (1817), Wallis's *Fashionable Puzzle* was bootlegged by American A. T. Goodrich and advertised in New York and Boston through 1822.

5. Slocum, *The Tangram Book*, 88.

6. Ibid., 85.

7. Knockoffs incorporating differently shaped pieces, like I. U. Mueller's "Puzzle Blocks," show a continued demand for the type of configurative puzzle that the tangram epitomized (U.S. Patent 37,763 [24 February 1863]). Between 1865 and 1875 there was even "more public interest in Tangrams, due primarily to the use of Tangrams in education, and numerous books and boxed sets were produced by several companies" (Slocum, *The Tangram Book*, 85). This is unsurprising, due to the rise in interest in spatial and geometric toys fostered by the kindergarten movement in the United States. The Froebel toys (cubes, pyramids, squares) advocated by this movement and mass produced by Milton Bradley at the time weren't far from the regular geometric shapes of tangrams, and encouraged similar habits of mind.

8. Phineas Taylor Barnum, *The Humbugs of the World* (Landisville: Coachwhip Publications, 2008), 15. Barnum's use of the phrase "outside show" refers to the inside/outside dynamic of nineteenth-century dime museums: "Generally the platform attractions [inside the museum] were described by the 'lecturer' or 'inside talker' (as opposed to the 'outside talker' who ground away at a prepared pitch on the sidewalk in front of the museum, drawing customers into the show)" (McNamara, 224). For more on the history of the dime museum, see Brooks McNamara, "'A Congress of Wonders': The Rise and Fall of the Dime Museum," *ESQ* 20.3 (1974): 216–232.

9. Quoted in Slocum, *The Tangram Book*, 55.

10. "Our Founder Sam Loyd," https://samloyd.com/about-sam-loyd/our-founder-sam -loyd/ (accessed 14 March 2017).

11. This moniker forms the title of a 1907 interview with Loyd in the *Strand Magazine*.

12. My use of "paratext" draws from that of Steven E. Jones in *The Meaning of Video Games*: "The paratext is a multilayered system of frames around a text that helps determine its reception, from naming the genre ('mystery') or implied audience ('trade paperback' or 'bestseller'), to advance reviews printed as blurbs, or the footnotes and index, even an author's photo, all of which affect how the book is read and interpreted" (7). Here, I'm less interested in the concept as applied exclusively to books and more interested in Jones's development of it as a way to think about the sociocultural/material embeddedness of games and other objects of material culture. Jones moves away from Gérard Genette's focus on verbal texts to include "extra-textual and non-verbal features, such as the technologies and material means of printing, publishing, page design, illustration, but also, relatively seamlessly, the machinery of marketing, previews, and reception, the whole *social* realm in which texts are given meanings by the transactions between their producers and their readers and critics" (8, emphasis original). See Jones, *The Meaning of Video Games* (New York: Routledge, 2008).

13. Phineas Taylor Barnum, *The Life of P. T. Barnum, Written by Himself* (Urbana: University of Illinois Press, 2000), 234–35.

14. Ibid., 231.

15. Ibid., 238.

16. Christopher Looby, "Introduction," in Robert Montgomery Bird, *Sheppard Lee: Written by Himself* (New York: New York Review Books, 2008): xviii–xix. For more on early national education, see Terence Martin, *The Instructed Vision: Scottish Common Sense Philosophy and the Origins of American Fiction* (Bloomington: Indiana University Press, 1961).

17. Lauren Berlant, "The Commons: Infrastructures for Troubling Times," *Environment and Planning D: Society and Space* 34.3 (2016): 393, 394.

18. Rosemarie Garland Thomson, "Introduction: From Wonder to Error—A Genealogy of Freak Discourse in Modernity," in *Freakery*, ed. Thomson (New York: NYU Press, 1996), 10.

19. Harris, *Humbug*, 79.

20. The general view of spectacle as an exercise in distancing oneself from otherness, with the effect of reimagining a clear line between subject and "territory," stems from Susan Stewart's important work in *On Longing: Narratives of the Miniature, the Gigantic, the Souvenir, the Collection* (Durham: Duke University Press, 1993), esp. 108–110. While I would not argue against this position on the whole, I believe, building from Judith Pascoe's reflections on Romantic-era collecting in *The Hummingbird Cabinet*, that there are other ways of understanding the social practices bound up in exhibitionary culture. See Pascoe, *The Hummingbird Cabinet: A Rare and Curious History of Romantic Collectors* (Ithaca: Cornell University Press, 2006).

21. Barnum, *Life*, 25.

22. Ibid., 26.

23. Ibid.

24. Eric Fretz, "P. T. Barnum's Theatrical Selfhood and the Nineteenth-Century Culture of Exhibition," in *Freakery*, ed. Thomson, 99.

25. James W. Cook, ed., *The Colossal P. T. Barnum Reader: Nothing Else Like It in the Universe* (Urbana: University of Illinois Press, 2005), 182.

26. Cook, *Reader*, 183–184; Barnum, *Life*, 152.

27. Barnum, *Life*, 157.

28. This is hinted at in Bluford Adams's gloss on Barnum's decision not to salvage objects from the American Museum after the fire that burned it to the ground (discussed later): "In the aftermath of the 1865 fire, it became clear that Barnum's stories were far more important than the objects they supposedly contextualized. The *New York Herald* attributed the showman's decision not to salvage any of his treasures from the Museum's ruins to the fact that 'it became rather a difficult matter to identify them or trace their history, as was so carefully marked out while on exhibition.' Rather than rewrite narratives around his old curiosities, Barnum apparently found it easier to generate new stories around new objects." See Bluford Adams, *E Pluribus Barnum: The Great Showman and the Making of U.S. Popular Culture* (Minneapolis: University of Minnesota Press, 1997), 86.

29. See Elizabeth Maddock Dillon's *New World Drama* for a wonderful example of an extended study that *does* attend to the coordinated effects of staging and racial performance, as well as Uri McMillan's *Embodied Avatars*, discussed below.

30. Barnum, *Life*, 143.

31. Benjamin Reiss, *The Showman and the Slave: Race, Death, and Memory in Barnum's America* (Cambridge, Mass.: Harvard University Press, 2001), 7.

32. Uri McMillan, "Mammy-Memory: Staging Joice Heth, or the Curious Phenomenon of

the 'Ancient Negress,'" *Women & Performance: A Journal of Feminist Theory* 22.1 (August 2012): 31. On the "ontic" dimensions of theatrical performance as distinct from the "mimetic" dimensions, see Dillon, *New World Drama*.

33. McMillan traces these alternative modes through a number of situational simultaneities: "[Heth existed] simultaneously as a well-rehearsed performer, a tactile object of display, and a commodity owned by her ostensible master P. T. Barnum" (McMillan, *Embodied Avatars*, 32).

34. Bernstein defines a "scriptive thing" as "an item of material culture that prompts meaningful bodily behaviors" (*Racial Innocence*, 71–72). This can get tricky when the "script" in play is emerging *from within a performance*, as is the case here. Nevertheless, as I discuss, I think it makes sense to say that Heth's particular being in the room—as a person of certain dimensions, inflections, and exhalations—prompts her audiences in ways that go beyond the staging of self and other that is explicitly arranged by Barnum.

35. Bernstein, *Racial Innocence*, 69–71.

36. Reiss, *The Showman and the Slave*, 219; McMillan, *Embodied Avatars*, 57–62.

37. This draws on Bernstein's redeployment of Roland Barthes in sketching a loose boundary between objects and things: "The difference between objects and things, then, is not essential but situational and subjective. The distinction between object and thing parallels Roland Barthes's distinction, in photography, between *studium* and *punctum*. The *studium* consists of a photograph's general visual field; it openly displays what the photographer photographed and thus enables a viewer to encounter the photographer's conscious intentions. The *punctum* is a small detail in the photograph that punctures the *studium*" (72).

38. Barnum, *Life*, 155.

39. Reiss sees Thorburn's fixation here as linked to his business connections among Southern tobacco planters (Reiss, *The Showman and the Slave*, 44–45). This seems plausible even as it doesn't change the *fact* of Heth smoking or explain away her own reasons for such prolific "inveteracy." Addiction or no, smokers are aware that their habit fills a room. The practices revolving around smoking might be fruitfully examined for their social and antisocial dimensions, though of course that's beyond my scope here.

40. David Claypoole Johnston, "Phrenology Exemplified and Illustrated," in *Scraps No. 7* (1837). American Antiquarian Society.

41. McMillan, *Embodied Avatars*, 28.

42. Thomson, *Freakery*, 10.

43. Addressing the potential for dementia in Heth, Reiss writes: "Even in delusion there is some shaping force, some motivation for the performance" (*The Showman and the Slave*, 223).

44. USPTO, "U.S. Patent Activity Calendar Years 1790 to the Present," http://www.uspto .gov/web/offices/ac/ido/oeip/taf/h_counts.htm (accessed 14 March 2017).

45. On the difficulties of using existing patent documentation, see B. Zorina Khan: "The major problems with patent statistics as a measure of inventive activity and technological change are that not all inventions are patented or can be patented; the propensity to patent differs across time, industries and activities; patents vary in terms of intrinsic and commercial value; patents might not be directly comparable across countries or time because of differences in institutional features and enforcement; and patents are a better gauge of inputs than productivity or output." Khan, *The Democratization of Invention: Patents and Copyrights in American Economic Development, 1790–1920* (Cambridge: Cambridge University Press, 2005), 27 n. 51. See also Christine MacLeod, *Inventing the Industrial Revolution: The English Patent System, 1660–1800* (Cambridge: Cambridge University Press, 2002). Khan argues that the pace of invention was accelerated in the United States because of its more "democratic" patent system: "Democratic objectives were

achieved through innovations such as reserving patent rights to the first and true inventor in the world, efficient centralized processing and examination of application, fees that were set at a low level, and countervailing checks and balances in the legal system. The public had ready access to patent specifications, which promoted the diffusion of inventions, and the system also facilitated extensive trade in patented technologies. These provisions encouraged inventors to obtain property rights in *incremental inventions* and small improvements in design and technique that could be applied across many industries" (29–30, emphasis added).

46. For more on the cultural impact of these concepts see Rosemarie Garland Thomson, "Introduction," in *Freakery*; Neil Harris, "The Operational Aesthetic," in *Humbug*; and Frances Ferguson, who argues that utilitarianism used disciplinary structures to exhibit "previously imperceptible kinds of action . . . to discern their value" via "constant comparisons of actions" (24, 30). See Ferguson, *Pornography, the Theory: What Utilitarianism Did to Action* (Chicago: University of Chicago Press, 2004), 24, 30.

47. Barnum, *Life*, 26.

48. MacLeod suggests that "it is . . . worth considering whether the rise in patent totals may bear witness less to an upsurge in inventive activity than to developments both in the patent system and in the economy at large that increased the propensity to patent" (*Inventing the Industrial Revolution*, 144). Abraham Lincoln put it in pithier terms, reflecting that, "The patent system added the fuel of interest to the fire of genius" (quoted in Khan, *The Democratization of Invention*, 182).

49. U.S. Constitution, Article I, Section 8, Clause 8: https://www.archives.gov/founding -docs/constitution-transcript (accessed 27 October 2017).

50. https://en.wikisource.org/wiki/United_States_Statutes_at_Large/Volume_1/1st_Congress /2nd_Session/Chapter_7 (accessed 27 October 2017).

51. Khan, *The Democratization of Invention*, 31, 43.

52. In 1861, the cost of a U.S. patent was raised slightly to $35; by contrast, the English system "reflected its origins in royal privilege," ensuring that none but the most elite (and rich) could obtain a patent by maintaining a baroque cluster of entrenched institutions in London (each with its own related gatekeepers and fees) and incredibly high costs: "Patent fees for England . . . amounted to £100–£120 ($585), or approximately four times per capita income in 1860" (ibid., 31). In France, costs were not as high as in England, but a lack of central organization (and aforementioned lack of inspection), meant that it was exceedingly difficult to develop knowledgeable improvements to existing ideas: "At least until the law of April 7, 1902, specifications were only available in manuscript form in the [provincial] office in which they had originally been lodged, and printed information was limited to brief titles in patent indexes" (ibid., 45).

53. Ibid., 59.

54. See Tony Bennett, *The Birth of the Museum: History, Theory, Politics* (New York: Routledge, 1995); and Les Harrison, *The Temple and the Forum: The American Museum and Cultural Authority in Hawthorne, Melville, Stowe, and Whitman* (Tuscaloosa: University of Alabama Press, 2007), xiii.

55. Shea and Mercer, *It's All in the Game*, 151.

56. A collector's photos of this game can be found at http://icollectpuzzles.com/Fun/724 .htm (accessed 14 March 2017).

57. Similarly, in 1870 an inventor named Benjamin Day—the son of the inventor of the penny press and himself later the inventor of the "Ben Day Dots" that would be a pop-art staple—received a patent for a "Grotesque Sectional Image" puzzle, in which the human face

was broken into ten sections (figure 10). Sets of blocks containing a range of facial features were arranged via a beveled mounting plate into a variety of physiognomically significant expressions. Day argues in the patent that "by means of this invention from a very few complete sets of features, a vast number of different images may be produced, and a great diversity of expressions studied by varying single or several features" (U.S. Patent #110,213). Here the face itself was subject to the possibility of expressive reinvention by means of incremental reconfiguration.

58. Shea and Mercer, *It's All in the* Game, 151–152.

59. In 1876, *Scientific American* claimed that the United States stayed ahead of the innovation curve "not because we are by nature more inventive than other men—every nationality becomes inventive the moment it comes under our laws—but because the poorest man here can patent his devices" (quoted in Khan, *The Democratization of Invention*, 9).

60. Quoted in Slocum, *The Tangram Book*, 88, emphasis original.

61. Leo Marx, *The Machine in the Garden: Technology and the Pastoral Ideal in America* (Oxford: Oxford University Press, 2000), 199.

62. Cook, *Reader*, 156, emphasis added.

63. Barnum, *Life*, 30.

64. Ibid., 31.

65. See Ted Cohen, *Jokes: Philosophical Thoughts on Joking Matters* (Chicago: University of Chicago Press, 1999). Cohen reflects: "When I first wrote about jokes, I thought of dividing them into the pure ones and the conditional ones. A conditional joke is one that can work only with certain audiences, and typically is meant only for those audiences. The audience must supply something in order to either get the joke or to be amused by it. That something is the *condition* on which the success of the joke depends. . . . A pure joke would be universal, would get through to everyone, because it presupposed nothing in the audience. It now seems clear to me that there is no such thing as a pure joke" (12, emphasis original). To Cohen's articulation of audience conditionality, I would add that jokes are also (of course) temporally conditional. That is, the success of joke, in addition to requiring certain knowledge and assumptions on behalf of its audience, also depends on the timing of the joke. Even the members of a suitably in-the-know audience may not laugh if the joke is, for instance, delivered to them upon abruptly awakening them from sleep or while they are fixated on a more serious matter. A joke's success may also be diminished if the audience feels that it was delivered too early to achieve maximum comic effect (shortchanging a later and bigger payoff).

66. Barnum, *Life*, 105.

67. Ibid., 107.

68. Ibid., 218.

69. Ibid., 218–219.

70. Interestingly, it seems that part of the talent Barnum displays here, and throughout his career, is to arrange his texts such that the *audience* appears to take the role that the "Mississippi operator" took in Melville's novel. Rather than fixing the variable values himself, he allows the audience to act as the operator, filling in the blanks and so gaining a pleasurable sense of agency in the course of the "humbug."

71. Ibid., 107.

72. Ibid., 143.

73. Ibid., 216.

74. See the *Oxford English Dictionary* online, s.v. "Tact," http://www.oed.com.

75. Slocum, *The Tangram Book*, 20.

76. See http://translate.google.com/#zh-cn|en|%e5%b7%a7. Though I hope I make it clear

in the proceeding analysis, I should note that I do not mean to imply a direct synonymy between "tact" and "ch'iao." "Ch'iao," as I understand from conversations with native speakers of Chinese, has a more typically passive connotation, particularly in its adjectival form—although it does connote an active skillfulness with one's hands and a seemingly *fated* way of *fitting* things together. My main intention here is to push our understanding of the English term "tact," using the Chinese term, and game, as a kind of backbeat, as it were.

77. Barnum, *Life*, 121–124.

78. Ibid., 121–122.

79. Ibid., 123.

80. Ibid., 123–124.

81. Pascoe, *The Hummingbird Cabinet*, 87.

82. Ibid., 94.

83. P. T. Barnum, *Dollars and Sense or How to Get On: The Whole Secret in a Nutshell* (Chicago: People's Publishing Company, 1890), 104.

84. Ibid.

85. See Harrison, *The Temple and the Forum* (x–xv). In addition to the ongoing historical debate Harrison notes between the function of the museum as populist *forum* on one side and culturally legitimized *temple* on the other, critics often cite the nineteenth century as the transitional point between the unruly collections that composed the "wonder cabinet" tradition with the controlled displays of later nineteenth-century museums. See also Harriet Ritvo, *The Platypus and the Mermaid and Other Figments of the Classifying Imagination* (Cambridge, Mass.: Harvard University Press, 1998). Judith Pascoe provides a useful analysis of these views in *The Hummingbird Cabinet* (esp. 60–61).

86. Cook, *Reader*, 215.

87. See Donna Haraway's "Teddy Bear Patriarchy: Taxidermy in the Garden of Eden, New York City, 1908–1936," in *Primate Visions: Gender, Race, and Nature in the World of Modern Science* (New York: Routledge, 1989). Discussing the ideology of the American Museum of Natural History, she writes: "One begins in the threatening chaos of the industrial city, part of a horde, but here one will come to belong, to find substance. No matter how many people crowd the Great Hall, the experience is of individual communion with nature. The sacrament will be enacted for each worshipper" (29). This communion is evoked through the realism of the exhibit, which is carefully controlled: "Unity must be *authored* in the Judeo-Christian myth system; just as nature has an Author, so does the organism or the realistic diorama" (40, emphasis original).

88. *Barnum's American Museum Illustrated* (New York: 1850), 21. In *The Lost Museum*, http://www.lostmuseum.cuny.edu/archives/guidecover.htm (accessed 15 March 2017).

89. Barnum, *Life*, 255.

90. *Barnum's American Museum*, 3, 4, 6, 9, 15, 28.

91. Cook, *Reader*, 193, 208.

92. Ibid., 212; "Disastrous Fire," *New York Times*, 14 July 1865.

93. Barnum, *Life*, 227.

94. Ibid., 216.

95. James Cook, *The Arts of Deception: Playing with Fraud in the Age of Barnum* (Cambridge, Mass.: Harvard University Press, 2001), 19.

96. Richard Butsch highlights the local and transitory nature of audiences, as opposed to crowds (spatial collections) and publics (discursive associations), in *The Citizen Audience*: "Audience is a situated role that people temporarily perform, and in their performance people produce

representations of audiences" (3). Butsch, *The Citizen Audience: Crowds, Publics and Individuals* (New York: Routledge, 2008).

97. *Barnum's American Museum*, 29.

98. "Disastrous Fire," *New York Times*, 14 July 1865.

99. Sutton-Smith, *The Ambiguity of Play*, 225.

CHAPTER 4

1. J. L. Magee, "A little game of bagatelle, between Old Abe the rail splitter & Little Mac the gunboat general" (Philadelphia: J. L. Magee, 1864).

2. In fact, the terms "billiards" and "bagatelle" were sometimes interchangeable in the nineteenth century, as attested in an anonymously attributed line in appendix of *The Game of Billiards* (1858; a revised edition of *Billiards without a Master* discussed below): "Vive la bagatelle! which, in English, means three cheers for Billiards!" (Phelan, *Game of Billiards*, 267). With a simpler gaming mechanic than popular forms of nine-ball billiards and "pool," bagatelle was more easily adapted to mechanical operation, as tracked in the U.S. patent archives. Enclosing the table and decreasing its size, inventors added spring-loaded cues, automatic ball return systems, and dinging pin obstructions designed to dazzle and delight. These improvements yielded the games we know today as "pinball" and "pachinko" (the latter of which is still massively popular in Japan). Michael Phelan, *The Game of Billiards* (New York: D. Appleton and Company, 1859).

3. Michael Phelan, *Billiards without a Master* (New York: D. D. Winant, 1850), 122.

4. Phelan, *Billiards*, 8.

5. My use of "targeting" in this chapter is indebted McKenzie Wark's discussion of this as a videogame practice in *Gamer Theory* (Cambridge, Mass.: Harvard University Press, 2007). Discussing the cult favorite "rail shooter" *Rez*, he writes, "To target is to identify an object of an action with an aim toward a goal" and goes on to observe, "The repetition of the act of targeting repeats the production of the gamer as fleetingly distinct and enhanced but permanently engaged and subsumed in the protocols of the network" (129, 148).

6. I should additionally note that though this sequential and operational distinction serves a heuristic purpose, it is obviously the case that these two terms have some degree of slippage in ordinary use. As a result, I have found it necessary to hold fast, throughout the chapter, to this specific distinction of terms as defined here, despite the fact that I am aware it can create some monotony on the level of style.

7. For an excellent account of the importance and emergence of reading as mode of social encounter (specifically within cities), see Henkin, *City Reading*. Using public reading encounters to situate general reading practices in a manner similar to the way I have used games, Henkin comes to similar conclusions: "The nineteenth-century urban public replaced the private reader with the promiscuous reader. By presupposing, inducing, and dramatizing countless rapid and disjointed acts of browsing, the street signs, placards, newspapers, and banknotes of everyday city life cultivated reading subjects whose sense of autonomy lay not in the ability to internalize and resolve exchanges among self-possessed speakers but rather in the ability to peruse, select, discard, and reassemble a range of messages and options" (12).

8. Louis Marin, *Utopics: The Semiological Play of Textual Spaces*, trans. Robert A. Vollrath (Amherst: Humanity Books, 1984), 163.

9. Nathaniel Hawthorne, *The Blithedale Romance* (New York: Penguin Books, 1986), 1.

10. F. O. Matthiessen, *American Renaissance: Art and Expression in the Age of Emerson and Whitman* (London: Oxford University Press, 1974), 277.

11. Hawthorne, *Blithedale,* 13.

12. Ibid., 37.

13. Ibid., 38.

14. Judges 4:16–23.

15. Or we might recall Coverdale's own image, from much later in the text, of "a bird with a string about its leg, gyrating round a small circumference," his "wanderings . . . confined within a very limited sphere" (Hawthorne, *Blithedale,* 195).

16. Richard Brodhead writes, "Did ever a book miss so much of the story it purports to tell? But this insistent *missing,* usually thought merely inept, is itself deeply interesting" (281, emphasis original). He goes on to argue that this missing-ness is a function of the novel's desire to construct a story emulating the way that theatrical show business was premised on a mix of presentation and a deliberate "shut[ting] the public out from the detailed knowledge of its motives or arts of contrivance" (283). As I note later in this chapter, these "arts of contrivance" are exactly what Hawthorne emphasizes through the various *mise en abyme* of the romance (framed stories or stories in embedded registers of scope). Brodhead, "Veiled Ladies: Toward a History of Antebellum Entertainment," *American Literary History* 1.2 (1989): 273–294.

17. Hawthorne, *Blithedale,* 46–47, 104, 107, 181.

18. The secret of utopia is that the answer is always one's own society, but in a different light. And the change of lighting suggests a different use of the materials, or suggests that the materials are somehow *already* different from what they were, despite no substantive change. (The shirt that will never be the same because it is now the shirt you wore the day you went into the hospital.) This residue has bearing, even if only in a comedic or memory-inducing way, on the use of that item as it reenters your everyday life. In tangram terms, the small square might always seem like a head once you've used it as such in a particularly suggestive figure. But at the same time, another particularly good figure might force you to always see that square as a chimney or another part of a larger composition. These things layer—they are additive, not exclusive.

19. Marin, *Utopics,* 163.

20. Hawthorne, *Blithedale,* 43, 56.

21. Ibid., 94, 135.

22. Ibid., 26, 49.

23. Hawthorne, *Blithedale,* 61. Marin uses "Greimas squares" to illustrate the role of this neutral idea space: while in opposing quadrants you might have "black" and its spectrum opposite "white," you must also take into consideration those things that are neither black nor white. The remaining two quadrants, "not-black" and "not-white," analytically encompass the alternative colorful areas between the two dialectic terms (Marin, *Utopics,* 3–28).

24. Hawthorne, *Blithedale,* 1.

25. Following the theatrical tropes of the novel that Hawthorne invokes with this turn of phrase, Richard Brodhead argues that Priscilla's stage appearances are "most essentially" about the "image of woman as public performer," in a directly historical way (evoking the performances of Jenny Lind, Fanny Elssler, and other women of the antebellum stage) (Brodhead, "Veiled Ladies," 276). While this is certainly true, I think that it also speaks to the more cultural forms of performance I have been discussing throughout this book. These social and limited (that is, broadly game-like) performances of character and agency, across genders, are indexed by the operational dynamics of pervasive games, such as billiards. I would argue that this is, as

Brodhead puts it, the "cultural situation a novelist would have had to address at this moment of American literary history," a supplement he might agree with given his sense that "what lies behind *Blithedale* is a development specific to the history of entertainment quite as much as any development in general social life" (273, 277). Brodhead sees this development as based on a somewhat passive spectatorial or "vicarious consumption" (286–289). I simply want to reinvest this consumption with more directed agential power, registered through the thematic of targeting or ridiculing. This is in line with Jordan Alexander Stein's recent observation that Coverdale's narrational styles should be understood "less as ideologies and more as improvisations," though I don't believe it is entirely necessary to imply an essential split between these two terms. Jordan Alexander Stein, "*The Blithedale Romance*'s Queer Style," *ESQ: A Journal of the American Renaissance* 55.3 (2009): 219.

26. Michael Colacurcio argues the opposite, claiming that "the book reads nothing like a utopian tract" (2). However, while I entirely agree that *Blithedale* does not have the hopefulness of the utopian genre in its earlier forms (it is undoubtedly more dystopic), I would argue that many of the problems Colacurcio reads into the text are in fact elements of utopian literature highlighted by Marin. Colacurcio notes, "Coverdale merely wanders, as it seems, in search of clues from the outside, finding some and missing many others, leaving us to make things out, little by little, the best we can" and registers that the reader or critical analyst has "to wonder, perhaps, why he has been put in the position of having to probe for the motives and to assemble the narrative of this tale of betrayal pretty much on his own" (7). As I argue here, being put in this position is precisely the point of the romance qua utopic as Hawthorne uses it. This is the text as platform for thinking and therefore, as Colacurcio himself understands, in a "fundamental sense, pre-political," where the prefix here denotes not naive absence but staging (1). Michael J. Colacurcio, "Nobody's Protest Novel: Art and Politics in *The Blithedale Romance*," *Nathaniel Hawthorne Review* 34.1 (2008): 1–39.

27. Marin, *Utopics*, 39.

28. Hawthorne, *Blithedale*, 3.

29. Ibid., 146.

30. Ibid., 40.

31. In its early form, bagatelles was played much like billiards, on a long table with depressions corresponding to various point values; players used a cue to send a ball down the table to settle in these divots.

32. See the database of patents available at http://uspto.gov.

33. Game designer Jane McGonigal highlights this in her book *Reality Is Broken: Why Games Make Us Better and How They Can Change the World* (New York: Penguin Books, 2011). Drawing on the findings of researchers in the psychophysiology of gaming, she writes: "Gamers spend nearly all of their time failing. Roughly four times out of five, gamers don't complete the mission, run out of time, don't solve the puzzle, lost the fight, fail to improve their score, crash and burn, or die. Which makes you wonder: do gamers actually *enjoy* failing. As it turns out, yes. . . . Failure doesn't disappoint us. It makes us happy in a very particular way: excited, interested, and most of all *optimistic*" (64, emphasis original).

34. Since games are inherently social, a victory that fails to consider the social paratexts surrounding gameplay is a particularly bad-faith kind of solipsism. This is not to say that people don't play this way—certainly many do. Yet when we understand games as a form of communication, we must concede that the community makes the "winner."

35. I should clarify that there are important ways in which it does or could matter. But the reduction of scope that occurs in gameplay, creating systems in which players can act *as if* the

outsides of the game were suspended, is exactly what can allow games of many sorts to play therapeutic and reparative roles for marginalized social actors. Without doubt, we can and do bring outsides into the chalk circle of gameplay—thinking through this interplay is the work of this chapter—but part of this has do with the potential for meaningful (if partial) suspensions of identity.

36. Of course, I am aware that "sphere" more typically implies domains of conventional action, and this is how Hawthorne often employs the term. But I'm not entirely certain he limits his view to a purely abstract notion of spheres. The model of billiards, present and prevalent during Hawthorne's composition, gives a somewhat different slant to *Blithedale*'s persistent invocation of netted pockets (the "reticules" or purses discussed later in this chapter), and "spheres." In the immediate aftermath of Coverdale's invocation of billiards, "Zenobia's sphere . . . impress[es] itself powerfully upon [his own]," and he proceeds to subject her to a "great deal of eye-shot" (Hawthorne, *Blithedale*, 46–47); in their forest interaction, "Zenobia repelled [Westervelt] . . . they mutually repelled each other—by some incompatibility of their spheres" (156); and Hollingsworth's monomaniac "sphere of philanthropic action" eventually impels Zenobia to the horrible moment when she "sank in the dark pool" (27, 235). A stretch? Undoubtedly. Meaningless? I'm not so sure. There is a kind of physics in Hawthorne's depiction of spheres that is not conveyed by the more airy connotations of the term.

37. Hawthorne, *Blithedale*, 194, 69.

38. Phelan, *Billiards*, 8.

39. Ibid.

40. Ibid.

41. Phelan, *Game of Billiards*, 259.

42. Ibid., 246.

43. Also like Bradley, Phelan emphasizes an "acute and mature judgment" that will be developed in the course of becoming better at the game: "Two players, of equal skill and facility of execution, may play together, and if one be superior to the other in point of judgment, he is sure to win, at least, three-fourths of the games played" (Phelan, *Billiards*, 11).

44. Hawthorne, *Blithedale*, 61.

45. Willard McCarty, "Knowing . . . : Modeling in Literary Studies," in *A Companion to Digital Literary Studies*, ed. Susan Schreibman and Ray Siemens (Oxford: Blackwell, 2008), 2.

46. Nathaniel Hawthorne, *The American Notebooks*, ed. Claude M. Simpson (Athens: Ohio University Press, 1972), 210.

47. Phelan, *Billiards*, 12.

48. See Kirschenbaum, *Mechanisms*, for more on the distinction between formal and forensic materiality, esp. 10–12.

49. Mintz, *Moralists and Modernizers*, 147.

50. Nathaniel Hawthorne, *A Wonder Book and Tanglewood Tales*, ed. William Charvat, Roy Harvey Pearce, and Claude M. Simpson (Athens: Ohio University Press, 1972), 378–379.

51. Ibid., 377.

52. Phelan, *Billiards*, 10–11, emphasis original.

53. Hawthorne, *Wonder Book*, 88.

54. Gérard Genette describes this technique as "a deliberate transgression of the threshold of embedding" and defines it as "when an author (or his reader) introduces himself into the fictive action of the narrative or when a character in that fiction intrudes into the extradiegetic existence of the author or reader" (*Narrative Discourse Revisited*, 88). Drawing on a parallel construction, Genette uses the term "metadiegetic" to describe narrations embedding themselves

within the primary narration, such that Eustace's stories are metadiegetic to the frame diegesis (91–93). For more, see Genette, *Narrative Discourse Revisited*, trans. Jane E. Levin (Ithaca: Cornell University Press, 1988). In what follows, I prefer to use the terminology of scope because it is not limited to Genette's "levels" of diegesis but can also include registers of attention that are more finely or widely delimited—for example, local character descriptions in a given chapter ("A Visitor from Town") versus relational descriptions of multiple characters ("Hollingsworth, Zenobia, Priscilla"). Scopic unsettling is both technique and content in *The Blithedale Romance*: it is surely no accident that the stage scenes that bookend the central action feature Professor Westervelt "looking like one of the enchanters of the Arabian Nights," a narrative that is itself a series of tales within tales (Hawthorne, *Blithedale*, 199).

55. Hawthorne, *Wonder Book*, 117.

56. Ibid., 169–170.

57. In her extensive study of Hawthorne in *The Anatomy of National Fantasy*, Lauren Berlant notes this: "Since [Hawthorne] sees the context of national identity as fundamental to his subjectivity, he is forced to identify and to devise spaces *within* the system, national 'heterotopias,' within which he might maintain a critical edge" (34, emphasis original). Lauren Berlant, *The Anatomy of National Fantasy* (Chicago: University of Chicago Press, 1991).

58. Hawthorne, *Blithedale*, 108.

59. Ibid., 108.

60. Ibid., 1.

61. Ibid., 116.

62. Ibid., 100.

63. Ibid., 98.

64. Ibid., 59, 73.

65. Ibid., 99.

66. This might also be connected to Coverdale's name, as one definition of "cover" has to do with "present[ing] a gun or pistol at (something) so as to have it directly in the line of fire; to aim directly at" (OED). While in his hermitage, Hawthorne's narrator literally covers, or targets, the dale (Blithedale).

67. Ibid., 100.

68. Ibid., 101.

69. Ibid., 46.

70. Ibid., 59.

71. Ibid., 101.

72. Ibid., 166.

73. Ibid., 165.

74. Ibid., 218.

75. Ibid., 94, 95, 126.

76. Ibid., 120.

77. Ibid., 195.

78. Ibid., 69.

79. It is also worth noting here that it is not the larger view *in itself* that creates this effect but the contact of the two registers of scope, hence the difference I am arguing for here between the operations of *scoping* and *targeting*. Targeting always puts at least two scopically contained objects into contact and in this way might be understood via the phenomenological idea of the *intentional object*, an object which is always already invested with the subjectivity of the viewer (in other words, all objects as experienced).

80. See the *Oxford English Dictionary* online, s.v. "Ridicule," http://www.oed.com.

81. Hawthorne, *Blithedale*, 35.

82. Ibid. Allan and Barbara Lefcowitz argue that Priscilla's purses "encompass at least two symbolic possibilities: covert sexuality and concealed guilt" and go on say that these align with "her association with the narrow, the clandestine, and the limited" ("Some Rents in the Veil," 266). While the implications of associating the limited/unlimited binary with domestic gender dynamics in the nineteenth century lie outside the scope of this chapter, I find their observation that Priscilla's purses are a symbol of "the limited" useful to my discussion of productive limitation. Priscilla's purses reticulate (grid up) as they enclose, but Priscilla stresses to Coverdale that they are for "use," contingent and sequential as in my discussion of ridicule, "not beauty," a transcendental and perhaps ridiculous-making device (Hawthorne, *Blithedale*, 51). Allan and Barbara Lefcowitz, "Some Rents in the Veil: New Light on Priscilla and Zenobia in *The Blithedale Romance*," *Nineteenth-Century Fiction* 21.3 (1966): 263–275. For a deeper discussion of gender's role in the representational practices of Hawthorne's novel, see Lauren Berlant, "Fantasies of Utopia in *The Blithedale Romance*," *American Literary History* 1.1 (1989): 30–62. For Berlant, the figure of the hymen acts as a threshold between knowledge of our implication in world history or ideology and a utopically liberating ignorance: "The veil is a powerful object because, as Zenobia's story of Theodore and 'The Silver Veil' tells us, it hides that which we do not want to uncover, just as the hymen (a figure of history here) is a fetish because it signifies a mystery that, for all its attractions, is better off left mysterious" (50).

83. Hawthorne, *Blithedale*, 198.

84. Ibid., 222, 247.

85. Hawthorne's working title for the novel was, in fact, "Hollingsworth: A Romance" (ibid., xiv), ironically foregrounding the dichotomy of concept and figure. It may be significant that, in this earlier draft of the novel, Hawthorne omitted the final chapter, "Miles Coverdale's Confession," ending on a more ambivalent note that may have better justified the irony of the original title.

86. Critical dialogue on the novel is, accordingly, filled with readings that index deep frustration with Coverdale's unsatisfying conceptualization of the story (often attempting to find alternatives, other targets for interpretation): Donald Ross suggests instead that "the central plot of the novel [is] the discovery and subsequent repression of [Coverdale's] sexual desire for Zenobia, adding that a "sensitive reading of the novel reveals no evidence of Coverdale's acting or speaking as if he loves Priscilla" ("Dreams and Sexual Repression," 1014); Allan and Barbara Lefcowitz contend, "He chooses Priscilla not because she is better than Zenobia, but because he too is afraid of Zenobia's power" ("Some Rents in the Veil," 275); Jennifer Fleischner notes, "[Coverdale's] production is sporadic and not, perhaps, what he would wish it to be" ("Female Eroticism," 530); and reinventing Hawthorne's final lines, Berlant claims: "Coverdale's real 'secret' . . . is that he—he himself—was in love—with—Hollingsworth" (Berlant, "Fantasies," 36). In a sense, readers appear "programmed" (or dispositionally habituated) to reject Coverdale's final explanation. Fleischner, "Female Eroticism, Confession, and Interpretation in Nathaniel Hawthorne," *Nineteenth-Century Literature* 44.4 (1990): 514–533; Ross, "Dreams and Sexual Repression in *The Blithedale Romance*," *PMLA* 86.5 (1971): 1014–1017.

87. Hawthorne, *Blithedale*, 165.

88. Ibid., 119.

CHAPTER 5

1. *Salem Register* (5 June 1843): 3; Charles E. Trow, "Parlor Games: 'The Old Corner Bookstore' and Its Associations," in *Prose and Verse with an Introspective View of the Massachusetts House of Representatives* (Salem: Barry Printing Co., 1900), 23.

2. A number of histories and anecdotal references to Abbot adopt either a common misspelling ("Abbott") or replicate the diminutive "Annie" (a nickname that would otherwise give no pause except for the fact that it is exclusively used by her male business associates). Throughout this chapter and book, I use Abbot's preferred name and spelling—"Anne W. Abbot"—as it appears in her copyright applications and in her signed copies of books.

3. Trow, "Parlor Games," 23; Michael Winship, "John Punchard Jewett, Publisher of *Uncle Tom's Cabin*: A Biographical Note with a Preliminary List of His Imprints," in *Roger Eliot Stoddard at Sixty-Five: A Celebration* (New York: Thornwillow Press, 2000).

4. Anne Wales Abbot, *Dr. Busby and His Neighbors* (Salem: W. & S. B. Ives, 1844), 2.

5. Ibid.

6. *Worcester Palladium*, quoted in *Salem Register* (26 December 1844).

7. Abbot, *Dr. Busby and His Neighbors*, 1–2. Though it's most plausible that one of the Ives brothers wrote this prefatory apology, the authorship isn't exactly certain. Abbot held the copyright for the book, and it's possible that she herself wrote the preface in a self-deprecating mode. I'd love to think this were the case, if simply for the profound ironies it would introduce. But without substantiating evidence, an Occam's razor approach would suggest that the publisher had the most to lose by leaving the book's "shocks" unacknowledged.

8. Bradley, "Uses," 225.

9. Patrick Jagoda, *Network Aesthetics* (Chicago: University of Chicago Press, 2016), 23.

10. U.S. Patent and Trademark Office, "Class 46: Games and Toys" (1872).

11. Trow, "Parlor Games," 23.

12. Bradley, "Uses," 225.

13. *Salem Register* (6 March 1843). Game makers after this, and indeed Ives in the time following *Dr. Busby*'s success, primarily ran advertisements in the fall to capitalize on buyers looking for Christmas and New Year's gifts. Though there are no exact dates given for the earlier conversation between Abbot and Ives, one might suspect that she had tried to get it published in the more advantageous holiday season of 1842–1843, but settled for the later date in order to have it published at all.

14. Trow, "Parlor Games," 23.

15. *Salem Register* (5 June 1843); Abbot, *Dr. Busby and His Neighbors*, i; *Salem Register* (26 December 1844).

16. *Salem Register* (26 December 1844). This discrepancy in sales is likely explained by the operational simplicity of *Mansion*. From the beginning, reviewers noted that this game was mainly for children, and not exactly enjoyable when played by adults.

17. Ibid.

18. Louisa C. Tuthill, *Characteristics of Distinguished Persons* (Salem: W. & S. B. Ives, 1843). American Antiquarian Society.

19. In *Putnam's Monthly Historical Magazine*, vol. 2 (Salem: Salem Press, 1893–1894), 36.

20. "Cornelia Wells Walter," from "Biographical Notes," in *The Poe Log: A Documentary Life of Edgar Allan Poe, 1809–1849*, ed. Dwight Thomas and David K. Jackson (Boston:

G. K. Hall, 1987). E. A. Poe Web, http://www.eapoe.org/papers/misc1921/tplg00na.htm (accessed 17 March 2017).

21. Though the record is slim by virtue of sexist market mechanics that produced a skewed documentary trail, Anne Abbot leaves some traces by virtue of the fact that she was unmarried and so, after the success of *Dr. Busby*, began seizing copyright for herself on future games. Many other games invented by women in the antebellum period credit their creators as simply "A Lady"—when they are attributed at all.

22. Anne Wales Abbot, *The Improved and Illustrated Game of Dr. Busby* (Salem: W. & S. B. Ives, 1843). Hereafter shortened to *Improved*, to distinguish these references from those related to the book.

23. Abbot, *Dr. Busby and His Neighbors,* i–ii (hereafter, *Neighbors*). Abbot would develop on this sensibility in a follow-up game called *Master Rodbury*, another pictorial card game with fascinating if less accessible rules.

24. Abbot, *Improved.*

25. *Dr. Busby* cards with handwritten markings can be found at both the New-York Historical Society and in the American Antiquarian Society's games collection.

26. Abbot, *Neighbors*, i–ii.

27. Abbot, *Improved.*

28. *New York Commercial Advertiser*, quoted in Abbot, *Neighbors*, i.

29. The liminality of gameplay situations, the sense of being always "both in and out of the game" in Whitman's terms, creates persistent opportunities for tactical "implicit coding," whether the stakes are high or not. Drawing on Joan N. Radner and Susan S. Lanser's work, Robin Bernstein describes implicit codes as those which convey meaning with and alongside other more obvious activities and meanings: "Implicit code differs from both complicit and explicit code in that the latter two forms communicate a single meaning in reference to a mutually understood key. Implicit coding, in contrast, communicates through multifaceted cultural references and thus opens manifold and often contradictory meanings . . . in implicit coding . . . all layers of meaning—including those conscious and unconscious—matter. Implicit coding is improvisational, creative, and expressive, often playful or joyful, and it creates a sense of control" (Bernstein, *Racial Innocence*, 84).

30. Abbot, *Neighbors*, 33–34. It might be merely convention, but I find it conspicuous that Abbot has her characters (erroneously) imagine that their creator is a man, especially considering that the Ives brothers are the only credited entity on the 1843 game box.

31. Abbot may have been trying to maximize exposure, since she hadn't be able to profit directly from *Dr. Busby*'s sale (having sold the copyright to the Ives brothers). As mentioned, following this initial success, she secures her own copyright. She also makes an effort to link her later ludic efforts to *Dr. Busby*. Published by William Crosby in 1844, *The Game of Races*, for example, explicitly markets itself as "By the Author of *The Improved Game of Dr. Busby*."

32. Abbot, *Neighbors*, 5.

33. Ibid., 33.

34. Ibid., 60–61.

35. Ibid., 1–2.

36. It's worth pointing out that *Dr. Busby and His Neighbors* was published more than two decades before Lewis Carroll would effect a similar maneuver in *Alice's Adventures in Wonderland.*

37. Abbot, *Neighbors*, 118.

38. Walter Aimwell, *Ella* (Boston: Gould & Lincoln, 1854): 171, emphasis added.

39. In his anecdotal history of Massachusetts parlor games, Charles Trow explicitly reminisces about the power of "higher order" card games to create social intimacy. His thoughts are worth quoting in full here: "These cards have brought into closer relation not only the members of the immediate household, but youths and maidens who have from time to time casually dropped in of an evening to widen and cheer the fireside circle of some neighboring family. The matching of cards on such occasions has not only been a source of amusement, but in some cases the outcome has been the making of matches of a more enduring nature. It has been said that the matches are made in heaven, but the writer is of the opinion that the terrestrial agencies have had more to do with forming matrimonial alliances than the spiritual. Be that as it may, we all know that social games have been a potent factor in drawing the sexes nearer to each other" ("Parlor Games," 22). After-the-fact reveries such as this are about as close as we can get to a confirmation of the broader implicit codes in action during gameplay of the past. Though I think we all know these sorts of things are meaningful in our own moment, it is often too easy to unsee similar modes of social irony in historical scenes.

40. Though suggestions like this are inevitably speculative, traces of reception can add to the plausibility here: I've seen a pack of *Master Rodbury* cards (Abbot's direct follow-up to *Dr. Busby*) at the New-York Historical Society with the following scrawled on the back, "How I love thee Charming Lizzie." This was trailed by the suggestive "Thursday Eve." A memory? A date? Either way, these cards were at play in temporal and social circles that were broader than the instructions alone could convey.

41. Abbot, *Neighbors*, 44.

42. Bradley, "Uses," 225.

43. *Southern Patriot* (22 April 1844): 1.

44. The Strong Museum of Play has a particularly rich selection of these later versions of *Dr. Busby*. For representative examples, see *The Game of Dr. Busby* (New York: J. H. Singer, ca. 1880–1890) and *The Game of Old Dr. Busby* (New York: J. Ottmann Litho. Co., ca. 1890). Some part of the perpetuation of minstrelized images can be traced to mobile labor: J. H. Singer is hired by J. Ottman Lithography Company and eventually moves to the Milton Bradley Company at the turn of the century (which uses directly copied images from his earlier, more offensive, game). The Parker Brothers do a faithful replication of Abbot's version around the turn of the century—seizing on the vogue for Salem history—but "update" the characters to draw racist excess into the portrayal of "Ninnycometwitch's Servant."

45. Milton Bradley attributes the game to "some young people of the city" in his 1886 *Good Housekeeping* article. In an expansion of this piece for a World's Fair exhibit on games, Bradley adds that *Authors* "was originated by a young man living in Salem, Mass., helped by some of his female acquaintances." Charles Trow gives greater credit to the unnamed women in question here, attributing the game to "a coterie of bright young ladies." Given the nature of publication, it seems somewhat likely a mixed-gender group originated the game, with the "young man" in question acting as a mouthpiece (in the best-case scenario). See Bradley, "Uses," 225; Stewart Culin, "The Exhibit of American Games at the Fair," in *Putnam's Monthly Historical Magazine*, vol. 2 (Salem: The Salem Press: 1893–1894), 35; and Trow, "Parlor Games," 24.

46. Bradley, "Uses," 225.

47. The Strong Museum of Play has an expansive and representative collection of this game as it radiated through different producers over time.

48. Bradley, "Uses," 226.

49. Louisa May Alcott, *Little Women: An Annotated Edition*, ed. Daniel Shealy (Cambridge, Mass.: Belknap Press of Harvard University Press, 2013): 191.

50. Extrapolating from the undersides his early games, Bradley's version of *Authors* went into production at least as early as 1863 and likely a bit earlier. Bradley secured a patent (always the engineer) for his improvements later in 1872. See *The Checkered Game of Life* (Springfield: Milton Bradley & Co., ca. 1863), Missouri Historical Society, and Milton Bradley, Improvement in Games of Cards, Patent 133,296 (26 November 1872), USPTO.

51. *Panorama of The Visit of Santa Claus to the Happy Children* (Springfield: Milton Bradley & Co., ca. 1868–70), 8.

52. Milton Bradley, "Home Amusements for the Winter Evenings" in box copy for *The Permutation Dissected Map of the United States* (Springfield: Milton Bradley & Co., ca. 1871–1872).

53. *Panorama of The Visit of Santa Claus to the Happy Children*, 8.

54. See the extensive Milton Bradley trade catalog collection at The Strong Museum of Play.

55. *Bradley's Holiday Annual of Home Amusements and Social Sports, 1872–3* (Springfield: Milton Bradley & Co., 1872), 6, 9, 28.

56. *Bradley's Catalogue, 1881–1882* (Springfield: Milton Bradley & Co., 1881): 25; *Bradley's Catalogue, 1890–1891* (Springfield: Milton Bradley & Co., 1890).

57. *Panorama of the Visit of Santa Claus to the Happy Children*, 8.

58. *One Hundred Years of Children's Books and a Presentation of Modern Style Trends in Juvenile Literature* (New York: McLoughlin Brothers, 1928), 7; see also Laura Wasowicz, "Brief History of the McLoughlin Brothers," at http://www.americanantiquarian.org/mcloughlin-bros (accessed 17 March 2017).

59. Chromolithography required complex hue overlays that resolved in combination to a full-color depth. A "chromiste" was a specialist in the stacking of hues necessary to create the multicolor effect. I am indebted to Lauren Hewes at the American Antiquarian Society for explaining the process to me with reference to the society's fabulous Louis Prang proof books.

60. An internal promotional sheet from 1880 narrates this move as follows: "For some years the business was divided between the store and two shops, in separate buildings [probably necessitating his work with Samuel Bowles on typesetting and engraving projects], but in 1870 the firm purchased land on the corner of Harrison Avenue and Dwight Street—100 by 120 feet— and erected thereon a five story brick building 90 by 40 feet with an L 75 by 25 feet, and four stories high, nearly all of the room being occupied by the firm in the prosecution of its business. From 50 to 100 hands are employed, varying with the season, the busiest time being from July to January, preparing for the holidays and winter evenings. The help permanently employed are mostly skilled artizans [*sic*] who command high wages. Mr. Milton Bradley and his father Mr. Lewis Bradley, are the active members of the firm, and they mainly devise and superintend the manufacture of the mechanical and mental novelties for which the house has become famous." *Milton Bradley & Co., Manufacturers of Home Games and Amusements, Kindergarten Gifts, etc.* (Springfield: Milton Bradley, 1880). Hasbro Company Archives.

61. *Panorama of The Visit of Santa Claus to the Happy Children*, 8.

62. *The Game of Bamboozle, Or the Enchanted Isle* (Springfield: Milton Bradley, ca. 1872– 1926). The Strong Museum.

63. Ibid.

64. There are some similarities here, however oblique and speculative, to the Melville sketches from which the game draws inspiration. To wit: "If you seek to ascend Rock Rodondo, take the following prescription. Go three voyages round the world as a main-royal-man of the tallest frigate that floats; then serve a year or two apprenticeship to the guides who conduct

strangers up the Peak of Teneriffe; and as many more, respectively, to a rope-dancer, an Indian Juggler, and a chamois. This done, come and be rewarded by a view from our tower. How we get there, we alone know." Herman Melville, "The Encantadas, Or Enchanted Isles," in *Billy Budd, Sailor and Selected Tales*, ed. Robert Milder (Oxford: Oxford University Press, 2009), 120.

65. Quoted in Augst, *The Clerk's Tale*, 52.

66. Comedy writers Leonard Stern and Roger Price first began self-publishing *Mad Libs* in 1958, inventing it without reference to *Peter Coddle*, according to Stern's version of events in "A Happy History of *Mad Libs*." Though it's possible neither had played *Peter Coddle* as a child, it's still interesting that their endeavor reestablished the genre of the absurdist word-replacement game precisely a century after Simonds had introduced his "New Pleasure" in *Jessie* (1858). See Roger Price and Leonard Stern, *50 Years of Mad Libs* (New York: Penguin Group, 2008).

67. In loose chronological order, see *Peter Coddle's Trip to New York* (Boston: Gould & Lincoln, 1858); *Peter Coddle's Trip to New York* (Cincinnati: Peter G. Thomson, ca. 1883); *Peter Coddles Esq. and His Trip to New York* (New York: J. H. Singer, ca. 1880–1890); *Game of Cousin Peter's Trip to New York* (New York: McLoughlin Brothers, 1898); *Peter Coddle's Trip to New York* (Springfield: Milton Bradley Co., ca. 1900).

68. Network media critic Patrick Jagoda is especially good on this in *Network Aesthetics*: "Technological infrastructures and protocols are surely important to any discussion of networks. These elements, however, make human experience secondary. They foreground control, management, and strategy over modes that are at least as common in network society—experiences of being ungoverned, disconnected, lost, laggy, intimately entangled, abandoned, frustrated, or broken down" (23). Though Jagoda is discussing networked life in the twenty-first century, I think the same shifts in emphases are imperative to keep in mind in earlier periods as well.

69. Henkin, *City Reading*, 14.

70. Friedrich Nietzsche, *Beyond Good and Evil: Prelude to a Philosophy of the Future*, trans. Walter Kaufmann (New York: Vintage Books, 1989), 80.

71. Lev Manovich, *The Language of New Media* (Cambridge, Mass.: MIT Press, 2001), 10.

72. Hawthorne, *The Blithedale Romance*, 165.

INDEX

Page numbers in italic type indicate illustrations

ACKNOWLEDGMENTS

This book has been the result of years of personally enriching entanglements, both serious and otherwise. I'm grateful first for the people and institutions that were willing to support my journeys with and to various tiny, "silly" things. Amber Gravett and David Tuma made possible an early archival adventure to Hasbro's Milton Bradley Company Archive, while George Burtch and the staff in East Longmeadow were kind enough to give me time and guidance while there. A fellowship from The Strong Museum and Brian Sutton-Smith Archives of Play was instrumental to the material focus of this project; I owe a deep debt to Nic Ricketts, who opened many doors and drawers for me. The Jay and Deborah Last Fellowship allowed me to spend a transformative month at the American Antiquarian Society, and I'm especially grateful to Laura Wasowicz, Lauren Hewes, and Paul Erickson for their guidance and conversation while I was there. Funds from the Dr. Nuala McGann Drescher Program administered by the New York State United University Professions and Joint Labor-Management Committee allowed a semester of leave that proved crucial in the final year of writing. I am thankful for the support I have received while at SUNY Oswego, both from the university as a whole and the Department of English and Creative Writing in particular.

I am indebted to the people who helped me understand my own writing and find purpose in it. Paul Jay, Christopher Kendrick, Christopher Castiglia, Pamela Caughie, and David Chinitz were each instrumental in helping me to find my way while at Loyola University Chicago. John (Jack) Kerkering taught me not only how to see the poetry in argument, but also how to take images and rhetorical figures seriously as models of thought. Steven E. Jones talked to me about video games, cartoons, textual studies, haptics, irresponsible dogs, and everything in between, offering an approach to rigor, intellectual capaciousness, and play that has remained an inspiration and aspiration. At SUNY Oswego, I feel lucky to have had access to the expert eyes and minds of Patricia Clark, Karol Cooper, Maureen Curtin, Christopher

LaLonde, Michael Murphy, Patrick Murphy, Bennet Schaber, Amy Shore, and Leigh Wilson. And I'm especially grateful to the wonderful folks of the junior faculty writing group—Fiona Coll, Roberta (Rosie) Hurtado, and Adin Lears—who did so much to help me understand how to introduce this book.

    This project is a product of so many conversations—whether at conferences over coffee and name badges or at archives while holding a wooden dowel with a pig on it. I'm grateful for the conversational generosity and (to my shy mind) downright impossible friendliness and support offered by Sari Altschuler, Diana Anselmo, Tom Augst, Stephanie Bacon, Lauren Barbeau, Rhae Lynn Barnes, Peter Bayers, Ariel Beaujot, Annette Becker, Keren Ben-Horin, Stephanie Blalock, Anne Blankenship, Jenny Brady, Nancy Caronia, Jim Casey, Darryl Cook, Paula Connolly, Emma Cormack, Stuart Davis, Laura Donnelly, Bob Dushay, Bob Early, Erin Eisenbarth, Lori and Maurice Forrester, Ritchie Garrison, Katherine C. Grier, Molly Hardy, John Hay, Cheryl Hicks, Rebecca Klassen, Heidi Kolk, Sarah Gold McBride, Amy Montz, Jacqueline O'Connor, Melissa Otis, Nora Rabins, Kelly Reddy-Best, Ashley Reed, Kyle Roberts, Michelle Sammons, Mark Schlemmer, Sarah Schuetze, Sarah Stern, Jose Vazquez, Justine Wells, Catherine Whalen, and Bruce Whitehill. The 2017 National Endowment for the Humanities Summer Seminar "American Material Culture: Nineteenth-Century New York" hosted by the Bard Graduate Center was a perfect place to calibrate my thinking about social space while I worked on the final revisions for this book. And I simply can't overestimate the value of my time at Penn State's First Book Institute. The kindness and unrelenting wisdom of codirectors Sean X. Goudie and Priscilla Wald—not to mention my "guest" reader, Hester Blum—were and remain my model of scholarly investment and mentorship. I am thankful to them and to all of the members of our cohort—Jesús Costantino, Sarah Ensor, Tara Fickle, Phil Maciak, Shaundra Myers, Jenny Rhee, and Andrew Rippeon—without whom this book would simply not be.

    At Penn Press, Jerry Singerman helped me navigate the publication process with wisdom, enthusiasm, and precision, while Hannah Blake and Noreen O'Connor-Abel were always quick and generous in fielding my endless questions about images and the fine intricacies of style. Early versions of parts of Chapters 1 and 2 were published as (respectively) "Forcibly Impressed: Reform Games and the Avatar Figure in Milton Bradley and Walt Whitman," *American Literature* 83.1 (March 2011): 1–27; and "Not Exactly Infinite: State Machines and Algorithms of the Interior in Herman Melville's *The Confidence-*

Man," *ESQ* 59.3 (December 2013): 484–518. I'm deeply appreciative to the anonymous readers at these journals and at Penn Press for their thoughtful, useful, and energizing suggestions.

I can't imagine caring so much for the little moments in life that are captured by games without the friends and family who filled those moments with meaning for me: my dad and stepmom, Rene and Anita Guerra, for finding the fun in the bold and blustery strategies of dominos, shuffleboard, and *Rook*; my mom, Diana Henson, who I used to love watching quietly lay out the cards for games of solitaire (and who reminds me to this day that I once aspired to the prestigious career of "video game counselor"); my sister, Lisa Guerra, for schooling me many a time in the art of singing while you annihilate someone in games of speed; my stepbrother, Kyle Rino, for putting up with my persistent and pestering color commentary during our countless games of tiny basketball on *Magic Johnson's Double Dunk;* Loren and Rhonda Wassell for ensuring that we always clean up on trivia anytime they're around (and for telling me about the game board that became the anchor for the opening of this book!); Bryan Blume for letting me pretend I was offering meaningful co-piloting during late-night run-throughs of *Doom;* Vijay Natarajan for his endearingly endless passion for *NHL Hockey '94* (despite winning maybe four out of two hundred games); Andrew Marchesseault, José Portuondo-Dember, and all of my improv theater friends at UChicago's Off-Off Campus, where it was always a pleasure to "find the game" in even the most absurd interaction, utterance, or gesture; and Michael Hasak for helping me to see the game in music—whether in the playing or simply in the desperate search to find a place to play. Finally, life, let alone this book, would not be the same without the unstoppable Courtney C. W. Guerra: partner, editor, arguer, expert, baloney dropper, business giver, artist, dancer, albondiga, friend. That's a pretty rare animal.